ALSO BY ADRIANA E. RAMÍREZ

Dead Boys

The Swallows

THE VIOLENCE

MY FAMILY'S COLOMBIAN WAR

ADRIANA E. RAMÍREZ

SCRIBNER
New York   Amsterdam/Antwerp   London
Toronto   Sydney/Melbourne   New Delhi

Scribner
An Imprint of Simon & Schuster, LLC
1230 Avenue of the Americas
New York, NY 10020

For more than 100 years, Simon & Schuster has championed authors and the stories they create. By respecting the copyright of an author's intellectual property, you enable Simon & Schuster and the author to continue publishing exceptional books for years to come. We thank you for supporting the author's copyright by purchasing an authorized edition of this book.

No amount of this book may be reproduced or stored in any format, nor may it be uploaded to any website, database, language-learning model, or other repository, retrieval, or artificial intelligence system without express permission. All rights reserved. Inquiries may be directed to Simon & Schuster, 1230 Avenue of the Americas, New York, NY 10020 or permissions@simonandschuster.com.

Copyright © 2026 by Adriana E. Ramírez

All rights reserved, including the right to reproduce this book or portions thereof in any form whatsoever. For information, address Scribner Subsidiary Rights Department, 1230 Avenue of the Americas, New York, NY 10020.

First Scribner hardcover edition April 2026

SCRIBNER and design are trademarks of Simon & Schuster, LLC

Simon & Schuster strongly believes in freedom of expression and stands against censorship in all its forms. For more information, visit BooksBelong.com.

For information about special discounts for bulk purchases, please contact Simon & Schuster Special Sales at 1-866-506-1949 or business@simonandschuster.com.

The Simon & Schuster Speakers Bureau can bring authors to your live event. For more information, or to book an event, contact the Simon & Schuster Speakers Bureau at 1-866-248-3049 or visit our website at www.simonspeakers.com.

Interior design by Kyle Kabel

Manufactured in the United States of America

1 3 5 7 9 10 8 6 4 2

Library of Congress Cataloging-in-Publication Data has been applied for.

ISBN 978-1-5011-4520-9
ISBN 978-1-5011-4522-3 (ebook)

Let's stay in touch! Scan here to get book recommendations, exclusive offers, and more delivered to your inbox.

*Para Esther
y Alberto*

Author's Note

The Violence is a work of nonfiction constructed from oral histories, namely the testimonies of people in my family and other stories I gathered over the years. Some names and details have been changed to protect the privacy of individuals. Translated dialogue is in italics. The information in this work comes from years of research as well as walking down the many roads described to interview the people who were there to witness this era in Colombia's history. Recollections will vary.

I would not be surprised if many of those people deny the stories in this book, even as they know them to be true. I would also not be surprised if many of them declare the flattering bits to be truest of all.

This work is rooted in research taken with great love and care. Unlike most historical documents, though, it will not always overlap with official narratives nor pretend to be all-encompassing in its scope. There is so much that is not included. I encourage the reader to dig deeper.

This book is the story as it was told to me, as I heard it, and as I understood it to be true. Still—Colombia is a land of many truths, and this is just one.

La Violencia has been one of the most fictionalized events in Colombia's history.

>—Robin Kirk,
>*More Terrible Than Death*

All Colombian literature has been made in the middle of war, all of it.

>—Ricardo Silva Romero, 2021

Some of the owner men were kind because they hated what they had to do, and some of them were angry because they hated to be cruel, and some of them were cold because they had long ago found that one could not be an owner unless one were cold.

>—John Steinbeck,
>*The Grapes of Wrath*

There are no young men in Colombia. They are all dead, abroad, or playing with guns.

>—El Jabón, 2007

Contents

Colombian History 1525–2025: A Brief Timeline xvii

Family Trees xx

Una Nota Sobre Mi Abuela (A Prologue of Cards) 1

PART I

How It All Began, Again (A Rhapsody in Gunpowder) 9

Thicker Than Water (A Recipe for Fingers) 14

All the Little Wars (A Story About Cows) 26

The Single Woman (A Study in Gossip) 31

The Condor (A Flight of Principle) 44

Election Day (A Deconstruction of Guns) 50

The Girl (A Consideration of Muscle) 64

PART II

An Eye for a Song (A Quarrel of Drunkards) 73

A Love Story (An Inquiry into Attraction) 81

CONTENTS

The Revolutionary (A Movement in Hiding) 92

The Ghost (A Fit of Severance) 97

The Cut (A Sonata in Rose Red) 108

A Wednesday in April (A Celebration in a Blue Dress) . . . 117

The Bird in Repose (A Gathering of Assassins) 128

Moon of Honey (A Sunrise in Vermilion) 133

The River Ran Through It (A Sediment of Fish) 144

PART III

Sureshot (A Fable of Names) 151

The Mother of the Groom (A Soup of Accusations) 157

The National Front (A Gathering of Old Gossips) 169

The Fracture (A Migration of Bones) 175

The Hidden Republic (A Utopia in Apocalypse) 190

The Land of Salt (A Whisper of Marsh) 198

The Guerrilla Priest (A Murder of Revolutions) 208

The Frozen Melt (A Bolero in Absentia) 212

Pablito (A Baptism of Fire) 223

PART IV

The Marlboro Kid (An Adolescence in Dollars) 233

The Impossible (A Requiem of Betrayal) 238

El Encanto (A Conference on Forestry) 250

CONTENTS

The Widow (An Experiment in Matter) 254

The Hacienda (A Swim in Burlap) 264

Our Lady of the Minefield (A Confidence of Gunshot) . . . 269

El Rey (A Rooftop in Staccato) 287

Looking for El Dorado (A Return to the Motherland) . . . 291

Those Dead Old Men (A Mall of Nostalgia) 296

La Dama (An Epilogue with the Sergeant) 300

Acknowledgments 305

Works Consulted 309

Colombian History 1525–2025
A BRIEF TIMELINE

1525   The Conquista Española arrives in Colombia.

1819   Simón Bolívar establishes the Republic of Gran Colombia, which includes present-day Panama, Ecuador, and Venezuela.

1849   Liberal and Conservative parties founded.

1861–1865   The Liberal Party rules, church is separated from state, and regions operate autonomously.

1885   A 45-year stretch of Conservative rule begins.

1899–1902   The War of a Thousand Days, where over 180,000 people die from combat, illness, and starvation. Panama, with U.S. support, declares independence from Colombia.

1930   Liberals return to power.

1946   Conservative Mariano Ospina Pérez wins the presidency.

1948   Jorge Eliécer Gaitán is assassinated. The civil war known as the Violence begins.

1957   Colombians go on a national strike to overthrow the dictatorship of Gustavo Rojas Pinilla.

1958   Conservatives and Liberals form the National Front to share power. The Violence ends.

1964–1971   The National Liberation Army (ELN), the Popular Liberation Army (EPL), the Revolutionary Armed Forces of Colombia (FARC), the National Popular Alliance (ANAPO), and the M-19 guerrilla groups are all founded.

1978   Drug trafficking declared a national problem.

1982   The FARC initiates a cease-fire as peace talks commence with Colombian government.

1984   War on cartels follows assassination of Minister of Justice Rodrigo Lara Bonilla.

1985–1988   Right-wing paramilitary groups fight left-wing death squads run by cartels. No accurate death tolls exist.

1989   M-19 becomes a political party.

1993   Pablo Escobar shot and killed while on the run.

1997   Far-right paramilitary group the United Self-Defense Forces of Colombia (AUC) founded.

2015 The government works with the FARC to set up amnesty and truth commissions, as well as special courts to try internal war crimes.

2016 The government and the FARC sign a peace accord, ending 52 years of conflict. Colombian voters reject the deal in a national referendum. A revised deal is signed months later, without a referendum. FARC dissidents remain fighting, despite the group formally ceasing to exist.

2017 The ELN agrees to a cease-fire.

2022 Gustavo Petro, former member of the M-19, is elected president.

Family Trees

ANGARITA FAMILY

Trinidad (Trino) Angarita — Evangelina (Eva) Sarmiento

10 CHILDREN

Francisco, Alfonso, Helena, Guillermo, Esther,
Trinito, Lucila,* Hilda, Socorro, Gerardo

70 GRANDCHILDREN, INCLUDING ESTHER'S 7 CHILDREN

Lourdes, Alba, José Alfredo, Edgar Anibal,
Alberto, Nidia, and Elsa Yolima

Cousins of Esther Angarita *include* Leonor Angarita.

* died in early childhood

RUEDA FAMILY

José Rueda — Rosa Guarín

18 CHILDREN, 10 OF WHOM LIVED TO ADULTHOOD, INCLUDING

Anibal, Inés, and Tito Edmundo

72 GRANDCHILDREN

Cousins of Anibal Rueda *include* Domingo Rueda, Benito Rueda, and Tecla Rueda.

Una Nota Sobre Mi Abuela
(A PROLOGUE OF CARDS)

As a child, I once asked my grandmother why she did not forgive or forget, given her fierce Catholicism. We were playing cards on the bed in her large, white bedroom in Barranquilla, surrounded by faded portraits of old saints and half-burned candles.

I think if Jesus had been Colombian, she said, *He wouldn't have been so much on forgiveness.*

She looked at me closely.

You're not Colombian, she said. *You wouldn't understand that.*

*   *   *

My mother left Colombia in her twenties after she met my Mexican father on vacation in Buenos Aires. A few years later, I was born in Mexico City and when I was three months old, my family moved to Houston, Texas.

I am not Colombian by accent, by passport, by nationality.

But I am Colombian by blood. My father, who is Very Mexican, has a Colombian American father (a whole other story), making three of my four grandparents Colombian. I am more genetically Colombian than anything else. Still—my mother's family has always been the connection to my Colombian self, and at the center of the storm that is my mother's family stands my grandmother.

*   *   *

I have been trying to make sense of my grandmother since I can remember.

The Colombian grandmother of my childhood summers was funny, mean, pious, and hard—despite being tremendously sensitive in her own way. My grandmother was silent. My grandmother offered hugs, but never longer than necessary. She was a woman of stillness and efficiency, on horseback or comfortably seated under an umbrella on the beach, the focus of every photograph.

Spending over half my childhood summers in Colombia, I was often a tourist on my family's coastal terrain, more camera than denizen, forever trying to reclaim something my mother left behind when she met and married my father.

To my deeply Colombian grandmother, I am her eldest and most foreign grandchild. I am the daughter of the one who left country and family. I am her only grandchild who speaks Colombian Spanish with a Mexican accent.

My mother has theories for everything. It is her way. She believes that because I grew up so far away from Colombia, I see her better than everyone. My eleven cousins on that side of the family all report different interactions with her, some in which she is far more tender. But unlike my cousins, I am out of her reach when it comes to day-to-day care and criticism. And because of this distance, my mother asserts, I interact with her as she is. But it is because of this distance, I argue back, that I don't know her, not really.

*   *   *

THE VIOLENCE

As my mother often points out, my grandmother set the example—she left her family first.

She and my grandfather took their children away from the small villages their ancestors had built back in the sixteenth century in the mountains of Santander, in northeast Colombia. She left and headed for the safety of the coast, along with untold thousands of other Santandereanos, doing whatever was necessary to survive, as Colombians always have since the beginning of time.

It was the aftermath of civil war that pushed my grandparents away from their homelands in the 1960s—a conflict so violent, they simply called it that: the Violence.

This is where her story begins, my mother once told me.

Not when she was born? I asked. *Her childhood?*

My mother laughed and left the answer to my questions, like so many others, just hanging in the air.

*   *   *

One night in the summer of 1995, relaxed in her overstuffed living room chair, one of my mother's sisters, Aunt Nidia, declared that during the Violence of 1948, my grandmother learned to internalize all her emotions, and she never stopped.

Don't underestimate trauma, Aunt Nidia said, *even if we don't call it trauma, it's still trauma.*

Even at twelve, I knew that Colombia was a dangerous place. I knew about the guerrilla.[*] I had heard about Pablo Escobar, cartels, and the cocaine trade. As a Colombian-by-blood trying to function in an American middle school, I was keenly aware of

---

[*] Here and throughout, the word "guerrilla," though singular in (English) form, is intended in the plural sense of Spanish "la guerrilla."

the association between Colombia and violence, as were most of my peers with their drug lord jokes.

But I never knew why so much conflict existed in Colombia particularly, or really anything else about the original disputes that yielded so much bloodshed. I certainly never knew that my grandparents had left the mountains where their ancestors had lived for hundreds of years because of a particularly awful conflict—which means something in a country that's had at least eight civil wars, more than a dozen local wars, three coups d'état, and countless uprisings.

My mother agreed with Nidia.

Your grandmother had dreams before the Violence. She was beautiful, smart, with long and wavy brown hair to her waist. When she was a girl—she wanted to be a doctor, something that wasn't impossible even during that time. If your grandmother had been born in another country or even another year . . . But she wasn't.

My grandmother lacked options, my mother asserted, *she is someone who is the way she is because of the circumstances that dictated her life. I know that not everyone who grew up during that time made the same choices, but given who she was, when she was, and how she was,* my mother insisted that my grandmother never really had a chance to be any different.

My aunt chimed in, *Colombians do not forgive, and your grandmother is the most Colombian of Colombians.*

My mother nodded vigorously.

My aunt continued: *She never forgave her country for forcing her to leave home—or her countrymen for not being more civilized. She never even forgave your grandfather.*

We sat in silence for a few seconds that felt like hours. The subject of my grandfather had that effect.

Eventually, I spoke.

Even blood cannot forgive, I said, quoting something my grandmother had once said, understanding maybe a little more about my motherland than I had before.

Exactly, said my mother. My aunt nodded.

My mother ruffled my hair a little bit, *You've never sounded more Colombian.*

* * *

My grandmother keeps a blade on her tongue, sharpened and meant to draw blood, even, or especially, when she expresses love. She speaks in aphorisms and with the weight of history.

There is a violence to my grandmother. Not a physical violence—she is not one to quickly raise a hand, although I've heard stories that she pinches harder than fate.

My grandmother's violence is more subtle than a fist. It dwells in her silence, in her absence, in what she won't say, in what she won't do. It will emerge, quietly, in a small statement, a little quip, a phrase—something designed to both harm and help, an expression of concern or an explanation that hurts a little too much.

My grandmother keeps her resentments just below boiling—somehow scarier when fully in control. My grandmother believes in Hell, and my grandmother also firmly believes that everyone that has ever wronged her belongs there, roasting slowly. My grandmother plans to outlive all her enemies, mostly all the men that wronged her, and so far, she's on track to bury them all.

* * *

Esther Angarita Sarmiento, called *Pita Esther* by her grandchildren (a corruption of "Abuelita"), is and has always been a survivor, beautiful and sharp, unknowable and impossible to fully grasp. Like her country. And like her country, she endures—through deceptions, woundings, and tremendous loss. Both my grandmother and Colombia are a puzzle I will never fully unravel—both parts of me that feel less like the facts of my origin and more like myths.

But I also know that she was once a girl. She was once a young woman with dreams of becoming a healer. She had crushes and went to dances. She walked along the mountainside with her friends, splashed her feet in creeks, gossiped relentlessly, and laughed at silly things the boys did.

She was only twenty when the Violence began.

* * *

Dreams change, my grandmother told me once after beating me at another hand of cards. *Dreams change when they have to*, she continued as I scooped up the cards.

"A lo hecho, pecho," she said, a common phrase that translates roughly to "what is done is done" with a tiny hint of resignation. I nodded. She shuffled the cards silently for a minute.

That's how life is, she said, before dealing another hand. She looked me over before finishing her thought. *At least in Colombia.*

PART I

*

I firmly believe that all of us here today, and all of us who belong to this unfortunate generation, can say with pride that we have witnessed Colombia's last civil war. Our grandchildren, who will be born after this cycle of horrors, will find it hard to understand what kind of insanity led to such bloodshed among brothers. But we will be able to tell them, from our old age, exactly how and why the last representatives of this cruel and intransigent political fanaticism had the sad privilege of witnessing the final hurricane in all its terrible devastation. It lasted over a thousand days and left nothing standing, either materially or morally, as it hurled Colombians into furious battle against one another. We may not find absolution from our descendants, but if the fatal inheritance does not reach them, it will be because we took all the blame upon ourselves, so to spare them.

—Rafael Uribe Uribe,
December 31, 1902

How It All Began, Again
(A RHAPSODY IN GUNPOWDER)

Bogotá, 1948

A nation has at least one crucial moment in every cycle of its history—a moment in which a hope is extinguished for a generation—the kind of rare moment that defines its history and the memory of its people. In Colombia, it was April 9, 1948: the assassination of Gaitán.

That April day, the newly minted leader of the Partido Liberal, and the projected winner of the upcoming presidential election, Jorge Eliécer Gaitán Ayala, left his law office to have lunch with friends in Bogotá. The day was cold, but Gaitán did not wear a hat, bareheaded as the clouds descended on the city.

*   *   *

Earlier that morning, the Ninth Pan-American Conference met in the north part of the capital to discuss and sign the charter for the Organization of American States, a political coalition of the Western Hemisphere sponsored by the United States. To welcome so many foreign dignitaries, a venerable who's who of North and South American politics, Colombian president Ospina Pérez ordered trash removed, streets washed, buildings painted, decorations placed, and new street signs positioned. Everyone sported fresh uniforms, from the president to the policemen to the shoeshine men on the street corners.

But underneath the facade of elegance and refinement, there remained the ugly realities of President Ospina's regime. His Conservative Party sponsored the flagrant corruption of the time, as had the Liberal Party when they held power years before—all to the benefit of large landowners, businessmen, and industrialists. Inflation and unemployment were high, which meant hunger for the jobless poor in the city. The threat of starvation, plus the idleness that can accompany lack of employment, led to angry and sustained protests for months before the conference.

People were energized enough to organize; a labor movement began to form—and they wanted Gaitán to lead the charge.

Jorge Eliécer Gaitán Ayala, affectionately called "the Doctor" for his doctorate in political science, represented a better option for the disenfranchised and for any kind of systemic change. Gaitán's speeches took the working poor into account, something few politicians had ever done in a country ruled by a wealthy elite.

In the weeks before the political Western Hemisphere descended on Bogotá, President Ospina responded to the street protests and speeches with summary executions of petty criminals. In justifying his public displays to the press, Ospina cited the inherent connection between assembly and riot, effectively convicting and killing the poor for protesting their conditions. The bodies of instigators hanged beneath freshly unfurled banners—a warning to anyone intent on disrupting the peace.

The crowds still gathered, for Gaitán and for change, despite the Conservative president's executions.

I am not a man, I am a people, Gaitán said before thousands, just days before his assassination.

*   *   *

It was a Friday and Gaitán was scheduled to stand before a delegation of political youth to explain that the struggle of the ordinary man was the struggle against the oligarchy, *and, boy, do we have an oligarchy.*

He didn't make his meeting. The bullets found him at 1:15 p.m. exiting a building, while speaking with friends, surrounded by dozens of admirers. Gaitán toppled mid-sentence before the third clap of bullets. As a woman shouted *the Doctor is gone, where is the Doctor, what has happened to the Doctor*, his words wilted into roasted leaves carried by the wind. The body-becoming-corpse was transported by compatriots to the hospital before Gaitán could touch concrete.

The remaining witnesses scanned the scene cinematically to the right toward the younger man holding the gun, the man in the faded taupe pinstripe suit, broken yellow shoes, and tattered felt hat—the man with the nervous eyes—Juan Roa Sierra. The clock displayed 1:16 p.m.

The man holding the discharged revolver in the face of an angry crowd—this man had a decision to make. Should he run? The crowd lined up, moved forward, ready for something.

As the smoke cleared, they screamed *assassin!*—and more and more bodies joined the throng, more and more whispers filled in the void, and more and more eyes fell on him as their fists sharpened. The bodies, so tightly packed together, ran toward the alleged gunman in an attempt to counter through flesh what had already been wrought with bullets. Sleeves were rolled up to intent elbows, rocks, and other makeshift weapons gathered in lightly tanned hands, sweat collected on furrowed brows; the sweet musk of surprise and purpose fueled the charge. The crowd paraded toward the gunman. Attempted to swallow him.

The police could not initially proceed through the swelling bodies, could not make their way to Juan Roa Sierra. The anxious little man holding the gun in his left hand shook. They—the cops, the people, the reporters—saw the gunpowder coating the lines where Juan Roa Sierra used to smile, his unwashed and unshaven face haloed with the black fire soot, the hint of an ashen snowstorm floating around him. No one asked for confirmation, no one doubted that he was the one who pulled the trigger.

The man tried to run, pushing his way through, but only got as far as the arms of the law. He screamed, *Don't let them kill me*.

It was 1:17 p.m.

* * *

The police did try to save him. They shoved the alleged killer into a pharmacy and hid the young man behind the countertop, behind shelves stocked with imported bottles of Coca-Cola and cream deodorants. They locked the door, took Juan Roa Sierra's gun, and tied his hands behind his back; they waited patiently for the crowd to disperse, watched the man pray.

But the crowd had no such intention. The iron-framed windows could only take so much pressure and soon the shutters and walls ceased to resist; the alleged assassin stood alone as the officers surrendered him to the masses.

They feasted. The crowd carried him outside, tore his limbs off, danced on his mutilated torso, and placed his body upon theirs, wearing the mask of what they had devoured. No one killed Juan Roa Sierra, because everyone killed him. The crowd's arms encircled him, even as they crushed him—the embrace of a nation.

And when it was over, even his shadow fractured and rendered unidentifiable by the overzealous mass, the crowd demanded more. A hunger for vengeance had ignited. Street vendors and radio stations began shouting recipes to satisfy the appetite: *¡We all know who did this! ¡The Conservatives! ¡The Liberals! ¡The Church! ¡El presidente nacional! ¡El presidente municipal! ¡Angarita! ¡Duarte! ¡García! Pérez! ¡Rueda! ¡Your neighbor!* And that's how Juan Roa Sierra found himself in the belly of Colombia—thousands infected with his madness; the memory of a generation imprinted with his scuffed, yellow shoes.

* * *

At a hospital several hundred yards away, medics worked on the candidate. But the task proved fruitless. Gaitán couldn't be saved either. He died, as did thousands more within hours, along with the dreams Gaitán inspired.

His death, and the death of the people's hope, unleashed a new wrath, blind and voracious, eager to consume.

The Violence had begun.

Thicker Than Water
(A RECIPE FOR FINGERS)

Santander, 1948

Esther Angarita Sarmiento did not imagine the nation in chaos when she decided to take a break from her accounting, but there it was—rioting thick on the airwaves. She listened to the death of Jorge Eliécer Gaitán Ayala announced on the radio, and soon after, a broadcast of the radio's call to arms in the capital, a long journey from where she sat. She twirled her pencil, hardly a machete.

Bogotá was under siege from within. As the Bogotazo, as it would be known afterward, raged, the twenty-year-old brunette contemplated what these deaths would mean to her and to her family. To the life she'd known. To the accounting she'd begun before she heard the news. That's when wars begin—on ordinary days for ordinary people busy with ordinary tasks.

Esther Angarita Sarmiento—the daughter of Trinidad Angarita and Evangelina Sarmiento—was a practical young woman. She was never known for her sentimentality. But she understood the passions necessary to lift a machete, even as she knew the impracticality of it. A fence broken in the name of a righteous cause still required work and time to fix—and this wasn't her first encounter with a broken fence.

THE VIOLENCE

My grandmother, like her three sisters, inherited the Angarita disposition. They were calm and watchful, communicating more with a glance than words. They kept their feelings close to the chest, a by-product of a culture where opinions voiced aloud could be deadly. She understood from a young age that every election cycle brought conflict—and survival in a country perpetually at war with itself rewarded the quiet and prudent. Esther learned this from her father, a man whose first memories were of the War of a Thousand Days at the turn of the last century, a different civil war. Don Trino had survived his fair share of conflicts with Conservatives by keeping his head down.

She turned off the radio before anyone else heard about the uprisings in Bogotá. She decided not to make a fuss out of the assassination. Politics churned her brothers' tempers—they had inherited the feisty Sarmiento disposition from her mother's side of the family. News of the presidential candidate's murder, the riots in Bogotá—all of that would be the talk of a hundred tomorrows. What moments of peace remained needed to be hers. If she kept quiet, she could perhaps delay history for a few minutes.

She continued making notes in the ledger. The accounting still demanded completion, and her father, Don Trino Angarita, depended on her. *Esthercita*, as he called her, was his *right hand*, a phrase he repeated often to her deep pleasure.

The most dextral of Don Trino's daughters frowned as she checked the births column. Too many were stillborn that month. She went back a few pages and started counting the number of dead calves in the previous month, and then the one before that. The numbers belied normalcy. She suspected the overseer of stealing the newborn cattle and reporting them dead, a popular scam and one that was hard to prove, especially once the evidence was sold for meat. She made a note on the ledger, "Revisar partos esta semana personalmente." She would go herself, although the note was for her father. She imagined he'd be distracted by the news from Bogotá and would let this theft go unpunished.

For Esther, even the possibility felt outrageous. A thief deserved a penalty. Some fences do require breaking, that they may be fixed stronger.

*   *   *

Esther continued her work well into the afternoon at the dining room table in Mancarique, the newest Angarita property and the family's home, just outside the hamlet of Cabrera. The closest big city was Socorro, deep in the mountains of the department (the equivalent to a state) of Santander—a half day's journey. It was a three-day journey to Bogotá in 1948. My grandmother often told me of the trips she would take to the capital—by land to Barrancabermeja and then down the Magdalena River on a barge until the train at La Esperanza. Bogotá seemed far away enough from her in Mancarique.

Mancarique had been her father's dream, and the care Don Trino lavished on it showed. Don Trino designed the main building at the finca himself and commissioned specialized tile for the roof from Bucaramanga, the capital of Santander. He oversaw the painting of the cement walls and the installation of wiring. He outfitted several rooms with water closets purchased in Bogotá and imported from England, a luxury few in rural Colombia could afford. He supervised the building of every annex and directed his own laborers on proper bricklaying technique.

Don Trino took pride in planning each stage of the homestead, refusing to rely on local architects or contract builders, as the methods commonly used in Cabrera hadn't changed much since the seventeenth century. He hated paying people for things he could do better himself. Don Trino was quick to give anyone a lesson on the newest techniques in masonry, plumbing, and engineering, all studied from imported magazines.

Every inch of the property was designed to produce, to grow, to feed. The tobacco he'd found growing naturally around the main corrals he transplanted into a large field behind the house and then planted sugarcane behind that. Lining the perimeter of every field were trees loaded with mandarin oranges. The pastures on either side belonged to the goats and, more importantly, the cows.

The Angaritas were dairy farmers by trade, although tobacco and sugarcane supported the family when the cows could not. Don Trino kept the household on animal time: a farmer's breakfast before dawn, a heavy lunch before noon, and a light dinner before retiring to a game of cards or dominoes in the evening. Seasons were divided up by rain patterns, the sugar burn, and the many ranching festivals that demanded Don Trino's attention.

Esther took the times in between meals to fulfill her duties, her afternoons busy with accounting and the small pleasures of balanced columns. She loved the sounds of the house, the clinking of the kitchen girls preparing small porcelain cups of black coffee, large burlap bags of corn flour scraping the floor of the walk-in pantry adjacent to the kitchen, and the symphony of insects warming up for the evening's performance. Esther heard everything and acknowledged nothing.

On that April day, she turned off the radio, blocked out sights and sounds, and settled into her favorite part of the afternoon, her posture perfect in the straight-backed wooden chair as she struggled to name the day's newborn calves—she wrote down "Flor" and quickly erased it, remembering that that was the name of the new kitchen girl, and she didn't want the new girl, who wasn't used to Esther's quirks, to think her rude for naming a cow after her.

As the afternoon began to fade, she thought about her country, despite her attempts not to. She felt the breath of history on her neck—she could sense how big the moment was. She chose to find haven in a ledger instead.

*   *   *

She rewrote the girl's name, Flor, on the ledger, having changed her mind and decided it wasn't rude at all—she would explain that it was in fact a welcoming sentiment—a habit Esther cultivated as a child, naming animals after the people that mattered in her life.

Cow number five hundred and fifty-four, a Holstein with a large black head, now named Flor. She rose to tell the girl the good news but found upon entering the kitchen that Flor the Person, who had been working since long before dawn, had retired before evening to the collection of small rooms behind the kitchen reserved for the house workers. Esther would not interrupt her; news of Flor the Cow could wait until morning.

Esther returned to the dining room where she continued naming beasts, waiting for her brothers and father to come home—to see what they'd say, how'd they take the news on the radio. The men in Santander were known for their fire. It was their reactions that mattered.

The Violence, like all wars before it, was a man's war.

*   *   *

The pickup truck hid in a cloud of dust as it traveled down the road into Mancarique, Don Trino at the wheel and his namesake, blue-eyed Trinito, hanging out the window, waving and hollering to Esther as she came out to meet them by the large wooden gate.

Her other brothers had been to town on horseback for business; yet, by the setting of the evening sun they trickled in: first Francisco, then Guillermo, and finally Alfonso with little Gerardo, who even at ten went out with his older brothers and helped with the finca's operations. All of them, down to Gerardito, were carbon-copied replicas of Don Trino—tall and angular, fair and stern, thin lips prone to stillness—future landowners and farmers in long pants, linen shirts, sharp-toed boots, and fedora hats.

Trinito and Alfonso brought out tables loaded with crates holding dusty, long-stored bottles of aguardiente, resting calmly on the long veranda that wrapped around two sides of the house—to my grandmother's relief, as this calm meant the men were yet unspoiled by the national news.

Friends, uncles, and beloved workmen arrived; horses used to bearing barrel-chested, sunburned men waited patiently as the day's heat relaxed into the cool of evening. The riders wiped the sweat from their brows before resting on quickly assembled hammocks and steel bar stools, rocking chairs, and turned-over crates, talking day-old politics from the morning's newspapers, and drinking water, coffee, and whatever other libation was within reach.

"Esther!" Don Trino called for her before he called for his wife; he knew his daughter would be closer and less fastidious about doing him a favor. Doña Eva was playing cards with her other daughters and womenfolk at this hour, and Esther moved quicker when summoned.

"Sí?"

"Unos dedos, por favor!"

Esther walked around the terrace wall into the outdoor kitchen, tying her shoulder-blade-length hair into a loose bun at the nape of her neck, knowing her curls refused to be dominated. Yet as the tight strands inevitably escaped the ribbon's hold, she smiled. *Hair is as stubborn as the head it rests on*, her mother would say.

She asked the older muchacha, Ubelina, to gather straw for the stove and to fetch the flint lighter as Esther rolled up her sleeves and tied an apron tightly around her twenty-three-inch waist. She would make the dedos quicker than the old woman, and she knew the men needed food soon at the rate they drank.

The fresh, wet cheese sliced easily as she rolled it into small-sized portions, lightly coating them in corn flour and butter, until she quickly folded the bottom creating a perfectly detached digit. The old woman lit the stove and soon the pan was hot enough to drop in the forty cheese fingers, frying them lightly in their own fatty perspiration, the sour smell of the fresh cheese replaced with the warm and buttery smell of frying. A linen napkin on the plate to absorb the grease, and the merienda was done.

This is how Esther liked her life, quiet and normal in its routine, without the world intruding. She had little time before the news reached her brothers. But she remembers the calm of the kitchen after she plated the fried food, and she remembers thinking *maybe the war won't reach us here.*

* * *

The noise emanating from the veranda ceased for a minute and then the radio bellowed the day's news, and she heard it all again, this time listening to it differently: uprisings in Bogotá. Thousands plundering and pillaging throughout the city over the death of Gaitán. ¡Bogotazo!

Esther thought they used the same announcers on the radio for soccer games as they did for war—everyone so excitable, conspiracies and accusations filtered through the broadcaster's voice and the kitchen's steady hum. Hundreds dead and the toll rising. Estimates claimed thousands more would be dead by morning.

Esther worried about her brothers. Each on their own could be trouble, but together, they only amplified each other's volatility. The voices discussing the news soon overcame the volume of the bulletin.

Francisco, always with an explosive look in his eye, joined forces with the more reserved Guillermo in arguing with Don Trino, the energetic and efficient Trinito, and bookish Alfonso about whether Cabrera was safe. Francisco insisted that looting and civil war were the only options. *We should go to town!* Don Trino argued for composure—*It's not knocking on our front door yet.*

Don Trino reminded his sons that by staying patient, they had survived the fighting that took place after the last elections—and the even worse post-election violence of 1930. Things looked bad at the time, but they'd defended the homestead and the other two smaller properties with everything they had, gun and pitchfork alike, yet staying quiet until called upon to act. They could do it again if they had to.

The need for and price of milk would not drop, and the dairy cooperative didn't care about party affiliations—Liberal milk was just as good. And because of that, the family still ate.

But the boys were getting excited. *Too excited*, thought Esther, knowing how dangerous and contagious rioting could be in Santander. When Francisco began to yell "Muerte a los que mataron Gaitán! ¡Muerte a los Godos!" Esther quickly loaded the plates onto the tray and called for someone else to make the delivery. The conversation on the front terrace was too risky, she couldn't bear witness to her brothers' hot heads.

She sent the old woman Ubelina out with the dedos and headed across the courtyard to her bedroom on the other side of the main house, an addition built to lodge the older girls, completing the K-shaped complex of buildings.

She made her way through the maze of dressers and tables in the room she shared with her younger sisters to the far side where her bed stood beneath the window. She loved feeling the draft first on the hot evenings and the predawn breeze before her father rose in the morning.

Her sisters and her mother, Doña Evangelina, were in the sitting room down the hall, playing cards and drinking hot coffee as they complained about the coolness of the night. The women drank coffee like water, and water like medicine to stave off heat and dehydration. Esther could hear her older, married sister Helena's gruff laughter through the walls and considered joining the card game, but tonight she decided she didn't want to ruin their good time with the news. She preferred to linger in her worries—about the murder in the capital, the brewing panic in her stomach about the disasters to come, and the calves they'd lost.

Curiously, all the dead calves were male. That was good and bad. Not a loss of future milk revenue, but a hit to the slaughterhouse and stud income. And now with this violence popping up, that was another excuse for the overseer to "lose" cattle and fudge the numbers. She could hear the excuses: Because the family is Liberal, a stray bullet killed five calves, fences were knocked down, and half the herd wandered off the property. And who could argue? War gives an excuse for mischief. *No, this was not good at all*, thought Esther.

She decided to wake up early the next morning to make sure all the livestock had been properly and clearly branded with the initials of the Angarita Sarmiento family, a carefully marked and stylized A and S within a line drawing of the North Star, as well as each cow's number and weight recorded. She would make sure everything was counted and recounted before the day ended. That overseer would have no excuse for his losses, and she would deduct the cost of the calves from his pay if she had to. Someone had to foot the bill, and it wasn't going to be her father.

With that, Esther brushed her hair for half an hour, a hundred and fifty strokes as she did every night, changed into a long, breathing nightgown, and prayed, before she slid into her blankets and promptly fell asleep.

* * *

It was her younger sister Hilda's scream that woke her, along with the sound of her father's revolver being fired. Esther jumped out of bed and quickly changed out of her nightgown as she rushed outdoors to be of assistance. By the time she reached the front of the house, the whole family had gathered with the workers, crowding around the body of the overseer of the Angarita family's previous homestead, a smaller finca called El Parador. This was the overseer Esther had planned on monitoring, and now he was a tattered mess of a man.

He had been dragged, that much was obvious, the rope still wrapped around his wrists had been cut from a knot tied to the back of a truck. *Probably dragged for a while*, Don Trino offered to his sons, and then quickly asked the boys to push the women back inside the house. Doña Evangelina kissed her daughters on the forehead and pushed them back along the corridors. Esther remained to no one's protests.

Don Trino squatted to get a closer look and inspect the damage. There was no mistaking what had happened to the man attached: The overseer's eyes had been scooped out, his arms chopped off with a machete, his skin coated with rough salt crystals, and a piece of parchment clung to his chest by needle and thread. Francisco wondered aloud if the note had been sewn before or after the overseer had been killed. *Death to Liberals* scrawled neatly in Palmer-style handwriting.

Leave, Angaritas printed hastily underneath the elaborate cursive. The overseer was a warning, a warning from the Conservatives in Cabrera, a warning with no eyes and a preserved hide. As Esther read the note out loud, Doña Eva crossed herself.

"¡Queé desastre!"

* * *

Later that night, before the cocks crowed and the sunlight filtered in through the low clouds of Santander, Esther watched her mother sit the hysterical widow of the overseer in the rocking chair on the veranda, mere feet away from her disfigured husband. Esther heard her mother promise to care for the widow and the children left behind, saying there would always be work for her with the family at El Parador. They could offer a proper burial and a place at their table when they stopped by Mancarique, but no more than that. They were the owners of the land, but they were not the big landowners who yelled the loudest at the local meetings. Even with a handful of small fincas, the Angaritas did not have enough money to stop working the land themselves.

Don Trino, and his favorite son, Trinito, covered the body with the guest-room sheets. Guillermo and Francisco loaded the corpse into the bed of their own pickup, the dusty red Ford Don Trino loved more than drink and cards combined, and drove the body directly to the church. They knew, even that night, that the police would not help. Doña Eva recited a prayer for the dead and held the shoulders of the overseer's wife, as the woman contracted into herself.

*   *   *

This is the image my grandmother Esther described to me when I asked her what the Violence meant to her: the body of a man she didn't trust, covered in beautiful sheets she'd once helped embroider, dead because her father voted what Colombians designated Liberal red in a country with a Conservative blue administration.

These are the details that remain with her of the night the overseer died. She remembers staying up until dawn, wondering who the family would have to hire to replace the dragged man, before she changed into a proper shirt and calculated how much this loss was going to cost the family.

And, oh, my grandmother told me over sixty-five years later, *oh how angry* she was that she never caught that overseer stealing, never got to fire him for his thievery, never got to deliver him the comeuppance he deserved.

The Violence had robbed her of something—and at the risk of defending her insensitivity to the man's tragic death, I understood her reaction. To get what she wanted, the man would have to be alive, and the violence toward him would have to be undone. A civil war made that impossible. History took away her closure, her sense of satisfaction at solving a minor accounting mystery.

Pita Esther, I asked her, *do you remember the overseer's name?*

No, she will respond, stirring her coffee even though she hadn't added sugar or cream, simply preventing the sediment of grains from settling. *I don't remember his name—there is no point in honoring thieves and people who cause mischief, no matter how sadly or terribly they die.*

No, she'll repeat to herself before laughing like a thunderclap, *I only remember the names of my cows, and I never named one after him.*

All the Little Wars
(A STORY ABOUT COWS)

Bogotá, 1948

Ten hours after the riots began, Bogotá quieted enough to begin an inventory of its destruction. Over three thousand people died that evening. Small skirmishes in the next twenty-four hours would kill another untold hundreds. Funeral parlors could not take in so many bodies; ever resourceful, city officials ordered the digging of mass graves.

Reactions across the country varied. On the Caribbean coast, after some initial riots, the people returned to their rumbas, blithely indifferent to the happenings of the interior, as usual. In the large mountain cities, like Medellín and Cali, larger riots broke out, pointed referendums on the elite.

But in the rural Colombia interior—the farmlands of Santander and Antioquia and Valle del Cauca—the owners of the land began to worry.

* * *

On the morning of April 10, 1948, the owners of the land had something to say.

They came on horseback, or in pickup trucks, wide in their hat brims and gaits. Before anything could be said about politics or death or whatever happened in Bogotá, the cows had needs: to be milked, to be reunited with the calves, to be vaccinated, to be rotated from one enclosure to another, to be weighed, to be prepared for sale and transport, to be inspected for disease. Once the cattle had settled into their pastures and trucks were loaded with cantaros bound for the dairy cooperatives, then the discussions could begin.

Some of the owners were compassionate, because they hated war and politics, they hated the absurdity of it all, or they hated the inhumanity of the violence. Some of the owners were cold because they understood that war demanded it.

The workmen waited for the owners of the land to explain what they already knew—the landowners needed these men to protect what was there. Would they come to a meeting that evening? With their families?

But not until the end of the workday, of course.

Later, the workmen and their families gathered at the owner's home. Plates stacked high with sausages, ripe fruit, and rice dishes stood next to delicate pastries and trays of hot chocolate with fresh cheese ready for dipping. As the people enjoyed a free and fine meal, the owners of the land took their place next to the police. Both the owners and the law looked well fed and prosperous, polished, and slick with authority.

* * *

At Conservative meetings, behind the police and landowners stood the priests, ready to bless a cause so righteous. Part of the Conservative agenda was to create a "Catholic order," so the clergy, with some exceptions in a very Catholic nation, became natural allies.

The workmen watched carefully as the men in power fraternized in the cooling, evening air. When the speeches began, stories of Liberal aggression and overreach abounded.

Yes, the Liberals wanted to punish the Conservatives for the death of Gaitán. Yes, the Liberals in many towns had rioted, killed some Conservatives in retaliation. Yes, churches had burned. Yes, they should have another plate of food.

The working men nodded, agreeing with the landowners who determined their livelihood while filling their bellies with sancocho, yuca, and steak. The women listened carefully, and behind them stood the children—black-haired and brown-eyed, barefooted, and full of energy. The women and the children exchanged looks with their men. Soon, the Conservative landowners came to the crux of their arguments.

The speeches all sounded the same. The Liberals let socialism into Colombia. They took the country into a world war that had nothing to do with Colombia and that did nothing for Colombia. *We must fight to save the soul of our nation—a Catholic, God-fearing soul. The Liberals want our land—to take this land, where you live and work—and they want to take the fruits of your labor for lazy socialists.*

The workmen nodded yes and looked at their plates, a sign of the fertility of Colombian soil. Despite all the wars, the fruit (lulo, mora, maracuyá) still came, and the people still ate. No one starved in rural Colombia—the land had always provided for the people that lived there.

But even fresh fruit could be picked off the trees and carted off on new train lines to the cities. If the Liberals proved to be as terrible as the landowners had said, it would end their way of life.

Look what they did to the capital.

The owners calculated that the workmen probably had family in the city—family they could not reach in the immediate aftermath of the riots.

You know the old saying: Either they take us, or we take them.

The old refrain asserts that Colombians view the world as one for the taking. The workers immediately understood what the bosses meant—the Conservatives were not going to let the Liberals take anything, not even another breath.

The owners of the land implored their workers, *it was time to fight.*

A happy landowner could do a lot for an ordinary man—rent him a piece of property, let him grow and raise his own sustenance, change his life. Once a worker aligned with a Conservative family, they became Conservative by association, as did Liberals.

The workers looked to their wives and children for permission to sharpen their machetes, for permission to kill their neighbors, for permission to die, as they, like their fathers and their grandfathers, had done before. Immunity would be granted, both on earth and in heaven, confirmed the police and the clergy, for any incidental crimes that motivated Liberals to leave. Small stipends would also be granted, confirmed the landowners, for anyone willing to take up the cause. For many in Colombia, those "small stipends" could mean education, and thus, upward mobility for their children.

The thousands of workers who said *yes* were given pay, weapon, and purpose, but they were denied uniform or recognition, rechristened "paramilitaries." Official sanction meant something else entirely—no, the Conservatives wanted an army they could deny to international eyes, a counterrevolution, working hands against working hands.

* * *

Before the destruction in Bogotá calmed, the wealthy and nervous Liberal landowners began to leave their lands. They understood that the riots started after Gaitán's death would inevitably provoke a violent Conservative backlash—there was always a violent Conservative backlash.

The workmen watched as their bosses packed up everything of value. They watched as the new sedans and pickup trucks, imported from the United States and Europe, departed, leaving behind expansive fincas. They watched as the sleek cars drove away toward the safety that cities granted the wealthy.

Before they left, the Liberal owners explained to their workmen, to the workmen's wives and children (just as black-haired and brown-eyed and barefooted as the Conservative ones), that they had to make a choice—stay on the property or venture out on their own. The workers nodded and began doing complex augury.

Staying on Liberal land carried great risk. Access to weapons was inconsistent; some fought with sticks, others with military-grade weaponry. Most fincas were hours away from any type of doctor or reinforcements.

The workers' wives—who often labored in the owner's homes, cleaning and cooking and raising the children of others, children who would one day also own the land—made their own calculations. As the owners planned their travels down the mountain roads, these women considered the logistics of leaving during a time of violence with their own children and whatever possessions they carried. Some followed the owners into the cities, others stayed.

Some of the owners were good and wanted to stay to help defend their fincas. Other owners could not afford to leave, having too small an operation and not enough cash to start life anew. Those owners took up arms, next to the workers, ready to defend whatever was theirs.

This was a war of waiting, but it was clear enough in Santander: The Conservatives would come.

The Single Woman
(A STUDY IN GOSSIP)

Santander, 1949

The gossips gathered in front of the church. That was the whole point of arriving early, to congregate before congregating.

The church in Cabrera had new pews installed in 1946. By early 1949, almost a year into the Violence, the color had deepened into a rich brown. Families etched their good names into little gold plaques that were attached to the sides facing the aisles. The building's humble stone exterior belied the gilded baroque altar within, much like the families themselves, humble and respectful in their attire and worship, even as their humbler servants stood in the back. Generations of violence had taught most people to be circumspect about their wealth, a muted luxury initially indistinguishable from the ordinary—old Colombian money has always hidden itself well.

The old church pews had been reconfigured into benches that lined the path between the church and the post office. My grandmother loved these benches, a place to sit and listen to gossip without having to participate. No one liked a single woman with too many opinions, but a single woman who simply wanted to sit in the shade was less noticeable, even as she couldn't help but overhear the gossip. She arrived early for precisely this reason.

My grandmother Esther heard the name Oliva Gómez Camargo as soon as she stepped into the conversation before mass. She didn't even make it to the bench; as she stepped her foot off the car, Leonor (second cousin, twice removed), greeted Esther breathlessly with the latest updates on local deaths and disappearances. Oliva Gómez Camargo had gone missing.

* * *

Oliva Gómez Camargo was not a stranger. She was my grandmother's confidant and childhood playmate, someone Esther sat next to in Sunday school until third grade.

Oliva and my grandmother shared secrets, braided one another's hair, and exchanged the looks and laughter of intimate friendship. *If Oliva Gómez Camargo could disappear*, my grandmother told me, *it meant that I could disappear. We came from the same place and walked the same paths and loved the same movie stars.*

As soon as she heard the news of Oliva's disappearance, Esther decided to say nothing about Oliva and her secret boyfriend—to keep her mouth firmly shut. If she told anyone that Oliva had a boyfriend, who knew what would happen to him? What would happen to Oliva's reputation? What damage Esther could accidentally do?

During a civil war gossip had deadly consequences. My grandmother has always said, "por la boca muere." In considering how fish die—hooked by their greedy, gaping mouths—one can hopefully avoid the same fate by remaining tight-lipped.

* * *

Oliva Gómez Camargo disappeared on an ordinary morning. She'd gone to fetch a shawl on her front porch and never returned.

The ensuing week had been fraught with search parties and rumors. The men in the Gómez Camargo family had ridden from door to door, gate to gate, elaborate homestead to rural shack, trying to find her or any information related to her disappearance.

The family offered money. The family offered land. The family offered jewelry. No one knew what happened, even though everyone believed the worst.

Women were being taken by Conservatives those days—it wasn't safe to be a woman alone. Especially from a good Liberal family. Days after Oliva Gómez Camargo disappeared, all anyone could do during mass was cast their eyes at her family's empty pew.

Cabrera was a predominantly Liberal town, but just barely so. The Conservatives that lived in the area attended mass early in the morning, and the Liberals attended the services well after the Godos, as the Conservatives were called, had gone home for their breakfasts. The Conservatives, while backed by the Catholic Church, dared not infringe on worship, even in the middle of armed conflict, so Esther made it to mass safely enough to hear the latest news.

Even if she didn't want to be a part of the idling tongues, gossip provided Esther one of the crucial links she needed to the world at large. The press, forever the enemy of the politician, had a harder time sharing the news than the old women standing on the cobblestones.

Word in the courtyard after the service was that Oliva's two brothers had gone missing too. The Gómez Camargo boys had run off to San Vicente de Chucurí, a few days' ride up the mountain, to find the bastards who took their sister—at least that's what the gossips said.

*   *   *

Esther worried about what the disappearance meant for her.

The entire walk after church—through the park, and around the plaza, underneath the red-blooming tree the locals called lorito—the gossips dissected the Gómez Camargo family and the vanishing of their unmarried daughter. The old aunts and distant cousins who gathered around the Angaritas after services would not shake the subject.

My grandmother remembers Cousin Leonor stating loudly and clearly, *you're an old maid, Esther, and if you're not careful and don't find a man to protect you, you're going to end up like Oliva.* At the time, my almost-twenty-two-year-old grandmother had no prospects of marriage. None that were serious. Something her extended family felt the need to constantly mention, appropriately or not.

Esther replied to her cousin. She had to say something—it wasn't in my grandmother's nature to take insults without defending herself. Her father had stayed inside the church to listen to some mayor from another town talk to all the landowners after mass, and the heat, combined with the uncertainty of how long she had to stand with said cousin, made it impossible to walk away or turn the other cheek.

I would rather be single than married to a man as ugly as your husband.

There was a second of quiet before Leonor replied.

Oh, he's ugly, she said, *but he's mine, a good person, and real—who do you have again? A pen pal?*

Twice burned, my grandmother fell silent and turned away, pretending to examine the carmine petals on a nearby branch.

Being single during a civil war was highly inconvenient. It required one to let go of certain standards, compromise on certain ideals—something my grandmother had never done and never wanted to do, unlike poor Cousin Leonor. But Leonor had a point too: The pool of eligible bachelors got smaller and smaller with every Conservative bullet. Most girls she knew had married by eighteen.

Of the men that remained, Esther found most of the ones she encountered utterly unappealing. There were few opportunities to meet anyone new. Any party or social event posed the risk of death. Music and sound attracted danger, as did walking without an armed chaperone. Even that didn't always help. And to not marry a Liberal? Well, that would risk alienating the whole family. The only place to really meet an eligible bachelor was church, but all the gossips whispering and *can-you-imagine*-ing indignities on kidnapped young women did not increase Esther's appetite for polite society.

The last ten months had been full of tension and temerity, relying on reports from friends and neighboring farms about when it was safe to venture outside. The Angaritas weren't immune from intimidation. But after the first night, no additional deaths were reported on Angarita lands, and Don Trino managed to keep everyone from reacting. Still—three more horrible notes had arrived on near-dead livestock.

Doña Evangelina and Don Trino had done their best to secure the safety of their children. Weeks after the assassination in Bogotá, all my grandmother's sisters, married or not, were covertly shipped off to relatives in Bucaramanga, the largest city in Santander, where urban density provided anonymity and security. The younger Angarita Sarmiento boys were sent to a boarding school far from conflict, where seclusion and a religious order protected them. Only Esther, Francisco, and the younger Trino remained on the finca, all essential to the operation that kept food on the table—all drilled on what to do in case of a Conservative raid. Attacks by the Godos had become the new weather, a subject of endless discussion and impossible to predict.

As she waited for her father to finish his post-church gathering, Esther decided to go back to the post office. Despite intense political violence, the post office continued to function—open on Sundays for the ranchers who only came weekly. Some things were sacred to everyone, including communication with the outside world as well as communication with the divine. With a curt "con permiso," she left Leonor talking to the trees.

* * *

Instead of going the direct route to the post office, she walked by the bench-lined pathway that often soothed her temper. As she made her way, she passed by the church's open door. But before she traveled the width of the building's facade, she heard something that made her pause.

She peered in. The noise continued, a male voice. Esther didn't recognize the simple thirty-something-year-old man standing below that gilded altar, but she did not like what she heard.

The speaker wasn't tall. He was pale-skinned, with a strong chin coupled with an even larger nose. Esther would not have thought twice about the man if she saw him on the street. But when he opened his mouth, everything changed. His voice, loud and tinny, had a compelling quality about it. One that couldn't help but draw the listener in. He spoke plainly and clearly about the hurt that the Liberals had been dealt at the hands of the greedy Conservatives. About Conservative land grabs. About banditry sanctioned by law. He talked about his days as the mayor of Barrancabermeja, an important transportation hub in the department of Santander, about a ten-day standoff with the Conservative police that resulted in a small victory for his battalion, demands met before a counterstrike, and then an extended retreat into the tropical mountains and small towns of Santander.

Liberals had not organized the way Conservatives had, and it was up to each farmer to defend themselves. This man proposed a solution for the small landowners of Santander. *It is time to form our own army. It's time to fight for ourselves, for the life of the Liberal Party in Santander.*

Esther did not like that idea at all. What mattered now wasn't creating soldiers, carting off more men—leaving more women alone and vulnerable and single. The last thing she wanted was for her father, or her brothers, to die. It was not time for a fight, it was time to ensure one's survival.

She'd heard him reference his own name, *Rafael Rangel Gómez*, and almost went in to ask if he was distantly related to the missing girl. She didn't. She kept to the path, bound for the post office.

*   *   *

Outside the post office, she ran into her brother Francisco and his friend Carlos Bermúdez, a schoolmate from their childhood boarding school about sixty miles away. Esther knew him before the Violence—he'd come to dinner at the finca during breaks from school, the Angarita Sarmientos being closer than Carlos's own home. With all the risk, he hadn't come to dinner in months, even this trip into town, to do some business for his father, was dangerous.

Who is this Rangel idiot? she asked Francisco, avoiding Carlos for the moment.

He's trying to start an army, he replied.

I heard that much, she said. The name still didn't resonate with her, but Francisco clearly knew it and got excited at the mention, his eyes lighting up.

He's a dangerous guy, Francisco said after a long pause, *he wants to go down to San Vicente and make a stand.*

Is he related to the Gómez Camargo family?

Maybe, but probably not. Why do you want to know all this, Esther?

Because he's talking in the church right now. And Papa is in there listening to him.

Francisco took a long look at Carlos and nodded. Carlos nodded back and looked down on the ground. Francisco smiled and ran off. He did not want to miss a chance to see the revolutionary speak.

Carlos lingered by the post office door, half blocking Esther's way into the building. He was tall, fair of complexion, with jet-black hair that looked blue in the sun. She waited for him to either move or speak, but he did neither.

"Bueno, ¿Carlos Eduardo Bermúdez Fuentes, como está?" My grandmother enjoys using people's full names as a tool to unnerve them. It was, and is, startlingly effective.

"Bien, Esther."

"Me debes una carta, no?"

He pulled the envelope out of his coat pocket and handed it to her.

She carefully tucked it into a little fold in her skirt—a hidden pocket for precisely such items.

"Mejor me voy."

"Sí, Esther." He smiled at her, quietly adding, *Thanks for saving me the stamp.*

And with that, Esther turned away, having never even entered the post office, and hurried back to the truck. She was in time to see her mother settle into the front seat and the aunts begin to disperse, Cousin Leonor vanishing into the labyrinth of streets surrounding the plaza. Don Trino had been spotted leaving the church with Francisco and Trinito nearby, all with scowls on their faces and ready for the bumpy ride home.

* * *

Francisco would not stop complaining once they'd all settled into the truck. When he arrived at the church door to see Rangel speak,

Don Trino stood up, which made all the other old men stand up, effectively cutting off Rangel. Don Trino had grabbed Francisco by the arm as he walked out of the building, forcing Francisco to move away from Rangel, out of the church, and toward the truck. Francisco didn't even get to hear Rangel's voice.

Francisco wanted to understand why his father would not allow him to listen to the revolutionary—why did Don Trino get to hear the speech, but not Francisco or Trinito? After waiting out Francisco's complaints for a few minutes, Don Trino only offered a platitude.

The Devil knows more because he's old than because he's the Devil. And this Devil thought it better to walk away.

Francisco disagreed. So did Trinito. Their old man, they argued, should have let them listen.

For months, young men had spread the word about Rangel, and Rangel's army—a Liberal guerrilla movement that was pushing Conservative violence away from Liberal strongholds. Just because my grandmother had not heard of the man didn't mean that her brothers were ignorant. Both Francisco and Trinito were exhausted from living with the perpetual uncertainty of war and itched to do something, *anything*, to defend their land. In Rangel, they saw an opportunity for action, but Don Trino only cautioned patience.

Don't you get it, offered Esther, *Papa doesn't want you to go and die like an idiot.*

Francisco turned on Esther. He didn't like this version of his sister, who usually did a good job of staying out of things.

I didn't hear you calling me back after I left you alone with Carlos Bermúdez.

At this, everyone in the truck grew silent, most with broad grins on their faces, while Esther grimaced at her brother's audacity. She hadn't been left alone-alone, they had stood outside the post office, about as public as could be and for only a moment—and she considered saying as much to her brother. But to argue was to extend the matter.

Carlos Bermúdez was one of her not-so-serious options in matters of love, and her whole family knew it. Nothing was secret in a large Colombian family, certainly not the letters between them that had been going back and forth for a few years. Secrecy and privacy were privileges afforded the few and wily. My grandmother preferred silence instead of equivocation or explanation.

It was complicated, having a courtship that was mostly about physiology and biology. Carlos and Esther had never openly exchanged any affection for one another, only for the information contained in textbooks and lectures beyond Esther's reach.

Carlos Bermúdez Fuentes was studying to be a doctor in Bucaramanga. His mother's people, the Fuentes half, were all doctors, so he found his family's legacy in the white halls of the medical school campus. How could Esther explain to her family that she mostly maintained a diligent correspondence with him for one reason—medicine. She waited breathlessly for each letter and its descriptions of procedures, cadavers, and remedies.

His most recent letter burned in her pocket. She wanted to know what he had to say, but she also knew that reading it on the way home tempted too many eyes and ears. She would wait until she was finally, impossibly, alone.

Her thoughts were interrupted by her mother asking what she and Carlos had discussed. Esther cleared her throat.

Oh, we just greeted one another and then I came back to the truck.

Doña Evangelina didn't stop there and quietly asked Esther if there was any hope of marriage in her future with Carlos.

Questions like this caught Esther off guard—even though this exact question had been posed to her hundreds of times by now. Every time she met a boy, talked to a boy, or even looked at a boy, someone—usually her mother—asked if he seemed like a good prospect for marriage. Most girls her age had several children by now. To be almost twenty-two and single was unseemly. To be almost twenty-two, beautiful, and from a good family while remaining obstinately single seemed like a tragedy. Or a personality defect.

I don't think I'm going to marry Carlos, Madre. He lives far, and I cannot leave you and Papa.

Doña Evangelina began to protest, to say that she was happy to send Esther away if it would help her prospects, when Don Trino interrupted her.

Esther is my right hand. She can stay with me forever if she wants to.

Which seemed to settle the matter of Esther. But Don Trino hadn't forgotten the original concern. As the pickup made its way up and down the gravel paths and rock-strewn roads, Don Trino deciphered the desire for bloodshed he saw in both of his sons. No one spoke as Don Trino considered his options. He tapped his daughter's knee with his free hand, smiling first at her, and then at his wife, who sat next to Esther in the passenger seat—Doña Evangelina's arm perpetually outside the window, riding the breeze. Through the open rear window just behind his head, sitting angrily in the bed of the truck, ears pressed against the glass, he could feel his two sons, Francisco and Trino, ready for a fight.

There was too much work to be done. That was the truth of it all. With the younger boys and most of his daughters away, with the reasonable defection of workers after the overseer's death, there were fewer people working the land. When those workers took their wives and children with them, there were fewer hands working the kitchens that fed those working.

In ten months since the overseer died, the five of them, with the help of another four, had done the work of twenty people. Don Trino had consolidated all his livestock into Mancarique and emptied the other fincas of anything that required too much labor.

He and the boys maintained the grass and the water reservoir levels of the empty lands, lined their perimeters in barbed wire, and often prayed for, more than defended, their gates. But Don Trino had to send money to the city and to the boarding schools for his absent children's upkeep, which meant keeping Mancarique working as close to full capacity as was possible. The months of hard work taught him he could spare very little—certainly not Esther, and more crucially, not the boys. He looked at his sons in the rearview mirror, slowly picking his way up a steep hill. The young men braced themselves against the grade, mumbling at one another about their father's unfairness.

Francisco. Trino. You're in charge of the milking tomorrow.

Trinito spoke up.

No, Papa. Francisco and I are going to San Vicente tomorrow. With Rangel, as a part of his army. We're going to take a stand.

Don Trino said nothing for the remainder of the slow ride. For half an hour, the family drove quietly through the mountain, stopping at one point to clear some tropical foliage from the road, Don Trino striking branches with his machete, arm and blade working together in one smooth motion. Even as the truck pulled up to Mancarique, Don Trino only looked at Francisco—who took the meaning clearly, hopped out, and quickly opened the gate, waiting for the truck to go through before closing it behind him. The silence continued until after merienda, when Francisco, unable to hold his tongue any longer, tried to explain.

We want to do something, Papa.

Don Trino looked at his sons.

You will do something. You're in charge of the milking tomorrow. Francisco. Trino.

With that, he stood up and retired to his bedroom.

Esther looked at her brothers and finally broke the tension.

What are you going to do?

Trinito looked at Francisco. Francisco looked at Trinito and shrugged. They both stood up.

I suppose we must go to bed, said Francisco. *We're in charge of the milking tomorrow.*

*   *   *

Esther wanted to do something too.

My grandmother once told me that female intelligence was both a blessing and a curse. Women had to be smart enough to avoid getting trapped, raped, or killed, but not too smart. Daughters and wives were liabilities for landowners in those days—objects of love that could be taken, that could be broken. How could Esther convince her father she was safe, if Oliva, from the Gómez Camargo finca down the road, had been taken from her own front porch? When so many people like her had been kidnapped or killed?

At times like this, my grandmother often wished she had been born a man. A man could make choices, could decide who he wanted to marry, could become a doctor or a warrior, could heal a body or wage war—a man could do *something*. But her brothers' frustrations proved that wasn't true either. Everyone was beholden to someone.

So she did what she always did. She readied herself for bed, even though it was quite early in the evening. Still, she had work to do in the morning.

The Condor
(A FLIGHT OF PRINCIPLE)

Tuluá, 1949

A Colombian aphorism says that to understand tomorrow, you need to make sense of yesterday. Like a long line of dominoes, one moment in time topples another, which topples another, until soon nothing stands.

In a city called Tuluá, about two hundred miles from Bogotá in the opposite direction from Santander, the owners of the land, Conservative to their core, called a meeting about reprisals on Conservatives by Liberal defense squads. One of the men in the crowd stood up and spoke about the need to aggressively avenge these attacks. He was a local cheesemonger who went by the name "the Condor."

Without hesitation, the Condor was appointed Defender of the Land by the landowners near Tuluá and Ceilán, a neighboring city. A small act with big consequences.

The Condor was no ordinary cheese salesman. His skill with a cheese wire was legendary, and kids in Tuluá had whispered that the Condor was a long-retired child assassin, responsible for the deaths of hundreds. No one could confirm, but no one chose to deny. He commanded respect and an army inspired by his commitment to both the Church and a Conservative Colombia.

Nothing about León María Lozano said "rogue paramilitary leader." Lozano was not a tall man. He was pale of complexion, rather square-headed, and boasted a thick neck from a muscled torso. He had no facial hair and a hard, thin-lipped expression in what few photographs exist. He favored white button-up shirts, worn with the top button undone, undershirt visible, as well as thick blazers, even in the scorching heat. Years later, when he met the president, he refused to concede his style, always demanding to be seen as a simple man. He preferred his nickname: the Condor.

*   *   *

Soon after the meeting, Lozano began to execute his plan, on behalf of the Conservative Party, to intimidate people in the mountains where he lived. Despite receiving a small stipend from local party leadership for his services, it was clear that the Condor had no aspirations or desires to acquire wealth. He did not claim any of the lands the Conservatives occupied after he'd personally intimidated their former tenants into relocation. He relinquished all material acquisitions—and chose humility even as he became a weapon of the Conservative state that operated outside of the established law or order. He operated on ideology alone.

León María Lozano was said to be a man of principle (so claimed the English title of his 1984 biopic, *A Man of Principle*). His main principles, as far as anyone could tell, were that the Church and Conservatives dictated all morality—and all Liberals were savage Communists in need of eradication.

This man of principle appealed to a certain demographic, and men started to join him by the dozens—some the third and fourth non-inheriting sons of landowners, some workers deeply allied with their bosses and communities, some fervent followers of the Church. It's not hard for a hero to become a monster. A monster with a small army of Birds. "Pájaros," they were called, for their quick ability to disperse—*how they took flight!* Within seconds, the perpetrators of killings, rapes, horrific assaults, destruction of property, and violent harassment disappeared, conveniently before any police could show up to pretend to investigate.

The Condor, like so many others, had spent the last eighteen months perfecting the art of civil disruption and forceful eviction. His goal was to herd all Liberals into cities far from his own, to declare the region where he lived purely Conservative, as he knew it was meant to be. Similar people with similar values existing together. He also realized that asking Liberals to leave was not the most efficient solution. Making a threat, and then following through on that threat, well, that required two visits. Massacring everyone from the beginning streamlined travel, or so his corporate logic went.

Civil wars usually involve clearly demarked regions. A north against a south, an east against a west. But the Violence had no delineations. There were mostly Liberal towns, mostly Conservative towns, but few were purely one or the other. The Violence became a war of intimidation—*leave*, the Conservatives said. *No*, the Liberals fought back.

And so, neighbors killed neighbors, after years of potlucks, worn shot glasses, and dominoes on shaded terraces. Families waved at each other on the roads into the church plaza, each moving in different directions between services, only to find themselves dead at the other's hands the next day. The Violence was as sporadic as it was planned, as orchestrated as it was randomized. It was chaos, unleashed. And the Condor was gifted at unleashing that chaos.

* * *

At 6 a.m., days before the November 1949 election, the dynamite went off in three locations in the Liberal town of Ceilán.

Even though the people expected Conservative violence, even though they'd been holding their collective breath for months and months of civil war, the dynamite was a surprise.

Over three hundred paramilitary Birds invaded like a horde, wrote one survivor. Without weapons training and numbering fewer than two hundred, the Liberal people of Ceilán stood no chance.

What the survivors remembered the most was the noise—the loud bang of the attack, the shaking of the buildings around them, the explosion of glass and the crunch of a building collapsing. The memory of such noises would rob the sleep of survivors for years.

We never imagined our homes could become ruins. We didn't imagine the destruction after the fire, the way the beams collapsed upon themselves, rendering the familiar into a nightmare.

What was a city, if not an erasable dot on an outdated map?

The fire spread, following small trails of gasoline—an inferno's promenade through town, consuming everything it touched.

Most people chose to run, it was perhaps the best option—better to risk the bullet than the flame. A survivor just had to get by the hundreds of revolver- and machete-wielding Conservative paramilitary Birds outside.

Horses ran through the streets, freed by the blaze as much as panicked by it. People ran outside, but the Birds quickly corralled them. Some citizens tried to escape into nearby water, only to find machetes buried upright below the surface, gun sights trained along the shore. The Bugalagrande River flowed red down the mountain.

Men were castrated on sight. Imagine worse for the women. Children were not spared, but I will keep from you what the Birds did to them—our hearts can only take so much.

Twenty-five years later, one of the survivors described the event like a religious painting of Hell—the arrival of Satan on earth and the conversion of men into furious beasts. A version of God was certainly represented. Because of the Conservative Party's deep ties to the Colombian Catholic Church, a priest had been sent along to bless the paramilitary in its execution of (equally Catholic) political heathens.

According to the testimony of several survivors, the priest stood on top of a jeep and performed a warped version of last rites on those dying, absolving them of their Liberal crimes and sinful existence, even as he denied their entreaties for clemency.

In Colombia, to defile the body of your enemy is to deny it dignity and honor in death. Colombian death rituals have mattered from the beginning of the country's recorded history, and the Birds perfected the art of human desecration.

They severed heads from bodies in the town square, and eventually a horrific tableau mort emerged: The Birds arranged the headless corpses as if waiting for the bus, heads substituted for suitcases, a raging fire in the background.

As dozens continued to burn to the death in their homes, half the Birds drove away with bound captives in their truck beds and laughter in their throats. The rest stayed behind to conscript any survivors to their cause. Within minutes, the clouds gathered and a rainstorm began—part of the damage quelled, some of the would-be-dead spared. One survivor called it a reprieve from God. The final toll came to 150 dead, only 92 identifiable.

By 9 a.m., most of Ceilán had burned.

* * *

Far away enough to remain unscathed, at the Happy Bar in Tuluá, the Condor looked at his watch, waiting for word of his victory to arrive. He had instructed his men to kill anyone who would not join their cause—there were to be no Liberals left alive.

Some still managed to scatter into the hills. One of those men, Pedro Marín, was a traveling meat salesman passing through, when he found himself caught up in the slaughter of Ceilán. He initially agreed to join the Conservatives, but as soon as he was granted any leniency, he ran. The Birds chased him, and any other deserters, fanning out into the neighboring towns, starting with Génova, the place Marín listed on his conscription paperwork as his hometown.

The Condor knew better than most men that one domino topples another. But even the Condor could not predict how those three hours would affect the next seventy years of Colombian history.

Election Day

(A DECONSTRUCTION OF GUNS)

Santander, 1949

Every day, Don Trino counted his cows and how many liters of milk they produced. It didn't take him too long to realize that someone had been stealing from him. At first, it was milk, then it was the cows.

He was lucky—it was a relatively small price to pay for being a Liberal.

Occasionally people would disappear or turn up in a bad situation. Don Trino got good at consoling widows; Doña Evangelina got better at finding them new work. Local Conservatives respected him enough to leave him alone, but not enough to keep him out of the conflict entirely.

Still, knowing that proximity mattered during war, Don Trino had changed their sleeping arrangements. He, Francisco, and Trinito now slept in the main living area, better to hear any movements in the front of the house, while Esther, Doña Evangelina, and the minimal house staff all lived in the largest bedroom in the center of the building, as far from any doors to the outside as possible, while still having access to a window or two for a quick escape.

Doña Evangelina made Esther wear all her best jewelry to bed every night. If anything happened during their slumber, she could leave with enough valuables on her person to get to Bucaramanga or the coast. She slept in layers of good dresses for the same reason. Although, the weight of it all was getting to her. Between the earrings pinned to her hemline, and the anxiety, sleep found my grandmother rarely—and not just because it became such a formal affair.

Carlos kept writing to her, and in the six months since she had spoken to him at church, her feelings had begun to grow in earnest. She'd kept his most recent letter hidden for a week before she finally manufactured a moment for herself.

She read through his words quickly. Then read it again. She folded it back into a small square and tucked it away—only to quickly unfold it and read through it once more. Carlos detailed his first autopsy—a fascinating matter for my grandmother.

None of his letters survived into my grandmother's old age. But even now, as she describes him, it's clear that Carlos knew of my grandmother's ambitions to be a doctor, that he cared for her and admired her, bringing her snapshots of a world beyond her reach. The care with which she recalls the smallest details of his penmanship and skill with a scalpel speak to my grandmother's affections. Engaging with her dreams proved to be the greatest seduction of all.

Since she was a child, she loved the idea of curing illness, of making the world better through action, study, and competence. My grandmother can still stitch a wound, knows which herbs help with inflammation, and can massage someone's stomach pains away. She believes in the power of pressure points, purgatives, and prayer. There is nothing, Esther believes, that a body cannot eliminate with enough perseverance.

An autopsy! *How exciting*, she thought, *to unravel the mysteries of life preserved even in death.*

His letters brought her much joy, but underneath the joy lurked a sadness. A regret at the limitations of gender, time, location, and fate. She knew that if any of her brothers had expressed an interest in medicine, Don Trino would have supported them. But she shook away the thought.

Esther loved reading about Marie Curie and Florence Nightingale. She loved knowing there were women, right now, somewhere in the world, learning medicine, nursing, biology—all the things that seemed unreachable to her.

But something was different about this letter. That she could tell. His handwriting felt smaller and tighter. The strokes were deeper somehow, as if he'd been pushing on the pen. At the end, an unusual request: *I would love to come visit you soon, perhaps to meet with your father and discuss things with you.*

She stared at that sentence for a long time. Her heart began a tremendous race against her questioning mind. *What could he mean? What did he want? Surely he didn't—*

Esther heard her mother stirring in the bedroom and hurried back to her bed.

There was time, she hoped, to think all this through.

She whispered to her guardian angels: *What on earth does Carlos Bermúdez mean? And please, God, let Oliva Gómez Camargo be safe.* The girl had been missing since March 1949, and it was now November; even Esther knew that, at this point, her prayers were in vain. She prayed for the girl every night, nonetheless.

*   *   *

Days later, two boys found the body of Oliva Gómez Camargo in a dried creek outside Barichara, just off the main thoroughfare. Word traveled up and down the mountainside quickly. The body, thanks to the minerals and dryness of the bed where it was found, had been well preserved despite being long dead.

The poor thing, Cousin Leonor intoned outside church the next Sunday. *Rips on the clothes. Probably raped. Left for dead.*

Esther and Doña Evangelina crossed themselves. It felt disrespectful to even say that word so near the church steps.

Everyone is saying it was those Conservatives, added another cousin. *Well, everyone that's still here.*

At least two families had left for Bucaramanga recently, selling their land to another Liberal family, *thank goodness*, defying the Conservatives' plan. There were about six completely empty pews in the church in Cabrera that week. Underscoring every pause in the conversation was the unasked question: *How long can we hold out?*

The gossip about the Gómez Camargo girl continued, building from fact and rumor. She was seen walking along the main road with someone once, perhaps a man—information suddenly outpouring after minor eternities of silence. Then, months later, she was found dead in a nearby creek. The tongues wagged—*she was not fresh.* She'd probably been killed soon after she disappeared.

Adding to the mystery were other disappearances. A cousin of Oliva Gómez Camargo, it was reported, hadn't been seen in weeks either. Also, her brothers had left for San Vicente two months after her disappearance, but no one had had word of them since. Old Man Gómez and his wife, the beautiful Estrella Camargo, had gone to Bucaramanga with their daughter's body to see the coroner, to figure out what ended their daughter's life.

I hope they know what happened to her, whispered Doña Evangelina.

Oh yes, replied one of the old aunts, *better they know. Better to know than to live with false hope.*

*   *   *

After Oliva Gómez Camargo was found, there were many hushed conversations in the Angarita Sarmiento household, all behind thick wooden doors. Esther knew they were discussing the safety of their children, especially their daughter.

Don Trino and Doña Eva spoke at length, weighing different possibilities. There was no real chance that he would leave the finca or his wife would leave his side—at least not yet. Doña Eva could not imagine a life without him. Her hazel eyes still lit up at the mention of his name. They loved each other tremendously, in a time when love was a luxury. There was no talk of separation between them.

But something had to be done about Esther, Trino, and Francisco. It wasn't safe anymore for them to remain at the finca.

The next Saturday, Don Trino and Doña Evangelina sat at the dining room table and asked their remaining children to leave home. Cities granted protection, if they promised to stay clear of politics. The two planned to stick it out on the finca together, maybe selling off some of their lands, but they could no longer bear the idea of any their children getting taken or killed.

Esther, they decided, would join her sisters in Bucaramanga, the largest city in Santander, about six hours away along the new highway. Francisco and Trino would head up to Socorro, a mid-sized city only about fifteen miles away, roughly three hours on horseback, one-and-a-half hours in the truck, slowly picking its way up and down the mountain paths. They would be under the watchful eye of relatives, but close enough to home to return when needed.

Esther hated the plan. Trinito and Francisco loved it.

Esther did not want to depend on phone calls and letters for news on the finca and her parents—she wanted to remain at home with them. She began thinking of every reason why she should stay. She promised her father she was careful, she promised that she'd never walk alone. *Please, Papa. Please. I'm your right hand, remember?*

Trino and Francisco knew that Socorro had bars, nightclubs, old friends, and unknown women. Both, full of energy and revolution in their early twenties, longed for freedom from the oppressive Don Trino and the ever-praying Doña Eva. When Esther finished making her case, the boys did the opposite, thanking their father for the opportunity, promising they would be safe and out of harm's way.

It had been over a year and a half since Gaitán died. So many had died, so many more would die. The upcoming national elections did not bode well. The bloodshed in Santander only grew, day to day, as did Rangel's local army, seducing farm boys from good, Liberal families with promises of heroism and martyrdom. Don Trino recognized and admitted he could not stop a civil war, could not offer basic protection anymore, not even to his own family.

The old man wished that he too could leave the land behind, but someone had to make sure the cows were milked and keep food on the table. Don Trino let himself get lost in his work, in his cattle—but he understood that revenge mattered too. He was Colombian. His sons had lost friends and people they'd known since childhood to the paid vigilantes of the Conservative Party.

That's how it went. Not just for his family.

Word was that hundreds of men were moving up the river and the mountainside to San Vicente for a standoff. Rangel's Liberal army—the little mayor turned out to be a good recruiter—itched for battle, as did many Liberal young men. Socorro was a safer bet.

The family had spent the last year living whisper-to-newscast. Sometimes the radio news was inaccurate, but they still gathered to hear it, to know who in what towns were slaughtered, what criminals had been apprehended, what inefficient moves the government tried to make in the face of all the bloodshed.

In some parts of the country, the Caribbean coast, little to no violence existed. People drank and danced freely and gaily into the night. But in the mountains, the nighttime carried a grave threat—drinking and dancing could easily get a man killed. The government served the Conservatives and operated as though nothing were amiss. Liberal politicians gave speeches, decrying and decrying into the winds heard whistling after dark.

Families listened to broadcasts as Congress attempted to impeach the Conservative president. They listened as the president shut down the Congress. They listened as the country prepared for another election. They listened as the leaders of the Liberal Party called for a boycott of the election.

Meanwhile, the gossips in front of church broadcast all the local dead and disappeared. The family listened to them too, dissecting truth from fiction together over the evening's coffee, because there was nothing else to do.

No one wanted to leave, everyone wanted to leave. The uncertainty felt crippling. But Don Trino knew how spooked cows behaved and understood that the moment to act was now. He said as much at the dining room table.

The idea of separating felt like a different kind of defeat to Esther.

As she got up to prepare for bed, Esther took a hard look at her father. She spoke clearly and with great resolution.

I will not be going as far as Bucaramanga. I will not. You cannot make me. And if you do, I'll come home on foot if I have to.

Don Trino nodded at his daughter. He understood her threat. He just wasn't sure he could grant her wish.

* * *

On Election Day, November 27, 1949, the Angarita Sarmientos, like most other Liberal families across Colombia, boycotted the vote.

Earlier in the year, Conservative assassins attempted to kill another Liberal candidate for the presidency, Darío Echandía Olaya, killing his brother Vicente instead. After that, and in light of continued and extreme Conservative aggression, the Liberal Party decided to sit this one out. What was the point of participating in a sham? Their goal was to both ensure the safety of their electorate—rumors abounded of a Conservative plot to kill Liberal voters at the polls—and to give zero credibility to the election of Conservative Party leader Laureano Gómez Castro (no relation to the Gómez Camargo family). The boycott worked: Of 1.1 million votes cast nationally that election, only 23 votes went to the opposition party.

President Gómez called it a landslide, a national mandate. The Liberal news stations called it a dictatorship. The United States government declared the Conservative Party their allies in the fight against Communism.

Esther, tired of listening to the radio analyze the ridiculous results, considered her choices. She'd written her reply to Carlos Bermúdez that morning, after hesitating long enough, describing her enthusiasm for both a visit and for the generous description of the autopsy. She wasn't sure what tone to strike, so settled for optimistic and friendly. She remembers writing the letter, her hands shaking, unsure of what he wanted or what she would reply if he made anything concrete. She planned to mail the letter that afternoon, but her brothers stopped her.

Too close to Election Day said Francisco.

She understood. She tucked the letter into her skirt pocket.

* * *

That afternoon—she grabbed Francisco's revolver from the drawer by the entrance to the main house and handed it to him. He looked at her, surprise in his eyes.

I think you should show me how this thing works.

He nodded and got up, not before glancing at her dress.

Wear something with longer sleeves. Until you know what you're doing. Go change and meet me outside.

Outside, she walked next to her brother. Esther and Francisco physically and spiritually resembled one another the most, the male and female versions of a body and soul split. They had been close from birth; Francisco understood Esther the most of all his siblings, and the feeling was mutual.

He didn't have to ask her why she wanted to learn to shoot a gun. Francisco had danced with Oliva at parties, flirted with her at the punch bowl, and knew her brothers well. Oliva's death hurt in a way that few other deaths would—*she was one of us,* my grandmother told me, *she could have been me—in almost every way she was me.*

Oliva had been beautiful, kind, with a dreamy look in her eye. She and Esther had done their First Communions together, had graduated from elementary together, had played in the schoolyard and at each other's homes. Oliva was not just a name in the news, not just a collection of anecdotes for the gossips to spit out. Esther refused to become a ghost attached to a rumor.

They settled by a pasture, near the stables. Francisco pulled out the weapon and an oily rag.

He began his instruction exactly as Don Trino had with him years ago—by taking the gun apart. Here are the parts that assembled to fire the bullet. His sister needed to know it the way he did—as a tool.

As he cleaned the pieces, Francisco explained how it worked, how the various mechanisms created enough pressure and tension to hold the bullet in place, until the trigger released that which could never be taken back.

But before Esther could even touch the gun, she heard a horse coming up the path behind her. It was Oscar Becerra Garza, a boy she knew from town, breathlessly heading toward Francisco and Esther in the open pasture.

You . . . have . . . to get . . . Don Trino, the boy finally said when he arrived at their feet.

Esther asked what happened, but the boy refused to speak until Don Trino was summoned.

Francisco ran off to get their father, and Esther walked Oscar toward the house, thinking it better to meet them halfway.

Oscar explained a little of what happened as they moved. The Gómez Camargo brothers were in San Vicente, and so were 398 other Liberal boys, fighting with Rafael Rangel Gómez and the Rangel army to take the town away from the Conservative police.

But that wasn't the news, Oscar explained, or why Don Trino was wanted. The Gómez Camargo boys had caught the man, had caught the Conservative bastard that killed their sister. Don Trino was being summoned to testify at the man's trial, a character witness for the Gómez Camargo clan.

As soon as he arrived, Don Trino expressed some skepticism. He didn't understand why he had been summoned, why the accusers needed a character witness, why anyone cared about a trial in the middle of a political takeover. None of it made sense, something Don Trino didn't mind saying to his wife and children, even as he packed up his saddlebag. He'd decided it would be faster to pick his way up the mountain on horseback—some paths were not ready for even the strongest trucks.

If I don't return in three days by nightfall, he told his wife, *you leave the next morning. You take what you can and leave. Just go.*

Doña Evangelina crossed herself and then choked back a sob as she hugged and kissed her husband goodbye. She held him hard just in case she would never get the chance to do so again. It's how they always said goodbye.

*   *   *

The day after her father left, Esther made a big deal of helping, of making herself somehow more indispensable to her mother. *See*, every action seemed to say, *you* need *me, you don't want to send me away.*

Doña Eva asked Francisco to go into Cabrera on the afternoon of the second day, to gather any news, and Esther took advantage. She asked her brother to stop by the post office with her reply to Carlos. The "yes" she'd written to his request had been burning a hole in her skirt, and she was glad to be rid of the paper, her response now in the hands of fate, or at least her brother and the somehow still dependable Colombian postal service.

Doña Eva, typically strong and stoic, had spent the hours after her husband's departure oscillating between determined leadership and an anxiety-driven need to run to the window every few minutes. Doña Eva lit candles and muttered prayers in Latin and an old language she'd been taught as a child by her mother, Ladino, calling on all translations of God for help.

Esther thought she wanted the kind of love her parents had. But perhaps it wasn't worth it—to love someone so much, to live with worry over a missing half—was that what Esther wanted?

The thought passed through her mind that she was perhaps taking Carlos's request for a visit too seriously. Maybe Carlos just wanted to meet her father for completely different reasons? Francisco returned from town; her letter was in the post, beyond her recall and in the hands of God. She tried to let it go and focus on work—work gave her something to do, somewhere to be.

It was Esther who organized the milking that morning. Esther who kept up the ledger, who supervised the storage and transportation of the milk, who sent Trinito out to fix the north pasture fence. By the evening of the second day, Doña Eva was back to her formidable self, softly directing the finca, grateful to her daughter for stepping up when needed, grateful to her sons for returning from town with all the necessary items, fences literally mended.

On the morning of the third day, both women ran to the window every hour, scouring the horizon for a horse, a truck, a pigeon, or a ghost—whatever turned up. At midday, Don Trino rode up on the same old roan he'd taken to San Vicente, just before true panic would have set in.

After he dismounted, Don Trino hugged his wife and daughter for a long time, called for his sons, and hugged them as well.

The news he brought wasn't good. At first, he'd only shake his head, until he finally began to tell his story.

Poor Oscar Becerra—that kid got the whole thing wrong—we all did.

* * *

The Gómez Camargo boys had not run off to San Vicente. Their father, Old Man Gómez, had sent them there, to keep them from avenging or discussing their sister.

The initial story, the one that the family did not want the public to know, is that Oliva had indeed possibly gone on a walk with a boy that day months ago, as she had snuck out to do many times. In the first few hours after she vanished, the family contended with a scandal involving an elopement. But then a day later, the dead body of the boy turned up in a stack of corpses after a Conservative raid in another town, nowhere near Oliva's home. Maybe she'd never been with the boy at all? But then where could she be?

Confusion quickly dissipated into even greater anxiety as time creeped on. *Where was Oliva?* When her body turned up months later, strangely preserved, the family had fewer answers than before.

Then war came to their sons. During the Rangel army's occupation of San Vicente, the Gómez Camargo boys emerged from hiding to fight for the Liberal guerrilla, sneaking away from their guardians, grateful to do *something*. In the heat of battle, they'd come upon a Conservative bandit who taunted them with the death of their sister.

The Conservative bandit told a gruesome story. Of coming across Oliva sitting on her front porch, of how beautiful she was, how easy to take. The bandit killed her first, then violated her corpse (as it wasn't the sin of rape if the woman was dead), eventually leaving the body in a shallow creek that soon became a dried-up ditch.

After the Conservatives conceded San Vicente to the Liberals, the bandit took off running. The Gómez Camargo brothers chased him to the River Chucurí, the river that separated Liberal turf from Conservative. And when the Gómez Camargo brothers chased that man across the river, the demographics shifted. Suddenly, the Conservatives had enough numbers that the boys' lives became worthless, without anyone to help or hear their cries. It was the bandit who had the last laugh, first killing Oliva, and, eventually, her brothers: an entire generation of a family extinguished by one hand.

When the bodies of the boys emerged in the river, Don Trino had been called, not as a witness for a trial, but to identify the corpses of the Gómez Camargo boys and to tell Old Man Gómez what happened. Some news is best delivered by a friend.

Don Trino finally caught up with his friend on the horseback ride between Socorro and Cabrera. When he delivered the news, Gómez took it well, stoically even. But it was clear the conflict wouldn't end there. The old man had asked to borrow Don Trino's revolver—a request that Don Trino denied.

This will never end, Don Trino sighed. *And poor Oliva, what a terrible way to die.*

Esther and her brothers crossed themselves. Doña Eva brought out the family Bible. Everyone took the time to hold one another and grieve.

At length, Don Trino mentioned that he would have been home earlier in the day, had he not stopped in Cabrera to watch the fire.

What fire? asked Doña Eva.

Oh, haven't you heard? It's all anyone could talk about. The post office burned down last night.

Esther gasped, imagining her letter to Carlos, much like her prospects for love, engulfed in flames.

The Girl

(A CONSIDERATION OF MUSCLE)

Génova, 1949

In the body, there is memory. We remember without thinking—the susurrated feel of a ribbon absently unknotted, hands disconnected from thought. The girl unbraids her hair, brushes it, and re-braids it each morning, her fingers dancing, her ruminations elsewhere. Her limbs simply know the steps—there is no need for presence.

Bernarda Garza Correa had been *the girl* since she was thirteen years old, and in the seven years since, she'd perfected the art of detachment.

The girl will fetch you a glass of water, the old woman had said. And Bernarda's mother had pushed the teenager forward, re-christening her daughter. *The girl.*

The girl didn't mind. She wasn't particularly fond of the name "Bernarda," for some forgotten saint her mother liked. No, at work she liked "the girl." It justified the infrequent and distracted way the old woman spoke to her. How most of the Señora's requests were filtered through bequests to others. *The girl will take your coat. The girl will clean that up. The girl will show you the way.*

The Señora made promises, and the girl fulfilled them. She didn't advocate for the system—but she slept in a comfortable bed, she hummed the latest boleros on the radio, and she spent Sunday mornings with her family. Her salary had paid for schooling, a new roof, and a wooden floor; her siblings, especially her youngest sister, had benefited greatly from the arrangement. It was more than most got.

After seven years, she could perform most tasks the Señora required thoroughly, mechanically, and to the old woman's impossible standards. She didn't have to give it her full attention though. Some things belonged to the girl, and the girl alone.

* * *

The girl walked at a notably steady pace. It took her exactly twenty-three minutes to walk back to her parents' house after the breakfast service on Sunday. Every week, never a minute late, never a minute early. Her family joked that they set their clocks by the girl's pace, and she loved this about herself.

There was never a reason for it to be anything other than twenty-three minutes. The girl woke at dawn, braided her hair, made a large farm breakfast for the Señor and Señora, said goodbye to the other girls (she wasn't the only one; some girls were twice her age!), swept the driveway as she exited the property, and walked across the main plaza to the southern part of their town—where she would spend six hours with her family. She did all this with metronymic precision.

In her many years walking home from the Señora's house, the girl missed her measure only once, on a foggy Sunday in early December 1949. When she finally arrived at home, fourteen minutes later than expected, her parents stood by the door, worrying themselves statues. There was no reason for the girl to have dallied, not during a civil war, no matter how peaceful things might seem.

The girl, shaken, explained the delay to her parents. She'd been stopped by the police at a checkpoint—Conservative police on a manhunt.

*   *   *

Detachment maintains a blur. The girl thought about songs and boys and who would be out in the plaza after church. Her feet moved free of her thoughts, but when the girl reached the police checkpoint, her feet stopped. Her attention, unaccustomed to engaging with the task at hand, focused too sharply and too quickly on the interruption. For the first time in a long time, the girl looked carefully at her surroundings.

Six men, all cradling guns, stood behind a barricade. The girl studied them, confused. Génova, a village accessible by old horse paths, had mostly stayed out of the Violence. No one in Génova had ever walked around openly carrying a gun. It was small, Liberal, and isolated from most of the world.

Génova, and her citizens, enjoyed its remoteness. Ceilán, one of the closest towns, was twenty miles away as the crow flies. But, to get there, one had to travel over four days and forty miles of unmarked roads and trails.

Ceilán! Suddenly the girl understood. At church last week, the priest mentioned that Ceilán had burned down the week before. And now the Conservative machine was here, in the form of the National Police, deep in the mountains in a Liberal town mostly untouched by riot or bullet.

The girl's face changed. The blankness of her expression disappeared, replaced with razor awareness and terror. She smiled the smile of someone used to serving.

The men approached her. The questions began.

Had she left town recently? Had she seen a man, an eighteen-year-old, running around the countryside? Had she spoken to anyone fitting the description? Did she know Pedro Marín, a man calling himself a "survivor"? Was she aware that he had participated in the burning of Ceilán? That it had all been an operation to discredit the Conservatives? (The girl knew this to be a lie.) Did she have any identification? How did she vote in the last election? Could she read? Did she believe Liberal reports of Conservative massacres? Or did she believe the Conservative reports of Liberal massacres? What color did she prefer—red or blue? Who was she? What else did she believe? Where was she going? What kind of family did she come from? Did she want to live?

The girl knew Pedro Marín, but only in passing. He was a year above her in school, but she had left school long ago. Her sister had had a crush on him. But Marín left Génova when he was thirteen to go work as a roving meat salesman, and the girl hadn't heard of him in over five years. Still, the girl did not say this to the police. To the police, she gave the truth that best worked as a lie.

I am a girl. I work for the Señora down the way. I have no politics, I can read a little and sign my name . . . I don't socialize with anyone that's not in my family, I don't speak to strangers, and I don't think very much about anyone at all. I cook and I clean. I am just a girl.

"A girl," an accepted abbreviation for "house girl," a maid, a muchacha, a person who knows everything and can say nothing. She is discreet, detached, inoffensive, and impotent. *A girl. The girl. At your service.*

The men with guns let her go. And for the first time in years, she quickened her pace home.

* * *

As the girl told the story to her parents, her sister, the youngest, the one who knew Marín, turned red.

What is it? the girl asked.

Her sister paused too long before she whispered, *I know where he's hiding. He's in a box on his uncle's land. My friend's brother helps him get out once a week for exercise.*

The girl looked at her sister. The girl worked hard, sending home her entire wages so that the sister could stay in the small church-run school, could avoid becoming another *girl* to another wealthy family that reduced her to the human equivalent of a mop.

You need to forget what you just said. The girl looked at her sister first, and then at their parents. *We all need to forget everything you just said about this and about him. You need to keep your head down and learn to unlearn. Forget what you see, even as you see it.*

The girl asked her family for promises. Her parents agreed too quickly, her sister too slowly.

The family stayed home from church that Sunday, and the girl started back to work early, taking the long way, avoiding any checkpoints. Thirty-two minutes—but at least her thoughts hadn't been interrupted en route.

* * *

The searches began the next night. Houses were picked at random, scoured top to bottom by armed Conservative policemen, looking for the "murderer of Ceilán." The exact men who had burned down the town now persecuted one of its survivors for the crime. The logic of violence defies reason.

The girl's family were perfect in the art of denial. Their poverty provided a shield; there can be advantages to being unseen. But the Señor and Señora in the big house, they were another story.

The search began with the Señora's *How dare you!* It ended with her exclamation of *Under whose authority?* The staff all remained quiet as the Conservative police roughed up the Señora a little (not too much, as she was very rich and from a very old family) and then took the Señor in for questioning after he declared *I wouldn't tell you if I did know where that boy was hiding.* There was nothing that armed Conservatives loved more than old, wealthy Liberals, all bluster and inaction.

As soon as she was alone, with only her many servants around, the Señora began making plans. She gathered her jewelry and started writing lists of people she would call when the telecom office opened at 9 a.m. She barked orders and had the entire house reinforced in case of another *incursion*.

The next morning at dawn, the Señor's body was found near the town square. The police declared it an accident, brought on by unsure feet and drinking. Everyone knew the Señor did not drink outside his home. Everyone accepted the explanation anyway.

* * *

"Siempre es mejor sobrevivir," the girl was fond of saying, but *always* and *survive* meant different things to different people.

The girl did what she knew. She cooked, she cleaned, she proved herself indispensable. The Señora reduced the household after the old man's death, but among those she kept, she kept *the girl Bernarda, the little one who worked well and stayed quiet.* The girl served small plates at the gathering after the Señor's funeral mass. The girl took coats and hats, carefully placing them to avoid wrinkles. The girl made the coffee exactly the way the Señora liked it. The girl cut the corners of the meat at the same angle every time. The girl listened, but never spoke. She heard, but never remembered, more than necessary.

Marín left town. Before or after the police stopped searching for him—it didn't matter. Weeks after, word in that part of the mountains was that Marín was gathering an army, traveling hundreds of miles northeast, toward the bloodshed and not away. The girl's sister had many friends join this burgeoning battalion. But the girl implored her sister to stay, so she did.

As did her parents and the Señora. They weren't the type to run to the cities. It felt defiant to remain, to live in the face of opposition.

There was a quiet revolution in choosing to be normal in times of chaos, thought the girl. She thought this as she walked from the big house down to her family's small one every Sunday, for exactly twenty-three minutes. She thought this as she braided and unbraided her hair every morning, tightly knotting a fraying ribbon.

She wanted so much to forget, but her dreams told a different story. When the nightmares came, her body fought. Her muscles tensed, and she woke to strange postures and memories of interrogation. For years, no matter how much the girl practiced the art of forgetting, one truth emerged again and again: Her body remembered it all.

PART II

*

He dug so deeply into her sentiments that in search of interest he found love, because by trying to make her love him, he ended up falling in love with her.

—Gabriel García Márquez,
One Hundred Years of Solitude

An Eye for a Song
(A QUARREL OF DRUNKARDS)

Urumita, 1950

There's a saying about Valledupar: No one there knows how to tell their shames; they only know how to sing them. And vallenato, the Colombian music born there, aligns with this: anecdotes, morality tales, and warnings wrapped into an energetic and dancing musical genre that sounds both tropical and medieval like a troubadour.

Like all Colombian truths, the accordion's arrival on her shores starts with a myth. A ship of German accordions washed ashore in the Guajira, the northeastern tip of the country. Or perhaps German sailors leaving the newly built Panama Canal stopped to trade. Or perhaps a group of Italians found themselves stranded nearby. But the drum of the enslaved Africans, the guacharaca (a raspy percussion instrument like the güiro) of the Wayuu people, and the diatonic accordions that may or may not have washed up onshore gave birth to a new sound.

Colombian music reflects its people: European, indigenous, and African.

*   *   *

Vallenato was also the people's music. The owners of the land turned up their Argentine boleros and Mexican rancheras to drown out the accordion's whiny insistence.

But vallenato worked its way from the rolling hills of Valledupar up the mountainsides of Colombia, and by 1950 it had snuck into the national consciousness. Parents warned children, do not heed this music of tall tales and banditry, stop listening to these songs of heartbreak and revenge. But their kids, trapped in their homes or at boarding schools, eager to join the fight or already in its thickness, loved these upbeat tales of darkness. The best vallenatos described duels and seductions, battles and defeats—which suited drunk and sentimental young men just fine.

* * *

I met a girl in a plaza, I fell in love at first sight, wrote her a song, and then I lost my eye. What more is there to say? Antonio Barrera Rodríguez chuckled with his entire body, his belly swinging underneath his starched, white shirt. He lifted the pirate-like eyepatch he wore and showed me the scarred eye socket.

Antonio was born in Cali, in southwest central Colombia, far from Santander, but still in the mountains, still surrounded by violence. But Antonio—even on the day of his birth in 1930, he was a poet. As he grew, he wrote ballads and tangos, sweet songs about doves and stolen kisses. When he was twenty, in the thick of the Violence, Antonio was a romantic during an impossible time to be a romantic. He believed that love was more revolutionary than violence.

If it isn't clear yet, he intoned almost sixty years later, *I was an idiot.*

* * *

He chose not to remember her name anymore. But he still could not help himself, in telling the story of a woman he loved for a night decades ago.

He met her one night, after he took a bus to a small village near Valledupar, Urumita, visiting a cousin in a region where the violence had died down. And that night, Antonio and his cousin gathered in the plaza like all the young people did, and they walked in circles, as was the fashion those days.

And there she was. A woman with long, black hair to her waist and a smile that could melt concrete.

* * *

From California down to Patagonia, there is a uniformity to colonization that cannot be denied. Every city founded by the Spanish has a plaza like the one Antonio visited. There's a church on one end, an administrative government building on the other, and a fountain or gazebo, along with a park, separating the two.

These plazas made for natural gathering spaces. During times of peace, young men and women of marrying age would meet here in the evenings, after dinner and chores were finished. At some point, a musician would arrive and begin to play songs, perhaps an accordionist accompanied by a friend or two on guitar.

Two circles would emerge. One of men and one of women. And as the song played, they would walk in opposite directions, until someone stopped. Then everyone stopped, facing a new or old friend, a socially acceptable way to speak to someone of the opposite gender alone, while surrounded, a form of public privacy, acceptable to the parental eyes nearby.

* * *

Antonio saw her as soon as he stood up to join the circle. She was on the opposite side from his spot, but he vowed to pause every time they faced each other. There was something about her, and he could not stop staring.

His cousin Tomás refused to join him in the circle, explaining how he had a girlfriend, and they kept it secret as their families did not approve. Tomás preferred to sit at the bar in a nearby café. He patted Antonio on the back before leaving him.

Be careful, cousin. These women are dangerous.

Antonio laughed. *All Colombian women are dangerous.*

As the circle began to move, he did his best to stop when the woman walked by him. But the momentum made it impossible. Enough of the dozen or so young men in line wished to keep moving, and so they did. Antonio did his best to make eye contact. She understood that he wanted her attention. She smiled. He smiled back.

Back in our day, that was enough to get married, Antonio explained. He memorized everything about her, and although she disappeared before he learned her name, he knew that his cousin would know her.

Even as he walked to the café, Antonio began composing a song for her. A vallenato set to a common rhythm and simple chords, expressing his feelings. She was the one, he knew it. All the saints his mother prayed to had finally listened and placed the right girl in his path. Antonio had no intention of getting things wrong—the song had to be perfect.

Perhaps if he had not been so worried about achieving perfection, he would have noticed that Tomás, who suddenly appeared by his side, was in his cups, *a little past himself*, as my mother would say.

Antonio described the woman thoroughly and Tomás eyed him suspiciously and asked, *Did she seem young and joyous or worried and distracted?*

We smiled big at each other, Antonio explained, and Tomás clasped him on the back.

Then I know exactly where she lives.

*   *   *

He hired the musicians who had played in the plaza as well as a rose vendor and an old man carrying a Spanish guitar.

Antonio prepared to give the greatest serenade womankind had ever heard.

Tomás, after securing a bottle of rum, scouted ahead, speaking to the girl's sister, who Antonio did not realize was Tomás's secret paramour. Everything was set up. Antonio, Tomás, and the band of romantics they'd hired headed toward the young woman's home on the edge of town, pressed against the mountainside. He would sing; if she approved, her light would turn on and eventually and demurely, she would emerge, and love would be professed by him and accepted by her. If all went well, there would be a serious discussion between himself and her parents within the week, perhaps a marriage within a year.

Tomás positioned the singers just so and stood behind Antonio in support. Just one glance at how much Antonio was sweating demonstrated the need. Tomás offered Antonio some of the rum, and Antonio accepted. His nerves had gotten the best of him, better another swig just to be certain.

After tossing the empty bottle on the ground, Antonio stood below the balcony Tomás indicated and pointed at the accordionist. They began with a popular song, which he dedicated to *the beautiful flower from the plaza*.

Two songs later and there was nothing. No lamp was turned on, no curtain parted. He knew what that meant. She wanted nothing to do with him. Her smile had been a polite ruse. Tomás produced another bottle of rum from his bag. Antonio nodded and asked the accordionist to keep playing popular songs. He wanted to give her as long as possible to emerge. He shared the bottle with the musicians as the rose vendor retired for the night.

After the sixth song, the men were all drunk. *Life without love had no meaning*, they sang, the accordionist not missing a note despite his obvious inebriation. It was time, Antonio conceded, to pack it up.

And then, just as he accepted his fate, a light turned on. The men stopped, as if seeing a holy vision. A curtain moved and a woman emerged. She was exactly as radiant and joyous as she had been hours ago in the plaza. Her hair was freshly braided and her smile contagious.

I'm sorry, she said. *My sister does not remember you. But we thank you for the entertainment.*

Antonio didn't waste a moment. *Oh, no, I came for you. Do you remember me?*

Yes, she said. *I thought you were quite handsome, my sister would have been lucky.*

The guitarist held his instrument, and Antonio cleared his throat. He pulled out his notebook and turned to the freshly penciled page. He nodded at the guitarist, asked for a simple chord progression, and then Antonio began to sing.

He sang of seeing a beautiful bird and wanting to chase it, only to find himself changed into a bird. Would she fly off with him, he wondered, would she explore the skies with him, until they found themselves too old for flight?

Yes, she said, breathless when he finished. But after a moment, she looked past him and changed her mind. *Of course I won't.*

Please, she said, *leave him be. I'm sorry.*

Antonio was confused. What was she saying? He turned to ask

Tomás what this all meant and found himself staring at the barrel of a revolver.

* * *

That's my woman, Tomás said quietly. The musicians took off running, the young woman went back in the house, and Antonio had to decide quickly whether to talk his way out of this or fight his cousin, potentially to death.

So I did both. I begged for my life, and when he refused to move his gun, I did what anyone would do, I punched him in the throat. He fired two shots. And it was so.

It cost Antonio an eye. It cost Tomás his spine. The young woman was never seen again.

* * *

And the two of us? Antonio gestured at Tomás, sitting in his wheelchair down the hall.

God gave us each other. Isn't that enough?

Antonio insisted that he saved Tomás's life, that Tomás had spoken of joining some jungle army, that so many young men were heeding the call of a meat vendor on the run from the law, a youngster named Marín, and that Tomás faced something far worse than paralysis. Antonio believed that the bullet that prevented his cousin from walking also kept his cousin from becoming another dead revolutionary. History has proven him right, Antonio said.

See, he pointed at his missing eye socket. *We're still alive.*

They still play my song, Antonio told me. *The one I composed for her, the woman on the balcony who cost me an eye. The accordionist learned it, played it everywhere. It caught on. But I never married,*

I never fell in love in again. Turns out, she was the only person who struck my heart like lightning.

It's almost cruel, he will lament, to know love like that can happen, only to have it never come again. He asked if I wanted to hear an old vallenato from a one-eyed man. I nodded.

He picked up his accordion and called to Tomás down the hall. *Come, cousin, it's time to sing our story.*

A Love Story
(AN INQUIRY INTO ATTRACTION)

Santander, 1950

After weeks of negotiations, Don Trino conceded. Esther would go to Socorro with her brothers and her mother. She would be close enough to the finca to come when needed.

It helped her case that most communications to the outside world had stopped. The radio towers near the finca were knocked down. The local newspapers had shuttered. The post offices in Cabrera, San Gil, Galán, and Barichara had all burned—which made Socorro the regional center of correspondence.

The idea of sending Esther on the long trip to Bucaramanga, without receiving any confirmation of her arrival, scared Don Trino enough. By the middle of the year, the violence in Cabrera had calmed down for a season, but it still felt like the clouds were gathering more than dispersing. Don Trino still didn't feel comfortable with his children, or wife, staying in the finca. If the Conservatives came, there was no one to hear a scream, no neighbor to help.

Don Trino drove the entire family to Socorro on a Saturday in July 1950. He decided to buy a small house near the edge of town—one with windows and a door reinforced by iron—close enough to the paved roadway and close enough to the city center, a compromise in safety and practicality, to ease Don Trino's anxiety. It was also in a Liberal neighborhood. Someone with sympathetic ears would hear his family's screams.

He'd consolidated his landholdings, buying adjoining properties, even as he sold the others he'd been forced to leave bare. For his newly enlarged finca, he hired one new overseer—it had taken him almost two years to find a good man he could trust, two years that felt both like six months and ten years. But with the new man, Don Trino could spend half his time in the city and half his time on his land, an arrangement that would have to do.

* * *

Esther found it all brutally unfair. So much had been taken from her youth—being a Liberal under Conservative pressure felt intolerable at times. The fake president in Bogotá, elected by only one party, did what all fake presidents did: worry about his legitimacy. But he also continued to support the Conservative paramilitary machine, which made it impossible for a young Liberal woman to have a life outside the house.

My grandmother has never been a fan of President Laureano Gómez. She has referred to him as *Franco's dog*, *the Monster*, and my personal favorite, *the false fascist*. She wasn't objectively wrong in any of these descriptions, as Gómez had used his newspaper, *El Siglo*, as a mouthpiece for fascism for twenty years before the Violence. He had, in many columns and interviews, expressed admiration for Franco. As far as the "monster" accusation, Scholar Vernon Fluharty once called Gómez's tactics "so wildly vitriolic that at times it seemed to border on insanity."

And Esther held the man personally responsible for everything she lacked.

She wanted dances and long conversations with friends over a glass of wine. She wanted to go to the finca and run her hands over the heads of cattle, feel the roughness of their hair, the warmth of their life. She wanted to oversee the milking herself. She wanted more, to be the owner of the land, to meet the right man, to have children. But still, she'd turned down some introductions to men that didn't seem right. Esther was never one to settle.

Between the relocation and getting her bearings, Esther had done a great job of distracting herself from concerns about marriage—but the topic was inevitable. She had sent dozens of new replies to Carlos since her last one burned in the post office, posted from anywhere she could convince her father to ride, but half of them had returned to her, unopened.

Months into her new life as a city girl, Esther finally received a letter from him. The envelope arrived tattered, covered in strange stamps and seals. She tore it open, only to find out Carlos had been sent to Spain by his father to keep him away from the Violence. (*Nothing like fascism to keep you safe*, remarked my grandmother.) He had tried to come see Esther before he left, but his father had offered him a year of study in Spain contingent on immediate departure, and he could not say no. *Would Esther keep writing to him? Would she wait for him to return?*

There it was. An implied declaration of . . . something. *Would she wait?*

* * *

By early summer 1950, the Angarita Sarmientos had adjusted to life in Socorro and now went to mass every Sunday at the big, Liberal church in the center of town, Nuestra Señora del Socorro. Usually, Doña Eva tried to introduce Esther to new families, new sons, new prospects. But as the days went by, fewer and fewer boys appeared for Sunday mass.

Several weeks later, Cousin Leonor eventually joined them. She'd been recently widowed—her husband had died making the milk delivery to the cooperative, stopped and killed by bandits along the way.

What is one to do? She asked Esther after church, as they walked back to the house, the two of them single women in a world with dying men.

Wait, said Esther, *something will come. Something must.*

*   *   *

They quickly established a routine. The week began with church on Sunday and ended every Saturday, when Esther walked to the center of town with her brothers, after lunch had been cleared but before dinner preparations started, to collect her father's messages at the telephone and telegraph office. The walk wasn't too long, about a half mile there and back along the red, stone road. If she hurried, she could be done with the whole endeavor in about thirty minutes, but usually she enjoyed the stroll, prolonging each footstep as she took in the cloudless sky, clear as the bottles of white rum her brother Francisco kept in a small cabinet. She shook her head in disapproval: Nothing good ever came of rum.

She looked older than twenty-three, the furrow in her brow beginning to set. Still—week in and week out, small adjustments were made to the quotidian, and routine took over as it always does. She filled her minutes, soon her days, and quickly enough months. Two years had passed since the death of Gaitán. And, to quote her mother, Esther continued to age without a husband, setting a poor example for her younger sisters.

* * *

One Saturday morning in late July 1950, she took her usual walk, cutting a stark figure on the cobblestone street. Esther was forever perfect in her posture, ruler-straight, hands pressed against her back, one hand firmly held in the other—her long, brown hair curling at the tips as the strands made loose contact with her hands. With each metronomic footstep she breathed in the sunlit scent of manure and grass, of cow and goat, even here in the city, a warm aroma Esther always loved.

But not as much as she loved the telephone and telegraph office, the small telecommunications office one block from the city's center. Her father always had a message or two, a family member confirming a safe arrival or departure, cousins from around the country asking for status reports, news from the milk cooperative's broker.

Esther rushed to collect the yellow notices; it gave her access to her father's business, his moods, his worries. And while she was there, she took advantage of the line out. She saved her centavos each week and paid the man for the privilege of accessing the greater world.

Her brothers would run off to the bar upon reaching the city center, and so Esther was left alone for the last few steps into the building. She relished this part of the walk, these moments without oversight, even if they were mere footsteps in broad daylight.

Esther gathered her long, mustard-colored skirt and stepped into the telecom, cleaning off her brown Chukka-cut leather boots, laced up tight around her thin ankles. She approached the clerk and asked for her messages. He handed her a small stack of paper; she thanked him and requested a booth.

He pointed her to the fourth screen on the right, and as Esther made her way to the back of the shop, she caught sight of Anibal Rueda Guarín, a school friend of her brothers. Anibal was handsome—a big man, with pale blue-green eyes and a childlike mischief to his face. Esther stopped in front of him and smiled when she caught his grin—it was quite infectious. He must have thought her insane for flirting; everyone in a fifty-mile radius knew Esther Angarita Sarmiento was not a flirt, but he stopped anyway and greeted her with a mock concerned look in his eye.

Good afternoon, Señorita Angarita.
Good afternoon, Señor Rueda.
How are you?
Quite well. All is good.
Good. Good.

Esther stood still, waiting for Anibal to say something else, even if just to excuse himself and move on. But he didn't. He simply stood there, blocking her way to the phone booth with banal pleasantries. He had recently been discharged from the army, rumor had it he had been in the president's personal guard, and it showed in the straightness of his posture and the directness of his gaze.

Your family? he finally said.
Well. Yours?
Well.

It was like talking to a child—a very handsome and imposing man-child, with a small vocabulary to match his beady eyes. But she knew he wasn't like a child in all things.

Anibal Rueda Guarín was a notorious womanizer and a gambler, with a twinkle in those aquamarine eyes and a belly to match his generosity and gregarious spirit. It was said that he never turned down a drink, a meal, or a woman. He lived by noble, yet outdated aphorisms as well as terrible jokes, turning a deeper shade of red with each euphonic chuckle. He was a different creature, that much she knew, even though she did not know him, not really.

Anibal Rueda was not known to be shy or short-spoken, and Esther could feel herself flushing at his sudden reticence toward discourse. She found herself without words, something that rarely happened to Esther.

"¿Señorita Angarita?" The clerk interrupted the long pause between Anibal and Esther.

"Sí?"

You have another message.

Esther walked back to the counter and added one more little yellow slip to her stack, thanking the clerk, who added a *see you next week* after his *you're welcome* and a reminder that she was in the fourth private telephone booth on the right.

Anibal excused himself as Esther tried to make her way to the booth a second time, saying that it was always a pleasure to see her. She thanked him and could not help but smile at him again, a rare gift from Esther.

She called her sisters first, and immediately after Helena picked up, Esther told her about the strange encounter with Anibal.

Esther left the telecom that day bemused—how crazy did Anibal Rueda think she was? Smiling to herself like a woman with a secret. She liked Anibal's look—he was thick and bulky in a way that made her feel small, protected. It made him seem manly, baroque in step and spirit. She would later write Helena a letter, telling her all about it in greater detail than the phone call—writing to her sister about how strange her day had been to encounter such a man.

When Esther met Francisco in the town square, her errands complete, she made the mistake of telling her brother who she'd bumped into. He found Esther's news quite amusing.

"Anibal Rueda."

"Sí."

"Anibal Rueda."

"Sí, Francisco. Anibal Rueda."

Francisco sang his name to Esther the entire walk home, but Esther was not having it. *Love is wonderful*, he sang, and she ignored him. She went into the kitchen as soon as they walked into the house, knowing her brother would not follow. Francisco was not interested in the domestic arts. He was more of a delegator. But he surprised Esther and did not relent in his pursuit.

Well, the occasion is such, teased Francisco, *that his sister has invited me for dinner. I should probably bring you along if I go, don't you think? I could use a chaperone after all.* Francisco ran in the same circles as Anibal's older sister Rosa.

Esther shook her head again in both excitement and confusion. But what Francisco remembered from that afternoon was my grandmother's smile. How the corners of her mouth fought her better intentions and won. He insisted she join him, and the matter was settled.

What Francisco did not remember to do was reply. Esther waited patiently for a day, and after her chores were done in the afternoon, she asked Francisco about the impending date, for scheduling reasons of course.

Oh, he said, *I only teased. Rosa Rueda only invited me to be polite.*

Francisco was distracted. He'd met a different girl in town, and he was trying to figure out who she was and how to see her again.

That night, Esther grabbed the stationery from the desk and wrote an enthusiastic reply to Rosa Rueda, gladly accepting her invitation, signing the note, *Francisco Angarita*. She included a brief mention, near the end, that Esther would come as well.

She sent the note via an uncle riding in their direction that evening. Rosa Rueda would know that she and Francisco were coming for dinner without delay.

As days went by, as she waited for a response, Esther began to pick up information about Anibal from the people who stopped by her home, innocent inquiries. She was told he'd returned from his government-mandated time in the military (something Don Trino paid for his sons to avoid) with a more serious demeanor—Anibal Rueda had stopped partying and womanizing as much. He was twenty-three, same as her. The gossips said he was looking for a wife. The armed forces, and two years of fighting on behalf of the government, had knocked some sense into him.

Esther liked this change in Anibal. Military meant order, meant discipline. Of course, the darker rumors also said this was not always true of him. But Esther put that aside as she sensed a deep compatibility—a complement to her own militaristic precision and ruler-perfect posture.

People in the family were starting to notice how often Esther casually asked about Anibal Rueda Guarín.

* * *

Soon enough, the confirmation from Rosa Rueda arrived and the date was set. Francisco would drive to the Rueda finca near the hamlet of La Fuente on August 8 for dinner with Rosa Rueda, his sister in tow. Esther wrote the date carefully in her leather-bound notebook.

Rosa Rueda met their truck in the hamlet's square. She got into the cabin with Esther and Francisco, after throwing some purchases in the back. As Rosa pointed out the hidden turns along the route, Esther calmed herself by naming the types of plants and animals spotted along the way. There was a chance, she knew, that Anibal wouldn't even be there, and all this anxiety was for nothing.

But he was there. Standing on the veranda of the Rueda homestead with his father, an uncle or two, and his cousins.

She decided to act as neutrally as possible despite her nerves. But as soon as she began her descent from the cab of the truck, Anibal appeared from nowhere and helped her down.

Halfway through the meal, it was clear that Anibal wanted Esther's attention. He would tell a joke and then look up at Esther expectantly. But my grandmother never rewarded him. The neutral line of her lips never wavered. Until, without warning, Anibal hit on a subject near to Esther's heart.

And that President Laureano Gómez . . .

The joke he told is lost to memory. But the laughter that peeled from her—the foreign sound of melodic amusement from a woman so serious—the story of her laughter was passed down through the generations.

Laughter can be a dangerous thing for a woman. Aside from the power of humiliation, laughter also carries with it the intimacy of joy. When a woman that rarely smiles gives a full-throated laugh, a certain amount of vulnerability becomes exposed. In making Esther laugh, Anibal Rueda Guarín had opened a door.

*   *   *

After dinner, Esther looked for her brother. Francisco had followed one of Anibal's cousins onto the veranda, a bottle of whiskey in hand. After having a few drinks, the two men left for Socorro together, leaving the Angarita family truck.

Esther knew her brother wouldn't be back that night. Francisco had been nursing a broken heart, as he'd fallen in love with the wrong woman. The girl he'd met in town turned out to be the daughter of a Conservative mayor on the other side of the river. Their brief and explosive love was forbidden and impossible. Francisco had spent most of the morning talking about how to convince the world that there was more to life than politics. No one listened to anything he had to say. Least of all Esther, who had to navigate her completely acceptable crush with dignity and composure.

THE VIOLENCE

After the meal and a game of cards, Esther decided to drive the truck home herself—she was never one to overstay her welcome. But Anibal volunteered to drive her truck back into town, to act as a noble escort through the confusing twists and turns of the mountainside. His double cousin (they were the children of two brothers who married two sisters) Domingo Rueda Guarín, someone she knew well from church, also needed a ride into town.

As he climbed into the truck, Esther made sure that Domingo sat in the center. She could feel her heartbeat and was terrified that Anibal would somehow hear it too. The entire drive, Esther made no eye contact with him. She responded to none of his comments or minor queries. Domingo filled in for her—laughing at jokes and providing appropriate anecdotes. The two Rueda Guaríns acted and looked like siblings, so the conversation flowed between them. Soon they'd reached Socorro, and after Anibal parked the car in front of Don Trino's home, he got out to walk with Domingo.

As Esther kissed both Rueda men on the cheek in polite farewell, she stopped for a second before turning up the walkway home. She wanted to say something but didn't know how or what would communicate her feelings best—especially in front of Anibal's cousin.

Can I write to you or call on you? Anibal asked her, interrupting her thoughts, a hopeful smile on his face.

I'll see you at church on Sunday, here in Socorro.

Which is a close to a *yes* as one can get from Esther Angarita.

The Revolutionary
(A MOVEMENT IN HIDING)

The Mountains, 1950

The Conservative regime began a campaign to encourage forgetting. Foreign dignitaries were beginning to ask too many questions about mass graves and rumors of government involvement. The Conservatives explained that it was all a Communist problem and turned up a Communist or two when needed.

One government massacre can be explained. The war between neighbors, between a government and its political opponents, did not suit the narrative. Survivors created a problem for the Conservative government as human rights groups began to form to address the disappearances and massacres.

Or as one Conservative politician wrote to another that year, *the Communists have created another committee to investigate their own deaths.*

The paramilitary commanders were given their orders: no survivors, no witnesses, no memories. The Colombian art of omission.

* * *

Entire villages would disappear overnight as territory changed hands.

When an entire village is killed, no one is left to remember them. They become places for disregard, confusing for researchers decades later and impossible to find no matter how many back roads are taken. Those who survived soon learned to forget for their own good, hometowns erased from thought and secrets hidden behind sealed lips. *In a closed mouth, no flies enter.*

The Condor, sitting back at the Happy Bar in Tuluá, kept a small list of Liberals who had managed to escape him—who remembered too much. Pedro Marín remained at the top. Three years of killing, and the old cheesemonger had not forgotten about the young man who survived his massacre in Ceilán.

He had good reason to remember the kid. Whispers had begun to circulate about someone from the western side of the Andes highlands, a former meat salesman who had started to gather his Liberal relatives and other like-minded folk, organizing them against the Conservative-funded paramilitary. Training camps had sprung up.

Pedro Marín, perpetually hunted by Conservatives, price firmly on his head, had begun to move his message east—far from what he thought was the Condor's reach.

But violence has no jurisdiction.

Paramilitaries, supported by the Conservative regime, spread from one region to another, changing names along the way, but sharing vendettas. Sometimes they were called Birds, sometimes Chulavitas, sometimes just los Godos. They were all the same—private armies that existed to drive out Liberals, exchanging kill lists and maintaining Conservative order.

Pedro Marín was wanted by them all.

* * *

Geography bears part of the blame. The Andes are at fault as much as the tempers of men provoked by rum and grievances alike. In Colombia, the mountains are green with life, with nooks and devious hiding places. The plants in these mountains—tobacco and coffee, fruit and fiber—survive its mood swings and temperature shifts, a reminder that to live here is to be hardened and ready for the fight.

When a man is on the run, the mountains welcome him with open arms, like the cool mist envelops the land in the morning. If a man happens to have the mountain's blood in his veins, then he'll know which exposed roots give cover in the night, which leaves collect hydrating dew, and how to bury himself to become the terrain. The mountains favor the hunted.

Somewhere on the roads between Bogotá and Santander, near the city of Tunja, there was a notorious paramilitary group called the Dogs, who were doing their best to sniff out the man.

But the Dogs had a problem. The Dogs were being systematically killed.

Men would disappear on patrols, found dead a few miles away the next morning, spears protruding from their distended abdomens. Men collapsed on the street, poison darts embedded in their skin. Within weeks, the Dogs went from being a large force interrupting departmental trade to an outfit barely able to muster enough men for routine banditry.

Stories circulated about ghosts, indigenous curses, and ancient revenge. The men had been trained to fight against revolvers and machetes, not arrows and sticks. Some claimed this was the work of the mountain—it hid too much. But leadership reminded them that men blow darts, men wield spears—not ghosts, not myths, not ancients. These were humans, men trained by Marín. And the Dogs would fight back.

* * *

Marín found it easy to recruit men to his cause as he traveled east.

Rebels, massacre survivors, and fed-up workers alike joined him. Younger sons from wealthy and middle-class Liberal families, who stood to inherit little (and who were more inclined to understand the unfairness of conditions established by birth) also allied themselves with him.

Marín fought for a Colombia that belonged to the workers—the dream of Gaitán. The people should be the owners of the land. Not these warmongering owners—didn't the land belong to the people who worked it? But most of these ideas came later. His first cause, the cause nearest to his heart, was the abolition of the Birds, the Chulavitas, the Godos, and—between Bogotá and Santander—the Dogs.

Marín used the wisdom of the old men to train the young. His grandfather, a veteran of the War of a Thousand Days, an earlier civil war between parties in 1899, showed him how to wage a different type of battle than the army-trained paramilitary. Marín recruited more veterans, and these warriors of older conflicts taught the younger combatants how to ambush, how to hide in the jungle, how to blow a poison dart—knowledge passed down by the indigenous over centuries and perfected by generations of irregular combat.

The newest techniques are also the oldest, Marín reiterated to his men.

His forces were patient, unlike most local reactionary brigades, which disappeared as soon as leadership collapsed. Marín wanted to plan, wanted to train, wanted to get uniforms.

Little by little, Marín began to amass his own army.

Raising weapons is the only way to survive, he would say to his men. *The time for justice has come.*

* * *

The Dogs in Santander found themselves facing an invisible enemy. Men would vanish from their homes in the middle of the night, their wives waking up next to an empty depression instead of a husband. In October 1950, five men went missing in one night in Tunja, and the Conservative leadership decided to act.

To secure funds to hire more men, the Conservative government began using a new word to describe men like Pedro Marín: revolutionaries. In the national government's estimation, these men may as well be Communists, with all their prattle about worker's rights.

And with that, the retaliations began. Paramilitary bosses established raiding parties, and small groups were sent to intimidate Liberal landowners—hoping to flush out the Revolutionary himself.

The Dogs were authorized to use any force required.

The Ghost
(A FIT OF SEVERANCE)

Santander, 1950

Francisco had a broken heart.
    His romance with a nearby village mayor's daughter continued for weeks, a back-and-forth of acceptance and rejection. The girl professed her undying love for Francisco but said it could not be. It was as simple as Romeo and Juliet, two houses, two political parties, two unwilling sets of parents.
    By December, she asked Francisco to leave her. To go back to his lands, Socorro and Cabrera. She had no intentions of ending up dead, she told Francisco.

*   *   *

Francisco, days before Christmas and drunk in the early evening after a bottle of whiskey with friends, had gone to the Conservative girl's house, had pleaded with her father for a chance at love, and upon receiving another denial (now with a threat of arrest and jail time), had subsequently drunk another bottle of whiskey at the local bar, and decided instead to concoct a plan.

Francisco had asked her to elope more times than the Devil tempted Christ—even after she told him to go. She was too scared of defying her family, too unwilling to take on the social and financial risks of not getting her parents' blessing. And that only deepened his obsession.

Francisco felt trapped. He was old enough to be married, old enough to make his own decisions. But the promise of family land kept him in Santander. In many ways, he was beholden to the same forces as the girl who now rejected him. He just had a father who remembered being young—and who indulged his sons more than he should.

There was a war going on, and Francisco considered joining the resistance. He considered starting his own gang of bandits. He considered moving to the city—any city. But he was tethered to Don Trino, and he knew it. He was all energy and no movement, a tea kettle burning to the touch, but yet to make steam. He wanted to destroy, to feel the power he'd been denied, to rage against her, her family, and the whole war that made their love impossible.

The logic of whiskey benefited the body count in those years, and why not? In a world where neighbors were raped and good workers lost their lives, a little scare could send a warning to the mayor. Obtaining the dynamite wasn't difficult. Plenty of urbanization projects and demolition supplies abounded in those days. He kept drinking, gathered more supplies, and waited out the day at a tavern. He headed for the small village after dusk, and kept the fire within him burning through another night.

Just before dawn, he positioned three sticks of dynamite over the fuel tank of her family's car. He lit the spark and ran, as the door opened and the girl's mother stepped out of the gate to pour out a bucket of water on the sidewalk. The slender wick burned down, as the woman watched Francisco run away. She recognized the boy and yelled for her husband, when something bright caught the corner of her eye.

The explosion killed her.

*   *   *

Francisco Angarita had not been quiet about his grudge, so it wasn't hard for the local police to imagine who could have done such a thing. Still, in the early hours, the gossips held their instrument. Was this just a crime of passion? Or had Francisco recently joined the new band of Liberal outlaws living in the mountains? Lists of enemies were drawn up and suspects removed or added.

Don Trino was respected enough by everyone that even the Conservatives worked slowly before charging his son with murder.

The woman's relatives retaliated in the immediate aftermath by forming a posse and randomly killing ten Liberals on the streets of Cabrera. Within an hour of Francisco's explosion, eleven bodies required rites and burial. None had anything to do with Francisco's fight, other than being background players in a much larger story.

Francisco, despite his claims of only wanting to scare the girl's father, was the party responsible. It didn't matter that it was an accident of fate and alcohol. It didn't matter that the family were Conservatives and had prospered as others died and faltered, sometimes at their behest. It didn't even matter that the old man was guilty of crimes against the hearts of youth in love. What mattered was that with his bomb, Francisco had not only killed the girl's mother, but also any possible chance at happiness with the girl.

He'd also killed his own chances at inheriting his father's land.

There was no way he could stay in Santander without facing justice for his crimes.

Francisco ran and walked for three hours along the road to the lands of Domingo Rueda Guarín, Anibal Rueda's double cousin, hiding in trees when he heard the sound of any car making its way through the winding roads. Francisco knew all the Rueda boys from school, enough so that he didn't worry about arriving in his current state. They had all drunk together, and Domingo Rueda Guarín had stayed up with Francisco to face too many sunrises. He knew his drinking buddy would forgive him everything, especially a crime of passion—isn't that why they drank together in the first place? To find forgiveness somewhere, even if only at the bottom of an opaque bottle.

Francisco reeked of whiskey and gunpowder. He looked like a revolutionary. Domingo heard two sentences of Francisco's story and stopped him. Domingo didn't want to know what happened—the less he knew, the easier it would be to help his friend. Right now, Domingo understood the basics. *The wife of a small-town Conservative mayor was dead. Francisco needed to hide.*

There were no rapprochements or talk of guilt and the necessary consequences. No one would mention the police. That would come later. The judgment of family and community can last much longer than the judgment of law. But where the law is rigid, so can a community be flexible. I imagine that when Francisco showed up, Domingo, knowing the political climate, did everything in his power to help. A fellow Liberal felt no need to turn over a good man, even if guilty, to severe Conservative justice.

No one could imagine the punishment that awaited Francisco if caught. A Liberal guilty of coldly murdering the wife of a village mayor, prominent Conservative, at that. Death would be a kindness compared to what Francisco expected if his escape proved unsuccessful.

Domingo hid Francisco in an alcove upstairs and left to go see Don José Rueda, his uncle and Anibal Rueda's father. Don José knew Don Trino, and as always, it's better when news like this comes from someone familiar.

* * *

Don José Rueda called on Don Trino within the hour. The old man was in Socorro, so it was easy for Don José to find him.

Don José explained the situation and the old man took it hard. Don Trino almost fell out of his rocking chair on the veranda, swaying back and forth as he tried to focus on a plan of action between bouts of crossing himself and adjusting the fedora he put on. He stopped after a minute or two, stood up and opened the front door into the house, called for Esther, and asked her to make some coffee—there were guests, after all.

When Esther left the room, Don José presented an idea: *Get Francisco to the coast. No one would look for him there; he could relocate and get out of this godforsaken battleground. If Francisco stays in these mountains, they will find him. Send your other son, the one with the temper, with him; sons are a liability. Let them start anew together.*

Don Trino had delivered news like this himself before. He knew that Don José was in possession of more information, information Don Trino could not know, like the location of his son. He knew there was wisdom in what Don José was saying. Trinito *was* a liability too. Any boy in his twenties was, during a civil war. And even though he knew all this, Don Trino still tried to figure out how to keep his sons next to him for as long as he could. There was no answer. There was no way.

Esther returned with the coffee, only to find Don Trino and Don José sitting quietly, each lost in their own contemplations. Esther knew something had happened—but she tried to separate her feelings from the sense that this was bigger than she could presently understand. It's not every day that Anibal Rueda's father showed up at her home.

She lingered in the kitchen, ready to be of service. When Don José finally asked for his coat, it was Esther who brought it to him.

And when the man delivered a muted greeting on behalf of his son Anibal, she had the good sense to nod in appreciation. She was not a foolish young woman, and she knew Don José was not at her home for lighthearted social reasons.

Don Trino informed Esther immediately of Francisco's fate and then grabbed his hat before he left to find Trinito. In the meantime, Esther was to stay put and keep the household on its regular schedule. It was imperative that she keep calm.

* * *

By evening, a large group of old men had descended on their home. And with them, a network of Liberals activated—some hid Francisco, others provided weapons, horses, and provisions, while others found clear paths and trails that would lead to Liberal enclaves and safety.

Benito Rueda, yet another Rueda cousin, gave Francisco copies of his papers—identification cards, passport, and checkbook ledger. The portly Benito was replaced with the wiry Francisco—photographs gently peeled over steam, as new ones were attached in their stead. These cards, certificates, and documents provided passage through any police or military checkpoints along the way—and should be enough to get Francisco to safety. Secrecy and back roads were of supreme importance. No one in this part of Santander would think Francisco a Rueda with his angular Angarita Sarmiento looks.

The next day, Don Trino called upon the local priest (a third cousin) to delete records of Francisco from the church house—any mention of his birth, or existence on paper had to be destroyed, transferred, and generally, impossible to find. The Francisco Angarita Sarmiento who existed in Santander could not be connected to the Benito Rueda living on the Caribbean shore. He had to be erased from everyone's memory and become a never-mentioned figment of the imagination, a ghost haunting the extended family portrait.

He would not be the first. My grandmother Esther will not tell me her own great-grandmothers' names. It doesn't matter how I ask; she tells me that no good will come of looking them up. That some histories are for the graveyards and the graveyards only. My mother tells me a name she once heard from another cousin or aunt several times removed. An uncle supplies another. The church where all the ancient family records were kept, the ones dating back to the sixteenth century, burned down in 1901, near the end of the War of a Thousand Days.

My grandmother's arguments for existence focus on the objectives to be met rather than the path already traveled. *Our ancestors brought us here, and here we are.* She does not mind the burned-down church, the lost records, the forgotten letters. *What's important*, she will tell me, *is that we're alive now. That is God's will.*

And it's true. She made it through the first couple years of the Violence relatively unscathed. Her siblings all lived, and her parents thrived despite the odds. Others, including too many of her cousins, were not so lucky. Part of it was Don Trino's wisdom in sending his children away. Part of it was the goodwill the family had fomented on their side of the mountains. Most of it was chance.

Eighty percent of the dead were impoverished, rural, unarmed civilians. People were quartered, decapitated, impaled, burned, stabbed, slashed, and drowned. Harvests were destroyed, homes demolished, goods stolen. The perpetrators were mostly impoverished and rural civilians as well.

Thousands of Liberals died, but tens of thousands more died who simply had Liberal bosses.

This is what happens, my grandmother noted to me once, *when the bullets are in charge.*

My great-grandfather had erased his family many times before, all that mattered was the deed to the land where he raised his children and his cows. History could burn down as many times as it wanted to, in his estimation. Don Trino's plan was to survive.

*   *   *

Francisco's best bets, everyone knew, were the big cities on the coast. Barranquilla had a quarter of a million people in 1950. Cartagena had 100,000. A person could get lost in a big city in a country where too many shared the same name. Francisco had a world of possibility before him, as long as he made it to the coast alive.

Before Francisco left, Don Trino, patriarch of the family, followed Don José's advice. Trinito, the younger, should go along with Francisco, *directly*.

It was for the best. Trinito had been acting out since the move to Socorro—getting into too many rum-inspired brawls for Don Trino's comfort. The two loose cannons would be safer from themselves on the beach than in the mountains.

Christmas was a quiet affair that year, with the boys in hiding and preparations for their departure under way. And then, a few days later, before the new year, on a day no one remembers or will speak about, my great-uncles Francisco and Trinito rode off, or drove off, or pushed off north, sleeping in cheap way stations and some clergy-sponsored halfway homes (a few coins tended to loosen some political alliances). They were lost in the throng of the displaced, seeking refuge from the violence that had torn through hamlets and villages throughout the nation, up and through Cesár, El Magdalena, and finally to the department of Bolívar, to the city of Cartagena.

The family waited weeks for word from the boys, and finally, in February 1951, a message arrived at the telecom office from one Benito Trinidad Rueda Angarita, informing Don Trino that the bulls he'd requested were healthy—happily acclimating to the relentless heat of the Caribbean. And for the first time since Don José had called at his house, Don Trino was able to breathe, to smile, to enjoy a sunset on his veranda. The old man had aged ten years in ten weeks, and for the first time in her life, Esther began to worry about her father, who was consumed by his sons.

Her family also found itself with a moral debt to the Ruedas—Don José, in particular. But like the good man Don José was, he simply shrugged off any mention of gratitude or compensation. *You would do the same for my boy*, he said to Don Trino. Plus, Don José was intrigued by the Magdalena River Valley, a few hours' journey southeast of Barranquilla. He'd heard good things about the coastal valley at the foot of the Sierra Nevada de Santa Marta and had some contacts in the region. Perhaps Francisco and Trinito could scout on Don José's behalf. More and more landowners were headed in that direction.

* * *

Liberals helped Liberals, or so the saying went. But no one could help the Angaritas once the Conservative police finally acted on the evidence connecting Francisco to the crime. The raids on the finca began days after Francisco disappeared.

As his cows died, a "tax" on his son's sins, Don Trino started hiding money in Esther's bedroom, stopped trusting the bank, and with great hostility submitted himself to daily inquiries by the Conservative police looking for Francisco and Trinito, who by association and conspicuous absence had now become a suspect in the bombing as well. Don Trino made sure to offend no one. As the weeks of aggression continued, he stopped drinking anywhere outside his home, rarely welcomed guests, and began attending the seven o'clock mass with the Conservatives. Esther and Evangelina were barricaded in the city house, only allowed to leave for church. The family had always been pious and Catholic, and it was time to demonstrate that an intelligent man could have faith and principles alongside any other.

Even after Don Trino told all his Liberal friends to stop visiting, Anibal Rueda continued to come, ostensibly on behalf of his father. Francisco and Trinito depended on the Rueda family's network of friends, and Don José sending his son to update Don Trino made perfect sense. But even after there was no new information, Anibal continued making social calls on Don Trino. The men began doing business with each other, trading cattle and borrowing equipment, as local farmers often do. Not even the police could question why Anibal stopped by the Angarita house in Socorro so often.

Until, of course, someone saw Anibal Rueda writing a love letter at a local café.

Gossip spread through the mountains of Santander that Anibal Rueda Guarín had fallen in love. When he spoke to Esther in public after church sometime later, the tongues began to vibrate in earnest. And when, a few weeks later, Anibal Rueda was seen riding from Cabrera toward Socorro, well, the old women collapsed from linguistic exhaustion, only to rise again—the pull of curiosity stronger than the limit of discussion.

No one understood how such a severe (albeit striking) woman could attract such a handsome and jovial man. What did she do to him? No one could assail her virtue, as she was pious in both her religious thought and filial obligation. But no one, except her dearest friends, found her particularly talkative or charming, which all old maids should be. Esther mostly grunted at strangers or snapped at their observations. There were plenty of single women with no prospects, women who were much more attractive than

Esther. Women abounded in a world where men were dying. But somehow my grandmother had beguiled the gregarious son of one of the most well-regarded small landowners in their part of Santander.

No one understood Anibal Rueda at all, except for maybe Esther Angarita.

The Cut

(A SONATA IN ROSE RED)

The Mountains, 1952

Deep in the mountains of Colombia, a woman and her husband stood in their finca's inoculation corral when a group of strangers approached. The woman and her husband had barely begun the day's work, when the men rode up, posse-style, brandishing weapons.

She stood upright with one of the workers, vaccinating, carefully plunging a syringe through the thick hides of the cows just like the veterinarian had taught her as the worker restrained the beast within the small pen. Her husband leaned on the other side of the corral, counting calves with the overseer. When the men rode up, everyone stopped their activity and stared. *It looked like a Western*, I was told, *something you'd pay a couple of pesetas to see on the trip into town, men on horseback waving guns.*

We are the Dogs, they had yelled, wearing blue face masks, holes cut out for the eyes and mouth, circling the woman, her husband, the overseer, and the farmhand. They carried machetes; one of them had a gun that clearly wasn't loaded, as he kept squeezing the trigger and making the *bang-bang* noises with his mouth. *Bang-bang!* he'd say.

The Dog who led the posse, indistinguishable from the rest, but riding in front, stopped before the husband.

"Franela, Florero, o Corbata?"

The husband stared at his wife. He voted Conservative but had married into a locally prominent Liberal family; therefore, by association, he had become a Liberal as well. Now he was to pick between a T-shirt Cut, a Flower Vase Cut, and a Necktie Cut.

* * *

Killing had become an art in the departments, and the several methods of slicing Liberals had turned into sculpture.

During these years, Colombians became infamous for the ritualized mutilation of their rivals. Everything that could be cut out, pulled out, and exhibited was: eyes, ears, heads, testicles, fetuses, breasts, intestines, hands, tongues, and hearts.

Looking through the photographic archives is difficult. But once one becomes numb to the horror, the creativity of Colombian murder cannot be denied. Over time, an elaborate manual of cuts evolved—each with its own name and method of execution. Particular killers defined themselves through their exclusive use of one style or another.

Some of the cuts showed a certain amount of whimsical disdain for human life: The Monkey Cut harkened back to an older custom of placing a decapitated pet monkey-head in a victim's lap; but in the Colombian version popular during the Violence, killers placed the decapitated heads of their victims in the victims' own laps. My mother will call this the John the Baptist Cut, and although nowhere else lists it that way, there is a savage poetry to serving one's own head on a platter. Other cuts relished in their cruelty: The Tamale Cut involved dicing a body, as if preparing for inclusion in a meal. The still living victims of the French Cut had the skin on their heads peeled back. The lists continue, each different "cut" eliciting a new disgust.

The impulse to turn the grotesque into something resembling art was not new. Worldwide and throughout all time, murderers have taken lives and created disturbing tableaus with what remains. Colombians excelled at this during the Violence, but the human impulse to display and make beauty from the unspeakably awful transcends geography or time. The stylizing of the dead body forces whoever comes upon it to stare. To divorce identity and soul and life from corpse and turn it into a different type of human object. These objects, in turn, denote the suffering of a victim as much as the perversity of the assassin; the strong metaphorical value reinforces the dehumanization of the victim. The artistry of the cut is meant to impart horror, revulsion, and astonishment. And it does. Absolutely. Horrifyingly.

This is how terror works. In violating the body, the killer ensures a closed-casket funeral—a certain final shame. At times, these displays made bodies harder to identify. A certain dignity is gone—forever attached to the story of the person's death is the story of how their body was found. These mutilations carry messages—warnings and histories as much as signatures.

Certain regions became known for particular cuts. Killers near riversides with bocachico fish engaged in a practice known as "bocachiquiar," wherein grooves were cut in the victim's back, imitating the scales of the fish. In Santander, the three most notorious cuts were the T-shirt, the Flower Vase, and the Necktie. When the man in the posse yelled out options for the husband's death, the husband would have known, would have been familiar with, what each cut entailed:

The T-shirt Cut involved a decapitation as well as the removal of the arms; the torso left looking like a long shirt, to be folded away and tucked in a wooden drawer. The Flower Vase Cut severed arms and legs and inserted them into a decapitated torso, the hole forcibly enlarged to accommodate the severed limbs, meant to look like a floral arrangement. The Necktie Cut, or as it is known today, "The Colombian Necktie," was characterized by a slit down the throat, with the tongue pulled out through the slit in the esophagus and placed over the chest, a mockery of the long ties worn by Liberal oligarchs on Sunday.

It was also, of the three, the husband's best chance for survival.

* * *

The husband didn't answer the Dog's question. He never removed his eyes from his wife as he addressed the man in a booming voice. *I am a Conservative. I am not a Liberal and I have done you no harm.* The blue-masked men laughed.

Oh, look at him, they said, he's so proper. *Let's give him a necktie. Something he can wear to town with his Liberal wife.*

The woman, who had frozen, screamed as the men advanced on horseback toward her husband. She screamed but did not move, her voice heavy and raspy, the shame of her frozen inaction imprinted on her vocal cords. The masked men turned toward her and slowly drew their machetes across their faces, a gesture of silence to the screaming woman. The worker, the farmhand, trying to save her or perhaps himself by forcing silence upon her, pushed her to the ground, where she landed on a spot of barbed wire, her left arm pressed beneath her, slowly bleeding as she bore her own weight upon the metal thorns meant to contain cattle.

As two of the Dogs dismounted, the husband pulled out his own machete, ready to fight. But there was no battle. Two more men approached from behind, knocking the machete out of his hands and tying back his arms.

They mocked the husband as they forced him to open his mouth, sticking the butt of the machete through his lips, breaking his teeth with their force. They wanted to watch his tongue be slowly pulled out through the slit they prepared to make along his throat. The husband had been so proud of his teeth, cleaning them daily with baking soda, boasting of their fortitude each morning. Yet bone and flesh succumb to metal and force too easily. One of the masked men went to the woman and sat on her, pushing her further into the barbed wire beneath her, making sure she faced her husband as they clumsily pulled his tongue through a gaping hole carved with a blunt and rusted blade.

If they had left, their niece told me, *if they had left right then, both could have survived intact; the family could have done something.* The men didn't stay long enough for them to both die. But they didn't leave soon enough for them to both survive. *Timing is destiny*, my mother would say.

*   *   *

They stayed until the husband died, watching him collapse in place, as they instructed the farmhand and overseer to surrender the property. *This finca*, one of them said, *is no longer yours. Leave.*

The husband was dead, and the woman was still subdued by the man sitting on top of her. The children had been sent to boarding schools, the closest relatives were an hour's ride away. The two workmen nodded, unsure what to do, knowing that they weren't important enough for a sculpted death, but in no way safe from the attackers until they proved they were simply hired hands. There was no space for loyalty here.

Your first job, said the man astride the woman to the farmhand, *is to vaccinate this cow. Give her a shot. Right in the arm.* The farmhand hesitated, so the masked rider took the thick syringe himself, squeezing his thighs to steady himself as he leaned back, gripping the large needle and turning the woman over just a bit, positioning himself for the penetration. Her skin gave quickly.

She felt the needle filled with bovine medicine and hormones go through her already swollen and bleeding arm. Felt the man on her back kick his heels into her stomach. *Take me to the house!* he commanded her, *Take me to the house, beast!*

She collapsed—released the arms that kept her head up even as she lay on the ground. She couldn't do it. She couldn't move. Her arm too numb, the man too heavy, her husband, or what was left of him, before her in the mud. The spines of her prized rosebushes pressing into her flesh along with the barbed wire of the corral. She did her best to speak to the man, the man that insisted on riding her, and simply asked to be killed. He spat on her.

We don't do anything a Liberal asks. We never will.

The man got off her. The farmhand came over to help her up, perhaps out of a sense of chivalry or history, a kindness to a fallen woman, but before he even touched her, one of the masked men tore the good man's stomach open with his blade, the rust-colored blood of the man who would have helped her instead spilled over her arm.

No aiding Liberals. The men laughed, a Greek chorus as she struggled to be still, to be silent, to be dead—or dead enough.

She stayed in the dirt after the men rode off and concentrated on dying as comfortably as she could. She tried to drag herself to her husband, to hold him, but the pain was too much. Her arm throbbed too much. Drawing a breath was too much.

After she was found, the doctors saved her, but not the arm. The amputation was quick, as painless as possible.

That evening, the doctor informed the woman that she was pregnant, and she imagined rubbing her stomach with her absent arm, the phantom limb reassuring, making sure the baby was all right. The baby was fine—a blessed miracle amid all this suffering.

Her family called the police, called the newspapers, called important men in town. All of them shook their heads, *there is nothing to be done*, said one. *We live in Conservative times*, said another. None offered solutions, simply advice: *Wait till your people are in power again. Then it will be your turn for justice.*

* * *

The bandits took the remaining man alive, the overseer from the finca, and tied him facedown onto the back of a horse behind their smallest rider. The Dogs rode for hours, crossing in and out of the mountains and valleys of Santander. By the time they stopped to let the horses drink from a stream, the overseer had no idea how to get home. The bandits knew this, so they finally removed their blue masks. The overseer remained tied to the horse, but the bandit in charge sauntered up and quickly cut the ropes binding the overseer. The commander posed a question to his captive.

Our bosses pay well. You want in?

The overseer shook his head. *I want to go home to my wife and children.*

We'll let you go if you swear on your family's life that you won't go back to working for Liberals.

The overseer nodded. There's little he would not have promised to see his children again.

Say it.

I swear on my family's life that I will not go work for any Liberals.

We'll need something more.

Anything.

The formerly masked man laughed as he swung his machete down, cutting off the man's left hand at the wrist. The other bandits watched with joy as the overseer kneeled in shock.

Sufficient. We know where you live. If you live and try to find us, we'll kill everyone you know. He looked at his men. *Let's go!*

The Dogs began to mount their horses as the overseer oscillated between scrambling for something to stop the bleeding and doing his best to stay conscious. The Dog that had only said "bang-bang" threw a rag at the overseer.

For your wound.

The man proved resourceful. He fashioned a tourniquet and sought help, slowly making his way, one impossible step at a time. An hour can contain an eternity; and after several eternities of wandering the mountain jungle, pretending he had a sense of direction, the overseer found a group of thirty men in a small clearing.

"Auxilio!" he managed to get out before language failed him. The pain was too much.

A young man, no older than twenty, stood and walked to the collapsed overseer.

"Ayúdenle."

Several men ran over and grabbed the fallen overseer. Another man pulled out a backpack and began looking for the right tools for the task.

This is going to hurt more before it gets better, the young man cautioned the overseer.

The overseer couldn't imagine a greater pain than the one he already felt. Suddenly, he realized that he didn't know these men. Were they Conservatives? Conservative paramilitary? Liberals? The overseer looked at the young man—he had a military bearing, clearly in charge of this group, but he wore no identifiable uniform. Pedro Marín, now twenty years old, answered the overseer's question before the overseer even had a chance to ask it.

Welcome to the People's Army.

The man with the medical supplies signaled to Marín. The young guerrilla told the overseer to prepare. The wound needed to be cauterized. The overseer nodded but looked confused.

Do you have any questions?

He only had one. *Who are the people this army fights for?*

You. Not the rich Conservatives, not the rich Liberals. You. My army—this army—fights for you.

A Wednesday in April
(A CELEBRATION IN A BLUE DRESS)

Santander, 1952

Anibal drove into town on a Sunday morning and found Esther leaving mass. He parked his truck, stepped out, and grabbed her arm—meeting her silence with his own. They walked together to a newly opened café on the other side of the plaza. Anibal was careful to open every door and pull out every chair, as manners pleased Esther, and he wanted very much to please her.

Anibal still visited Mancarique, ostensibly to discuss cattle prices with Don Trino, at least once a week. Don Trino found him agreeable and thought his daughter could do far worse. Not that anyone talked about love or intentions, but still—he wasn't blind, and Anibal's feelings toward Esther had always seemed clear.

A year of deep staring and chaperoned walks were a minor eternity for Esther and Anibal. People married young and quickly in those days—a courtship that bled from one year into the next was rare. Don Trino had begun talking about weddings, as had Doña Eva. My grandmother understood that Anibal would say something when it was time.

They had been lagging behind their chaperones for weeks, attempting to catch moments alone. Even this moment, a chance encounter leaving church, required some stealth. Two Angarita cousins stood outside, drinking their own coffees, occasionally glancing in, to make sure Esther's honor remained intact. There wasn't much time for them without familial company, and all she wanted was to be alone with Anibal Rueda. In a few minutes, her cousins would come get her and this moment, like so many others, would end.

*   *   *

In the café, Anibal ordered two slices of cake with accompanying tintos before clearing his throat to speak again.

We've been friends a long time.

She nodded. This was true.

I think it's time we got married.

Esther, not a muscle moving in her face, nodded. This too was true. Anibal waited for her to speak. He wasn't sure if she'd nodded in agreement or in acknowledgment of his question. He needed to hear an answer from her. She thought she'd answered the question and had already moved on to planning the wedding in her thoughts. The owner brought the food and drinks. Her silence finally got to him; Anibal cleared his throat twice more, bringing Esther back into the moment.

Will you marry me, Esther?

Yes, she said, *it's time.*

He procured a ring from his pocket, but it proved too big for Esther's thin fingers, so she held the ring in her left hand and nodded as Anibal told her how much he loved her, his large hand enveloping her smaller one. She stopped him soon enough. Her cousins might see.

When should we do this?

The question caught Anibal off guard. He hadn't thought about the *when*, only about whether or not she would say yes.

I don't know. When do you want to get married?

He imagined she would pick a date months away. Perhaps an October wedding, before the rains.

I'll need at least three days to make a dress and a few days for my sisters to travel. I have the fabric, though, for the dress. How's Wednesday?

At first, Anibal couldn't hide his surprise—he, of course, wanted a big party—but soon enough he agreed. A big Liberal wedding made little sense. That would tempt Conservatives a little too much. Wednesday would do just fine.

Anibal walked Esther home from the plaza after they'd finished the rest of their coffee in silence, and she matched her pace to his, a reasonable distance behind her cousins, quietly linking her arm through his. He reached over with his free arm and squeezed her hand.

She imagined their lives together. The children they would have. She wanted a large family and knew that he did too. And children would be the solution to the only dark cloud dotting their horizon—Anibal Rueda's mother, Doña Rosa Guarín. Esther had only met her a handful of times, mostly after church, and each time had been progressively more awkward.

She got on well enough with his old man, though. Anibal's father was kind and silent—the kind of man who worked hard and enjoyed a good game of dominoes. He was a man like her own father. Doña Rosa drank from a different well, as my grandmother once put it, and Esther hoped that time would emend her dislike.

After reaching the edge of town, where his truck was parked, Anibal drove her, and the cousins, back to her father's land. Esther considered how she would fit into the Rueda clan and how Anibal would work with her family. *You marry the family*, she said to me often. *When you say yes to another person, you are also taking their whole family with them. Don't forget.* Family was also a portent. *Look at how the father treats the mother, that's how the son will treat his wife,* my grandmother has always said. But she knew more than anyone that the love my grandparents shared, as strong as it was, could not survive without the approval, or at least tolerance, of family.

His parents could wait, though. The first hurdle to be cleared was her father, and as much as Don Trino seemed to like Anibal, that was no guarantee of his blessing. She looked in the rearview mirror as they pulled onto the last road.

After parking in front of the house in Mancarique, Anibal immediately asked for a quick meeting with Don Trino. As they settled into his large chairs, I imagine my great-grandfather found himself amused at the situation. Not two years ago, his daughter had been publicly called an old maid, doomed for life to be by his own side, something that didn't bother the old man at all. And now, a nervous young man prepared to ask for her hand. Don Trino gave Anibal the same answer that he gave the suitors of all his daughters, which was that he could only give a temporary response until Esther confirmed her desires. When Anibal responded that Esther had already said *yes* to him, Don Trino smiled. At least Anibal had the good sense to ask her first.

* * *

I don't know why my grandmother loved my grandfather. I just know that she did. And he loved her back. That even as the world around them burned, even as friends and family were killed and damaged, my grandparents found love and one another. That she chose him—not just because there was a war, or because she particularly felt she needed marrying. And I know he chose her, much to the confusion of many. My grandparents chose to love one another in the middle of an era when choosing was the biggest luxury of all.

Knowing Esther, she probably never ran to my grandfather in a field. She never jumped into his arms wearing a crown of flowers.

She never sang to him or wrote him poetry. She never acted seductively or held him in public. She danced with him (she *is* Colombian), rigor and rhythm in every step, but never with abandon.

I don't know if she hungered for him. I cannot speak to her thirst or longing or ardor. She did not speak of herself as a seductress; Esther would never be so vulgar. She was still a Colombian woman, though, and Colombian women tend to give themselves completely when in love.

* * *

Planning a wedding under the threat of paramilitaries and revolutionaries takes a great deal of caution. Certain kinds of joy, though, cannot be restrained.

Doña Eva, upgraded from mother-of-the-spinster to mother-of-the-bride, told everyone in the family the next morning that Esther would be getting married, thankfully leaving out the specifics. The telecom lines were soon carrying the news across their little region of Santander. *Esther Angarita Sarmiento and Anibal Rueda Guarín were getting married.* The lack of details fueled rumors.

Some errant tongues predicted a pregnancy, but those that knew Esther Angarita knew better. My great-uncle Francisco once told me she was "virtue incarnate—except for her devilish laugh" and nothing ever felt so true.

On Monday evening, Don Trino and Doña Eva received Anibal's parents; they would soon be family and it warranted joining together over bread. The two men knew each other well, but aside from a few cursory nods after church services, Doña Eva and Doña Rosa ran in different circles. Doña Eva played cards with her friends; Doña Rosa was a consummate reader.

Doña Eva had complained all afternoon that she had no time to prepare, having spent the morning in town making phone calls, only managing to plan and orchestrate a five-course meal for her guests. Her preoccupation with the matter of the meal meant that when Doña Rosa arrived, Doña Eva was completely unprepared for the effect a morning rampant in rumors could have on a woman's mood and demeanor.

Doña Rosa had some concerns. Concerns about the Angarita family, about their decorum, their ability to keep a secret under pressure. Everything was expressed aggressively, while wrapped in perfect manners. Doña Eva did not hear the education dripping from Doña Rosa's tongue. She did not hear the care and attention to feeling, did not catch the desire to please in the accusation. Doña Eva cut through to the heart of the matter the way she had always done—she was the daughter of a cattleman, the wife of a cattleman, the mother to many cattlemen, and wore that label with pride. She had the ability to be as upper-crust as necessary (she knew her forks and whatnot), but Doña Eva preferred to speak plainly.

We know how to behave, my dear Doña Rosa, we are not savages, Doña Eva is alleged to have remarked.

Doña Rosa looked at her son. Looked at her husband. Neither of them had her jet-black hair or tan skin, neither had ever been called a *savage* before. Neither even picked up on the phrase as unusual or worthy of remark. She considered her many options in replying. But, instead of saying something uncouth, my great-grandmother Doña Rosa decided to publicly forgive my other great-grandmother, Doña Eva, in the name of peace and excellent manners. *Decency is not cowardice*. Doña Rosa always did the decent thing.

Of course, she replied. *Let us move forward.*

My grandmother does not quite remember this anecdote, nor does she consider it the cause of her discomfort with Doña Rosa. But it was, in many ways, the reason her mother-in-law's house never felt like home to her. A fissure now existed where none had been before, a deep crack in the understanding between them. The family, both parents and betrothed, got through the remaining courses, complementing one another's stories and anecdotes with their own. After the meal, the men went outside to have a little whiskey, and the women sat in the living room, fanning themselves and talking about the menu for the post-wedding reception, and what could be assembled in the hours that remained.

Esther was a good match for Anibal. She came from a good family. Doña Rosa had too many children to be precious about all her children-in-law. She loved her son and knew that her son wanted to marry this woman. There was nothing worthy of objection—except maybe that Esther was a little older and more taciturn than most single women. But that was Anibal's choice, not Doña Rosa's. She wanted to see her son settled, and he could do a lot worse than Esther Angarita Sarmiento. She came with good land and good genes—none of the Sarmiento women had died in childbirth for a few generations, something that was known in town.

For Esther, the dinner felt like a success, minus a few interactions with Doña Rosa that were always clouded by anxiety, enough that she was always unsure where she stood with the woman. Still, by the end of the evening, she could not help but sigh in relief that neither of Anibal's parents seemed opposed to the marriage. Things could proceed. There would be time to get along, to fix whatever it was that could have been said and done incorrectly. She would be married to Anibal Rueda in two days. Doña Rosa had approved—or at the very least, she had not disapproved.

* * *

The next day, Esther did her best to finish the dress. But the white fabric was about a foot short of what she needed.

She decided to make herself a coffee—sometimes a little tinto is just a cup of calculated distraction, something to move the mind away from the problem and in a different direction. She looked at the pattern and considered what adding a large blue panel above the hemline would do. Most of the fabric in her sewing trunk had been pale blue linen, not white as she'd initially believed.

A body had been discovered that morning in front of the church, and everything in the plaza was closed out of respect for the dead. The banditry was decreasing, but it was not over. Were these Conservative bandits? Liberal revolutionaries? A dispute gone awry? There were too many reasons for a body to turn up.

My grandmother considered how much more numb she'd become to death over the years. There were only a few people whose demise would shock her, anyone and everyone else was fair game to the cruel hand of God and fate. She wanted to care, but caring sent her down a dangerous path. To care meant to think about all the people that had died in the last three years. Friends, rivals, gossips, a few cousins, a stranger she'd met one afternoon, the red-and-gray-haired man who worked at the telecom. All dead. Some for real offenses and grudges, others for simply existing. When she prayed in the evenings, if she didn't swallow the knot in her throat, she knew that all her entreaties to a complex God would turn into sobs. Some days it was too much. And when *the too much*, "el demasiado," got to her, she could only drink her tinto and hope for the best.

But she'd paid little attention to the temperature of the tinto when she poured it, and she suddenly found herself burning her lips and spitting out onto her hands some scalding coffee. While slightly cooled from boiling, the heat still shocked her, and she dropped the miniature saucer and plate service directly onto her dress-in-progress the day before her wedding.

THE VIOLENCE

It was not meant to be a white wedding, she supposed. She looked at her fabric trunk, and pulled out the only thing available, quickly running to get her sharpest shears.

* * *

Esther, twenty-four and too old, according to her and her mother, to wear white anyway, sewed a pale blue linen frock, with embroidered embellishments, in less than twelve hours to wear to church at 4 a.m. on Wednesday, April 29, 1952. The priest had suggested the time—no one was likely to disrupt a ceremony that early.

She hadn't slept in at least a day, or perhaps more. Time became fuzzy around the wedding. She knew that she was at the right place at the right time, in a pale blue dress that Anibal declared contrasted beautifully with her dark hair and eyes. Esther remembered smiling for photographs. She remembered squeezing his hand. She remembers kissing him in front of her whole family. She remembers the delight in taking his name and arm, walking out of the church transformed—a new person with a new life.

What she also remembered: She wished her brothers had been there.

* * *

By the time the sun rose she was Esther Angarita Sarmiento de Rueda, wife of Anibal Rueda Guarín. The ceremony had been small, only immediate family invited to the brief mass. Anibal's little sister Racquel, sixteen and just as striking as the men in her family, sang a song; Socorro, Esther's youngest sister, carried the flowers. Don Trino walked her down the aisle, passing empty row after empty row of seats, keeping his composure until the priest declared her someone else's. He'd always loved the idea of having

Esthercita by his side until the day he died, but that was the nature of children. *You raise them so they can leave you*, he often said.

The families agreed only on how unlikely they found the match. The groom seemed so different from the bride, always entertaining others, the life of the party. Esther enjoyed a good one-on-one conversation. The wedding's starkness suited her just fine. In fact, it was Anibal who seemed out of place, grinning so wide that most of his family suspected Esther had somehow managed to drug him.

There were more Angaritas at church that morning, but after a long break to ready the food and decorations, as day tumbled into evening, the Ruedas turned out en force for the imported whiskey and strong aguardiente of what was supposed to be an intimate gathering of family. The small reception in Mancarique filled with Anibal's brothers and cousins. Musicians appeared. As the couples swayed to the accordion music, shuffling their feet to the Cuban boleros, it was easy to forget the country at war. How could blood be shed on a night such as this? The workers joined the family and drank gaily into the evening, the women balancing glasses of rum or whiskey on their heads as they fanned out their great skirts beneath them, locked into the genetic rhythm of the Andean drum.

One Rueda cousin, Benito, drank merrily and asked for updates from Don Trino on his doppelgänger—Francisco had traveled with Benito's papers to the coast, after all.

Francisco and Trinito lived, *thrived*, Don Trino reported, and seemed happy on the Caribbean lowlands. Life was slower, more peaceful, and less driven by the politics of Bogotá. Don Trino himself considered a move away from Santander, although it seemed too far away from the tobacco and sugarcane that sustained them when milk prices dried up. Still, he thanked Benito, one of so many Ruedas that now formed part of the newly expanded Angarita family circle.

Talk of moving to the coast echoed throughout the mountainside in those years, the same feet that danced tonight would over the years move their bodies to different cities drinking Caribbean-tinged glasses of rum instead. As Don Trino plotted the potential northern expansion of his cattle empire, a kingdom of dairy from the mountains to the sea, the party turned away from talk of politics back to its loudest love: music.

Benito, everyone who attended the reception remembers, pulled out his guitar and as his eyes reddened from aguardiente, began singing sweet love ballads to the newlyweds. An accordionist accompanied him soon enough and Benito's young wife, Inés, sister to the groom, cried, she was so moved by her husband's voice and passion. The ballad ended, and everyone applauded Benito Rueda. Inés held hands with her new sister-in-law, Esther, and squeezed her palms tightly.

I'm so happy you're my sister now. My grandmother remembers this declaration well. Life proved it true in so many ways.

The music and celebration eventually drew notice. In the distance, that night, gunshots were fired into the air as a warning against making too much merry, and soon the party dispersed into smaller bands. Benito took the accordionist and a few bottles with him, perhaps to meet another cousin. Inés went home with her parents that night, still humming her husband's ballad. Esther changed from her wedding dress into one suitable for travel, gathering up her suitcase of belongings. She hugged her father goodbye. Kissed her mother on the cheek, and pinched her baby sister for good luck.

The new couple was leaving immediately. It was the last time Mancarique would be her home.

The Bird in Repose
(A GATHERING OF ASSASSINS)

Tuluá, 1952

Four years into running the Birds, the Condor thought himself a successful paramilitary leader. The fifty-three-year-old cheesemonger and unassuming mastermind walked through the streets of Tuluá to his office every day. On his walk, he thought about creating a new world with his army of mercenaries.

The Happy Bar was León María Lozano's place of business. But the building was quiet on this day in 1952, and the Condor was too caught up in his plans to notice that no one met him at the front door.

When he walked in, the bar was empty. But he went to his customary table anyway.

He waited.

No one came. Not a single Bird, not a single waiter, not even the regular vendors who sang the songs of their wares along the street.

At first, León María Lozano assumed there had been a massacre. But a massacre without sound seemed strange, and he had not heard a thing all morning. So he did what he always did: He prayed the Rosary.

When the door opened a few moments later, he was surprised to see the Conservative general of the National Army, Gustavo

Rojas Pinilla, enter alone. The Condor immediately put his rosary beads away. The general had traveled from Bogotá and demanded the Condor's complete attention.

*   *   *

He was asked to retire. The Condor refused. The general insisted. The Violence was going to end soon, he promised. There had been enough bloodshed.

The Condor, a man who had ordered the deaths of four thousand people, all from the Happy Bar, stood firm. There was no such thing as enough bloodshed. Every Liberal needed to be erased. Did the general not read the news? There were guerrillas in the mountains across Colombia. There were guerrillas in the Eastern Plains. It wasn't just Pedro Marín. There were new groups. And they were all Liberals.

But the general countered: Yes, they're Liberals, but most of them are Liberal workers. The campesinos. And all these different factions, if they started working together . . . Well, what did the Condor want? An actual Communist revolution in Colombia?

The general continued. León María Lozano needed to see that the tide was changing. The people were tired of war. They wanted televisions. They wanted to travel. They wanted to listen to American music and wear blue jeans and go dancing. The Conservative cause of relocating all Liberals into small enclaves had failed. There was a new enemy. Did León María Lozano not see the threat posed by these leftist guerrillas, these organized bandits who terrorized the paramilitary, who terrorized the landowners? The Pedro Maríns of the world? The revolutionaries mounting resistance? These peasants fighting back were worse than the Liberal landowners. Did the Condor not see how the rest of the world fought a Cold War? There were bigger things at stake.

The Condor did not care. He was a man on the path of righteous cleansing. His part of Colombia should be truly Conservative. He could not surrender.

The discussion continued for an hour. The Condor remained immovable. The general got up and left. No waiter ever appeared to take their order.

And before noon, *for his own good*, the authorities later said, León María Lozano was arrested and taken away.

* * *

The Condor never saw Tuluá again. He never saw the Happy Bar again. Five days after his arrest, the general freed him, on condition of relocation. He'd learned his lesson. Or would soon. But the general knew that the Condor was still useful.

León María Lozano was sent to the coast, but he hated it there. So he was sent to Bucaramanga, where he also disliked the anonymity of the city. Finally, the Conservatives put him in Pereira, only seventy miles away from his hometown, but not a step closer.

The wealthy child of one of his victims tried to sue him in court. In response, the Conservative president declared the Condor an extrajudicial entity. There was no recourse via the law. To convince the American government to help them fight the supposed Communists, 80 percent of cities of a certain size were intermittently under curfew, unable to venture outside their homes after 7 p.m. The Conservatives needed to demonstrate that they had the situation under control. Foreign aid depended on it. They couldn't have aggrieved citizens suing their operatives, exposing the pettiness of Conservative violence and tactics.

The Violence had begun to change cities too. As more and more internally displaced people moved into cities, a different kind of violence emerged: the violence of poverty. People who had had steady jobs for generations found themselves competing for whatever entry-level positions existed. Those denied the opportunities turned elsewhere. Robberies and carjackings increased in number.

The president had asked General Rojas Pinilla to take control of a situation that was quickly beginning to bear ugly consequences. But to control the cities, first he needed to control the countryside.

León María Lozano could walk in the darkness in Pereira without fear—who would dare hurt him? Still, *for his own good*, the authorities said, he was placed under house arrest, family and all.

León María Lozano did not like this. León María Lozano imagined his enemies laughing at him. He imagined all the secret Liberals of Tuluá, finally emerging from their hiding places.

León María Lozano did not like this at all.

* * *

Weeks later, the Birds entered Tuluá dressed in black, and soon the entire town heard the rumor: The Condor had died. They said he died in his sleep, peacefully, hands in prayer.

It was a little difficult to believe. At first. There were more rumors than facts, but often, rumors were the most accurate news around.

But the grief seemed real. At the church, the Birds were anguished, their mourning unmistakable, their grief palpable even to the most cataract-filled eyes. The people began to talk. Had the man really died? Was this an end to the constant news of massacre and desecration? Would the Birds disband?

But the people knew, they knew that once those young men tasted violence, they'd want to taste it again. A family aphorism says it perfectly: *Who tries to tell a shotgun to become a stick?*

Still, without the Condor pulling the strings, the city felt a little safer.

The people of Tuluá began to gather. They shared the news, the stories—anecdotes of how polite the Condor was, amazement at his brutality, sadness at the deaths attributed to him. Someone began playing music. Others cracked open beers. Suddenly, it was festive. The Witch was Dead.

And that's when the Birds descended, quietly entering any home that displayed mirth and disposing of it immediately. The bodies began to pile up in the town square. When all the music makers had been eliminated, the Birds gathered and performed a public count of over two hundred bodies.

A notice was left for those remaining: *This was a practice round. The Condor lives. Grieve better next time.*

* * *

The very alive Condor hated house arrest. He sent a letter to the General, offering his services. He could eliminate the guerrilla threat in less than a year, given a proper budget. The general declined. The general took away the military vehicles he'd loaned the Condor and his Birds. The Condor asked his men to steal horses and use the bus.

The Condor, pushing the limits of his house arrest, ordered the death of a judge, too sloppily executed and easily traced back to León María Lozano. He went to jail for another five days, a warning to stop ordering killings. This time, when the general freed him, the general whispered something in his ear—something the Condor heard well.

The next day, León María Lozano announced his retirement from political affairs. He was but a former cheesemonger, now living only a couple hours from where he grew up. Didn't the people in Pereira know? He was a peaceful man. He had never even owned a gun.

Moon of Honey
(A SUNRISE IN VERMILION)

Norte de Santander, 1952

They were due in Maracaibo, Venezuela, before sunset, and even though her neck still ached, Esther's entire body was shivering with excitement and relief. She was happy to finally be seated on the train; she was nervous about what would happen when they arrived at the hotel Anibal had reserved. She was thinking too much about his hands, trying to focus instead on her exhaustion and how long the journey had been from her father's lands to this train.

The car ride to Cúcuta had taken all night, and the newlyweds had slumbered while interlocking fingers in the backseat as a distant Rueda cousin took the wheel. My grandmother, always a light sleeper in the car, remembers waking several times to hear the man consulting with various people along the road about the safest route—free from both the Conservative bandits and the growing leftist army, who often collected "taxes" to fund their cause. The ordinarily ten-hour car ride from her father's house to the train station along clearly defined roadways became a fourteen-hour trek through back routes and dirt paths. But they arrived in Cúcuta, easternmost city in North Santander along the Venezuelan border, a place untouched by the Violence, intact and unbothered.

My grandfather and his cousin hugged at the train station, and then, finally and for the first time, Anibal and Esther were alone together as a married couple. They dropped their suitcases off in the luggage hold, took a bite to eat in a small café, politely chatting about their food, until Esther began to rub her neck with one hand. Anibal asked if something bothered her.

She had slept sideways in the backseat on the journey, and the stiffness on the right side of her neck had become unbearable. She complained to Anibal, and he stood up gallantly from the table, paid the bill, walked to her side, offered her an arm, and quickly escorted her to a quiet bench outside.

There, without thought of propriety, Anibal used his thumb to rub the knot at the base of her neck, while telling her that he'd learned this trick during his military service. It was the first time he had touched any part of her body that wasn't her hand or her eager lips at the conclusion of the marriage ceremony, the latter too brief and only when commanded by the priest. She tried to concentrate on looking elegant, but she inevitably surrendered to both his touch and his inane anecdotes about military life.

Suddenly, sitting on that bench with Anibal, the day felt eternal, and she simply longed to be comfortable and settled in a bed. With Anibal. But there were hours left in their journey. A train, another car, and—finally—the hotel.

When do we arrive in Maracaibo? she asked him in a voice barely above a whisper.

"Pronto, mi amor."

She murmured in agreement, happy to know that he would take care of everything, even and especially all the knots that plagued her.

*   *   *

After she claimed some relief, Anibal withdrew his hand, and they simply sat together silently, watching the people walk in and out of the train station, perpetually busy, some passing through even as others lingered with loved ones and friends. Cúcuta was a city—with all the bustle and anonymity involved. No one stared at Esther and Anibal. No one knew who they were. Border cities were safe havens during the Violence, the needs of commerce and trade trumping political violence.

There was time before the train left, and Anibal suggested visiting some parts of the city to pass the remaining hour. Esther agreed and they checked their luggage before walking down to the boulevard.

They took a taxi down to the main plaza and walked around it, visiting the church—Esther always loved visiting churches. In particular, she found herself gravitating toward each architect's interpretation of the Stations of the Cross, Christ's journey from when Jesus is condemned to death until the tomb. The variations of the walks, falls, and humiliations fascinated her, but they also grounded her in their fundamental sameness. She and Anibal came from the same kinds of people, Catholic and Santandereano, people who were fierce and hardened, in both their work and fight. They were also different.

She let her heart relax. She let her mind clear itself of all the worries that lingered. She was briefly at peace. Churches did that for her.

In the early afternoon, they returned by taxi to the Cúcuta train station and claimed their luggage from the porter. This station was bigger than the one in Bucaramanga, Esther noted. *The red-brick building resembled a dance hall*, she told me, *but the dancing was all porters wielding these massive luggage carts.*

They boarded the train bound for Maracaibo, and settled into their seats, preparing for the two-hour journey north along the border and then across into Venezuela. She leaned out the window, looking at the throng of families saying goodbye on the platform. Anibal squeezed her hand. He was her family now.

*   *   *

Esther had been to Venezuela a few times as a young girl; Don Trino encouraged all his daughters to travel as much as they could. She'd seen most of South America and had even been to Florida. Don Trino often quipped that he had to show his children the world in case they married people who never wanted to leave home. But Esther had never traveled without family, or at the very least her mother and her sisters.

She looked at Anibal, and when no one was glancing in their direction, she squeezed his hand again, this time with temerity.

You don't have to worry so much about what others see or hear, he said, reading her mind—something he did often. *You're my wife.*

I'm still a lady from a good family, Anibal.

I know, he said. *It's why I love you. I'm not sure I deserve you.*

Long before the train departed the station, Esther found herself drifting off to sleep, her head on Anibal's chest. She, once again, marveled at how their bodies complemented one another: Her waist without a curve and his forever round and accommodating. She privately chuckled to herself about life's incongruities—what she could not stand in herself, she loved in him. Anibal made her feel protected. It was, perhaps, even more important than the love she felt.

*   *   *

The crowd on the platform cheered, waking up Esther. She started, worried that a mob had formed seeking out Liberals. But no, the train had blown its whistle, and the crowd cheered as the engine sprung to life—for so many people in Colombia, trains were still a marvel.

Slowly, the crowd and station began to recede as the train picked up speed.

Children ran alongside the locomotive, a habit she found endearing, even after Anibal woke up to tell her they did it every day and it wasn't special at all. Still, she liked the idea that their marriage was blessed by children. And as they pulled away, she briefly wondered what her family would look like. How many children would God give her and Anibal?

She was almost twenty-five. At her age, most women were married and mothers several times over. The worry of her womb having dried up was not unfamiliar. Her grandmother was married quite young, and while norms had changed and no one was getting married before fifteen anymore, Esther knew she was behind the count, if not in her own estimation, then at least in the thoughts of most everyone she knew. What if they were right? She thought about what happened to infertile cattle, how they were cast away and left for slaughter.

She worried about her father, about leaving behind her old man, who suddenly found himself with all his children away from him. She had been his right hand—he had always said so. And now, she was gone too, the last of his children to leave home.

As if reading her thoughts, Anibal leaned her back into his chest, wrapping his arms around her.

There is so much time to worry, Esther. But we are only here now. A honeymoon is a lucky thing, he said. And the corollary to his phrase hung in the air between them: So many people, especially during a civil war, did not get to take two weeks together in Venezuela to begin their marriage. Don Trino and Don José had worked hard and quickly to make it happen for their children.

We should probably not waste it, Anibal continued, *and get to our labors.*

Esther blushed. The results of their labors would be children. And if Esther didn't come back from their days in Maracaibo pregnant, the tongues would be in need of reanimation from their collapse.

A few minutes later, Anibal drifted back to sleep. *That man, my grandmother told me, could sleep anywhere. On a horse or in a battle, he had no shame about closing his eyes.*

As Anibal slept, Esther pulled out a letter that her mother, Doña Eva, had pressed into her hands as she left Santander. *She reminded me again that I was too old, too mal-accustomed to my own habits, and that I had to learn to make his habits my own. That my job in marriage was to accommodate him. Men needed women in this regard.*

She read the letter again and again, as Anibal began to snore. And when an attendant came by with coffee, and a small bag for trash, my grandmother threw her mother's letter away. But she never forgot it. She told me as much every chance she got.

She was right: I was too mal-accustomed to my own habits.

* * *

When they arrived at the Venezuelan border checkpoint, usually a quick stop on the way to the city, a fastidious Venezuelan immigration officer climbed aboard with an assistant and a booklet.

I need everyone's passports.

As he approached their row, Anibal paused before handing them over.

Be sure to give them back, he joked to the immigration officer.

The officer did not laugh. Instead, he ordered my grandfather to stand and follow him off the train.

Esther tried to stand up. The assistant told her to sit.

Anibal looked back and gave her a hard stare.

She sat back down.

After an incredibly long half hour, Anibal returned, red in the face and too furious to speak. The train started up again, and Esther looked out the window, only to see the immigration officer wave the train off. She turned to Anibal.

Did you get our passports back?

He shook his head and remained silent for the first fifteen minutes of the journey. Then, emitting a great sigh, he turned to Esther with a twinkle in his eye.

Well, I guess our sightseeing will be limited to the lake and our hotel room.

Esther pinched his forearm in warning. The woman in the row behind had arched her eyebrows. Esther still wore her wedding ring on a chain around her neck, as there had not been time to resize it before the marriage.

Anibal laughed at Esther's quiet and wide-eyed shock at his banter.

Well, Esthercita, the Venezuelans have confiscated our passports until we return. We must re-enter Colombia through here. With the situation being what it is, we should probably just stay in Maracaibo. A HONEYMOON *on the lake.*

The woman in the row behind lowered her eyebrows. Esther breathed a sigh of relief only to have a whole new set of concerns arise.

Why did they confiscate them?

To make sure we return. There are too many Colombians crossing over to live in Venezuela and wait out all this violence.

She knew this, of course. On some level, she knew that the Violence had driven people from their homes for other places. It made sense that people would leave Colombia if they could, and Venezuela was closer and more stable then. *An arepa was an arepa,* and wasn't it Simón Bolívar's dream that Venezuela, Colombia, and the other Bolivarian states form one great country? Venezuela was more familiar than anywhere else.

Still, she hadn't considered what effect the emigration would mean for tourists.

They believed me, Anibal continued, *when I told them I would never leave my finca for too long.*

Of course, Esther offered, *the cows need you.*

Exactly.

He kissed her hand. *You understand me better than anyone, Esthercita.*

The woman in the row behind them sighed and then focused her stare on her own husband in the seat beside her, who was snoring louder than the train engine.

*   *   *

When I asked my grandmother about her two weeks in Maracaibo, she laughed softly.

Some things are for me alone . . .

Honeymoons are a beautiful way to really get to know someone, I offered. She thought for a minute before speaking.

The honeymoon is a perfect promise for everything a marriage can be.

She told me about the beauty of the lake, how it felt like an ocean, reflecting the sunset like a shifting mirror. She told me about the long walks they took around its edges, the ease of their conversations, the lightness of their laughter. She told me about learning my grandfather and his moods, waking up before him to prepare the day for him—only to find he'd already done the work the night before. She told me how perfectly he held her on the hotel's parquet dance floor, whisking her around as boleros played.

She told me about the luxury of their room, the chocolate mint on their pillow.

Your grandfather felt guilty leaving the hotel, it was so nice.

She smiled. *So we stayed in as much as possible.*

*   *   *

Two weeks later, they crossed the border again, back into Colombia, tan and happy, glowing with newlywed joy. A different immigration official handed them their passports without any hassle or comment. Anibal tucked their documents safely into his breast pocket.

At the train station in Cúcuta, a different cousin from a different side of the family met them with an urgent message to call his father, Don José. Anibal and Esther looked at one another in worry, a silent language of stares and hand squeezes having already developed between the two, as he made his way to the telecom booth.

Esther paced the entire time he was gone. Esther prayed. An urgent phone call could mean anything. The cousin walked back and forth with her and eventually turned and asked how the weeks in Maracaibo had gone. Esther blushed.

The days were beautiful, she said. *The views of the lake were beautiful. The hotel was beautiful.*

Soon you'll know how successful it was, the cousin offered with a wink and hearty chuckle.

My grandmother widened her eyes and did not reply. She didn't even know this man. But that hadn't stopped everyone at their hotel from making similar implications throughout their stay.

She prayed for a second, this time hoping the man was right. She did want a baby; she wanted more than just one, of course. But right now, she prayed for one. A boy, preferably, one that looked just like Anibal.

Then maybe everyone would stop commenting on things that no prudent person would ever even think to mention. She said as much to Anibal's cousin.

By the time Anibal returned, the silence between Esther and the unnamed cousin had grown to continental proportions. But Anibal didn't notice, he was in such a good mood.

Our fathers, Esthercita, have delivered unto us a bounty. Your father has given land, and my own has filled it with cattle.

Esther felt her heart grow in her chest. *Their own finca*, one that she and Anibal could manage together. Until the baby came, of course.

Her eyes lit up at the possibilities. She imagined herself, waking up in the morning to oversee the milking, counting out the inventory and tracking the names of all the cows in a ledger.

They got in the car and began the long drive back to Socorro. Anibal sat in the front seat this time, to help keep the driver awake through conversation, and Esther sat ruler-straight in the back, willing herself awake through the fourteen-hour ordeal, naming imaginary cows the entire journey.

When they arrived in Socorro, at the empty house on the edge of the city, as her mother had moved to the finca to live with her father, she shyly showed him the empty bedroom where they would be staying until a house, their home, could be built on the newly acquired land.

Later that evening, as they made themselves comfortable on the narrow mattress, Esther turned to Anibal with a thought: *I should name the first cow after Saint Rita, as praying to her has given us so much.*

Anibal said that he liked the idea, but after a second, he furrowed his brow.

Esthercita, he said into the darkness of their bedroom, *I adore you. But you should know, my love, that it's my job to name the cows. I am the man. It's your job to manage the home.*

Oh, Esther replied tentatively. *I always helped out with the bookkeeping for my father, and I'm happy to do the same work for our land.*

The land is my job, Esther. Anibal looked confused. *You don't have to worry about that anymore.*

They had spoken for hundreds of hours about everything under the sun. But somehow, Anibal didn't understand how much she wanted to be a part of running the finca. It was Esther's turn to be confused.

You'll be too busy, Anibal offered when Esther stared at him blankly for a minor eternity. *We're going to have at least twenty children. When will you have time to think about cows?*

Oh, Anibal. I hope so.

And in that moment, she gave herself away. Her dreams and desires became his—so quickly and without a thought.

The River Ran Through It
(A SEDIMENT OF FISH)

Bogotá, 1952

In April 1952, the newspapers reported that President Laureano Gómez, often called the fake president of Colombia, asked for daily reports on the river levels, as a recent increase in bloodshed had affected the waterways. His heart sank with every report, as the aftermath of massacres and mass graves began leaking into groundwater. Bodies were damming the rivers.

Without clean rivers with good water, there were no fish. Without fish, there was nothing to feed people living along the riversides and marshes. Entire towns began evacuating overnight, and cities became overcrowded, which meant less housing and even denser clusters of half-built homes on edges of the city. Crime increased. Everyone was thirsty. Everyone was hungry.

The Violence, they said, *is rising. The rivers*, they said, *are not.*

* * *

The rivers have always been sacred. Every president, every conquistador, every parched body that has ever stepped foot in Colombia understood the importance of her flowing waters.

THE VIOLENCE

The way the Muisca—the first people of Bogotá, before the Spanish arrived—tell it, before there was a country, Colombia was the tropical wild of the gods, caught between the Caribbean, the Pacific, and the Andes—all mountain and ocean and coast and fruit tree and condor.

But the gods thought something was missing. And so, high in the mountains, between the cliffs and valleys in a deep lake, Bachué, Mother of Us All, goddess of long black hair, emerged with a boy in her arms. The child was a gift to her from the other gods, a playmate in the jungle of creation.

She fed the boy her creations: rosettes and ferns, the savory meats and fried skins of birds and reptiles, sweet soups of earth, and bread of gold. The boy, a god himself, grew strong into a man. Bachué remained young, goddess that she was, beautiful and dark, elegant and capable.

When he was ready, virile and strong enough, they joined in union. Their coupling, so holy, so important, soon found her with children. For decades, she remained pregnant, birthing humanity to populate the lands around her.

In time, her children grew wise with her teachings, and Bachué finally began to age, sacrificing her eternal youth for a people to grow. Her face wrinkled, her breasts sagged, and her exhaustion showed through—giving birth to humanity was no easy feat. To regain her immortality, she had to leave the earthly plane along with her children, the People of Salt.

But first, she created the rivers, connecting her lake to the ocean, the mountains to the sea, that her children could always find her.

Satisfied with her labors, Bachué took her husband back to the lake from which they first emerged. They entered, and the lake consumed them, turning them into serpents as the water touched their skin.

When her children eventually succumbed to old age and the elements, Bachué could not bear to watch them suffer. She left the light-filled realm of the gods for her womanly form once more, shedding her snakeskin, choosing the dark path back to the edge between life and death. She could not return to them without risking death, but she could hold her children as they crossed into the world beyond, guiding them to their life after life.

It was their mother who greeted the Muisca in death, who died so that the People of Salt could live, who birthed humanity and loved them enough to forfeit her beauty, her vitality, and her time in the paradise that is Colombia. It was their mother who gave them the rivers.

* * *

The Spanish saw the Río Magdalena for the first time in 1501. Rodrigo de Bastidas could not pronounce her original, native name and so rechristened her "Magdalena" after the woman that a pope once called "Apostle of the apostles," which is to say, one who witnesses the witnesses.

Along the Caribbean, the natives first called her by a different name: Caripuaña ("great river"). In her central valleys, she was called Yuma ("river of friendly neighbors and mountains"), Arli ("river of fish), and Guacahayo ("river of tombs").

Her waters are well traveled, from the southwestern edge of the Colombian Andes to the Caribbean. Her tributaries begin on ancient peaks, trickling down, joining their brethren tributaries, and together forging her might. By the time she reaches the sea, in the Mouths of Ash, as her delta is called, the Magdalena River will have coursed through two-thirds of Colombia.

There are other rivers in Colombia—tributaries of the Amazon and the Orinoco south of the Andes, but less than 7 percent of the population inhabits that half of the country—full of dangerous and monsoon-prone savannas and jungles. Most live in the temperate highlands or north, between the mountains and the Caribbean, relying on the tributaries of the Magdalena and Cauca Rivers for water, with the latter joining the former on its way to the sea.

The Magdalena is the heart and artery of Colombia—and the river the Spanish first followed up the mountains to Bogotá.

The Conquistadores gave their men a task as they moved up from the coast into the central plateau: Clear the area of its people. The Muisca were to either become loyal subjects or face the end of a broadsword. The choice was stark: Either accept the Europeans' God, or prepare to meet their mother, Bachúe, whose kind smile would guide them home.

The conquerors threw the bodies in the rivers back then too.

* * *

President Laureano Gómez read the reports. In 1952, large sections of the river were choking with too many bodies, following a Conservative mandate to dispose of bodies in the water. But the Conservatives could not concede. This Violence was an opportunity to finally drive all Liberals into submission, they were only four years into what might take a lifetime. Still—the president knew what the reports said. The Mouths of Ash were more salt than water, and his own party was more apocalypse than human.

The drying riverbeds revealed fossils—*undrowned*, or "desahogados," as Colombians like to say. Bones from previous wars, bones from before war, bones turned to paper, bones turned to stone. A million little stories all asking for a witness, an apostle to bear their truth.

President Gómez knew the country was hemorrhaging people. And he had only his own party to blame. So he did what any politician would do—he blamed the Liberals. The logic of war prevailed: Even more had to die, so the carnage could finally end.

For the rivers, the president said. *We do this for the rivers.*

PART III

*

Colombia . . . has a brain for a heart and a heart for a brain and a furious and fierce gut. It has bloody breasts and brutal mounds.

—Silvana Paternostro,
My Colombian War

Sureshot

(A FABLE OF NAMES)

Neiva, 1953

Carlos Mauricio Restrepo Ochoa did not intend to become a teenaged guerrilla. He intended to become a butcher, like his father. Carlos adored his father, spent every day with him when he wasn't in school or playing soccer with his friends. His life in Neiva, in the southern part of the mountain range that cut through the center of Colombia, had quieted down. There was word that the revolutionaries lived in the nearby slopes, but Carlos hadn't seen anyone that fit that description—no strangers with guns, no men in fatigues.

One afternoon in late March 1953, Carlos came home from a soccer match in the park. His father was not home. He wasn't at the butcher shop either.

A week later, after the family had searched under every stone in the city, pale in anticipation of the worst, Carlos's father turned up in a ditch outside the local police station.

When a body was found outside the police station a week after a disappearance, it was either disposed of by the police or planted by an enemy of the police—private citizen with a grudge or organized revolutionary making a statement. Either way, bad people were involved. The National Police had a less than stellar reputation on issues like corruption and violence. They were worse at solving crimes against the working people.

This was a time to leave, Carlos's mother insisted. But he insisted on staying.

Someone had to run the carnicería.

* * *

The police turned up soon enough, asking him questions about his father and the "Communist guerrilla," as Pedro Marín's burgeoning army was now called by Conservative operatives, with no regard for the truth. Did the butcher supply meat to the guerrillas in the hills outside town? Carlos did not believe his father would. The questions continued, and Carlos grew angrier and angrier. Carlos knew his father respected the guerrillas philosophically, but he did not aid them or support them. Carlos had heard his old man say it a thousand times: *Agreeing is not the same as supporting.*

It only took the police a day to shut down the butcher shop—declaring it a criminal enterprise. His mother and sister left for the capital, begging Carlos to join them. He remained, dedicating his efforts to reopening his father's legacy. But in a span of two weeks, Carlos was alone and flat broke. His fate turned so dramatically that even decades later, in his seventies, he cannot fathom what kind of wrathful God would have done this to him. *Like Saint Job, don't you think?*

As he sold his family's belongings, doing anything he could to make some money before beginning the trip to join his mother and sisters in Bogotá, a longtime customer from the carnicería stopped by and said hello. Carlos chatted with the old man for a while, explaining his various heartaches and hardships. When the man suggested Carlos should just ask the guerrilla if his father had worked for them, Carlos thought: *Why not?*

*　　　*　　　*

He found someone who knew someone who knew someone who could facilitate an introduction; days later, Carlos found himself standing before a subcommander in Marín's army.

He learned that his father did not supply them meat. The government had killed him on this bogus charge to intimidate others. *The Cause*, the commander explained, was to right all the wrongs that had been committed against the People, including the death of Carlos's father.

That night, he and his fellow soldiers-in-training slept underneath the stars in green fatigues.

The guerrilla immediately offered him something no one else could—the opportunity for revenge. Carlos learned the lessons of guerrilla life quickly enough. He knew he'd have to go out on a reconnaissance mission to prove his loyalty. He knew he'd have to give them whatever money and possessions he had. He knew that he believed in *the Cause* more than anything except God.

He knew he'd need a new name. Every guerrilla has a nickname, a policy instituted by Marín himself, to shed former identities and be born anew. Marín was rechristened "Tirofijo," or Sureshot, in honor of his skill with a weapon.

"El chiste es nunca fallar," he once wrote. *The point is to never miss.*

As a new recruit, Carlos toyed with several possibilities—the Butcher, the Cleaver, Angel of Justice. Carlos began to memorize Marín's sayings. He also learned to sleep in a tree and on the ground. He learned to carry a gun. He learned to march through the jungle. He learned to camouflage himself. When it was time for his first mission months into his time with the guerrilla, a reconnaissance effort to gather intel on some local Conservative finca owners, Carlos felt ready.

Fifty-five years later, Carlos Mauricio Restrepo Ochoa, now an old man himself, cannot remember exactly what happened on his first mission back in 1953. He claims his mind has washed away the memories. He tells me that his head is protecting him from himself.

But truths are truths: Carlos killed a man.

During his very first training mission, he missed a shot, intending to hit a police horse. Carlos doesn't remember much else, except that the man his bullet found looked like a grandfather from the American movies. Carlos had killed an innocent worker, who, like Carlos's father, had nothing to do with anything.

* * *

His commander told him not to worry, but Carlos could not rest. *Did that man have a son, a daughter, a child, who like me, wanted an answer?*

His commander told him to remain quiet. The killing was being assessed, his commander promised, and soon, someone would tell them what to say and how to say it. There was a committee for everything in Marín's army, even for responding to and assessing unintentional deaths.

The committee made its determination. The death was officially attributed to the police. In killing Carlos's father, they determined, the police traumatized the comrade, which enabled him to act inopportunely, thus the police were ultimately to blame. The guerrillas took no credit for the killing.

Carlos could not live with this. *But destiny has a way of intervening*, Carlos still believes.

Pedro Marín arrived at their camp a week later. He toured all his micro-operations routinely. It kept his soldiers sharp and his pursuers at bay—a man who cannot stay still is harder to catch and harder to track. Marín had also been taught by his elders to mix ranks, which meant the newest recruits fought alongside the longest-serving veterans. And so it was that soon after his arrival, Marín decreed that the greenest man, the one who had discharged his weapon into a civilian, should join him for an afternoon. Carlos found himself walking next to the biggest guerrillero there was.

Marín, only twenty-three years old, denied being the leader, of course. He was a member of the directive, one of many in a committee, offering resistance to the oligarchy. But to Carlos and millions of other Colombians, Marín and the guerrilla were synonyms. If anyone could rectify the misinformation about his kill, Carlos thought, it was Marín, el jefe, Mr. Sureshot himself.

But Marín claimed he could do nothing about it—ascribing unintentional deaths to the police was a crucial tactic. A dead civilian helped recruit men exactly like Carlos. Armies need soldiers. And Marín's army needed soldiers to charge protection money from Liberal farmers and to generate kidnapping revenue from rich Conservatives. He needed revenue to buy guns and feed his men. The revolution is never cheap.

We do our best to balance things out, and we know that once we win, we'll ensure that no one ever needs to use these tactics again, Marín said. La Causa allowed Marín to justify anything done in its name. A guerrillero doesn't survive because of his idealism, after all—concessions must be made.

* * *

That night, I snuck away. Walked down the road for hours to the nearest bus terminal. Took off for Bogotá. I never told my mother or my sister what happened. I just went to work for another butcher in a city far from anyone I ever knew.

Carlos never returned to Neiva.

I suppose the Cause was not sufficient for me. I wasn't even there long enough to get a nickname. God and destiny made sure I remained Carlos, and just Carlos.

The Mother of the Groom
(A SOUP OF ACCUSATIONS)

Santander, 1954

Esther remembers their first fight. Not that they hadn't quibbled before, but it was the first fight where the depth of anger, for both parties, startled her. It was the first fight that tested the strength of their love.

They were on horseback, two years into their marriage, and they fought—of course—about his mother.

They never yelled. Anibal kept his demeanor calm and steady, a hint of anger in his smile, but he was always respectful. *Decency is not cowardice*—the Rueda family motto was a constant refrain on his lips, explaining his own disciplined calm in the face of Esther's quiet fury.

On horseback, trotting through the corrals on the property, moving from one pasture to another on the mountainside, she tried to find the words to explain herself. Doña Rosa had made comments at dinner the night before, and this morning, after breakfast, as they saddled up the horses to go inspect the corrals, Esther felt the need to say something to Anibal about his mother, about the snake that woman kept in her mouth.

Anibal did not take well to Esther's criticisms. His silence confirmed this disapproval, and after plenty of antagonistic contemplation on horseback, he finally uttered a simple phrase.

I cannot let anyone disrespect my mother, my love, not even you.

My grandmother kept her own silence for the length of the corral. When the horses reached the last post, she flashed sad eyes at my grandfather.

Yet you would let your mother disrespect your wife?

She rode back to the house.

* * *

A few months after returning from Maracaibo, they moved into the newly built house on the finca Don Trino had gifted them, a large parcel of land carved from one of his own. Don José delivered one hundred head of cattle as promised, Anibal named the finca Canaán—the Bible's Promised Land.

The honeymoon was over, but for Esther, these moments were better than their two weeks in Venezuela. They began to build. They designed the homestead together, discussing the best practices from their childhood homes. And when it was finished, they worked together to decorate it and make sure it was ready for all the needs of their family.

Esther's love for Anibal grew as she discovered how much he valued her. She'd always thought that men like her father were rare—men who listened to women and did not just dismiss them outright. Anibal, it turned out, had been worth the time it took to find him.

To hear my grandmother tell it, the beginning of her marriage proved to be both familiar and not—her daily life did not differ too much from her life in Mancarique. She organized, managed, and kept the books for the new finca just as she had done for her father's before. Anibal, despite his earlier claims, accepted her help as long as the household was also in order. They both knew this was to be temporary, until their first child arrived, anyway. Hopefully.

Evenings were spent together, slowly learning the language of one another. She wanted to be fluent in Anibal, and he returned the favor. These were the nights to be treasured, the two of them discovering each other in their multi-level house on the mountainside.

Still, as lost as Anibal and Esther were in the present, everyone in the family was focused on the future. Both sides waited for Esther to get pregnant, clearing their throats every time she showed up equally thin, if not thinner, than she'd been at the previous family engagement. No joyful news came, no baptism announcements circulated. The tongues clicked.

With time, the clicks grew louder, audible whispers that evolved into cruelties. A theory circulated in La Fuente, Rueda territory, that the water must be bad on the Angarita side of the mountain, as women from there were proving to be old and barren. No one even considered that Anibal could be the problem. But Esther, well, Esther was an unknown entity to most Ruedas, and she was almost twenty-five when they married and almost twenty-seven now—closer to sainthood through martyrdom than virginity.

Still, there were other concerns. Plenty of national news dominated discussion at dinner those years. Conservatives executed an intra-party coup against their fake Conservative president in 1953, which amused Esther to no end. The Spanish word for "coup" is synonymous with "punch." President Laureano Gómez was gone after three years in office. Good, Esther offered. He deserved a good smack in the face. The new Conservative president—the former lieutenant general of the army—could not be worse than Laureano Gómez.

Anibal warned her that she was wrong. *They're all Godos anyway, Conservatives to the bone. Every family has their disagreements.*

She understood. My grandmother was one of nine children. Her own mother was one of six, her father one of twelve. My grandfather Anibal was one of eighteen. Catholic dogma, a keen awareness of death and long, hot summers tended toward a fertile population. It was not unusual for an individual to be in possession of dozens of cousins on any given side of the family. Entire communities and villages in Colombia have grown from expanding homesteads—the kind of town where half the residents can be traced to one progenitor.

She was expected to have many children. Because life expectancies were relatively low (in some regions as low as forty-nine years old well into the twentieth century) and infant mortality rates were high, having as many children as possible made sense. Of my grandfather's seventeen siblings, only ten grew into adulthood. Only six of the initial eighteen lived to meet their grandchildren. And they fared better than previous generations.

Esther prayed, drank every tea prescribed, and did the stretches her mother recommended. *A healthy womb is a fertile womb.* She would close her eyes and imagine her child with Anibal. A child with his blue eyes and her long brown hair. Always a boy in her imagination, but at this point, even a girl would do, Esther thought. Anything to signal that she was more fertile than La Guajira. At least that desert sustained human life.

She prayed for her country, for a more peaceful world where children could live. She prayed for her husband and his love to remain with her, even as her body continued to fail to live up to its promise. And in the meantime, she endured. Her friends told her to be patient, her sisters counseled her on which scripture to read. She attended every family event and did not even narrow her eyes in self-hatred and judgment toward anyone who asked about her health with too much concern.

The weekends became structured around their families. Early Sunday afternoons, right after church, they went to Mancarique to visit her parents and siblings. And on Sunday evenings, they went to see Anibal's parents.

* * *

Doña Rosa was terrifying. She was beautiful, tiny, and fierce. Her hair was as black as obsidian—and her eyes matched.

And she made the worst sopa de ruyas in Santander.

Normally, a sopa de ruyas is difficult to get wrong. The basic ingredients are a delicious mixture of broth, meats, tubers, beans, cabbage, onion, garlic, guaca (creeping spotflower) leaves, cilantro, and grains. But at its core are the ruyas themselves: elongated threads of cornmeal pasta. Think penne pasta, but as thick as a pinky finger and made of corn. When prepared correctly, the soup is both hearty and healing.

But Doña Rosa Guarín did not concern herself with the flavor of the soup. It is rare for a bad recipe to be passed down the generations, so I'll never know exactly what she did to make it so unpleasant. I can only say that she made it every week for her many children and grandchildren, and that its effects on their palates were permanent. Every cousin from that side of the family attests to how horrible that soup really was.

I write this not to disparage my great-grandmother, but to note her power. Imagine making a soup so bad that generations of your family are aware of how painful it was to consume. Yet, every week, without fail, her children and grandchildren appeared and paid the price for her company: a full bowl of sopa de ruyas. Sometimes there were forty people at Sunday evening dinner, sometimes there were fifteen. Anibal and Esther were of the few who showed up religiously.

Now consider this: Esther liked the soup. She, alone, of all the family, truly enjoyed eating this soup of corn pasta and leaves. And yet, Doña Rosa still hated her.

* * *

Dinners at the Rueda house became more boisterous as they discussed all aspects of the new president, who most still thought of as the general who staged the coup against Gómez. But President Rojas Pinilla had surprised his critics and declared an amnesty as one of his first acts, in an attempt to end the Violence. He offered to buy back weapons from all sides, stopped Conservative government support for the paramilitary, and offered no prosecution for any war-related crimes committed since 1948.

Liberals worried it was a trap. On the Sunday evening before Anibal and Esther had their first big fight, sometime in August of 1954, a year after Rojas Pinilla took unelected power, the dinner conversation at Doña Rosa's table had begun innocuously enough. About twelve people gathered, a smaller crowd than usual, a mixture of Rueda siblings, cousins, and a handful of spouses. Pleasantries were exchanged, as well as news of family elsewhere. Esther sat down to enjoy her soup, while Anibal filled up on bread.

A cousin asked Esther about her family, and she happily confirmed that her parents were doing well. Attacks on their side of the mountains had decreased, milk production was up—perhaps amnesty was working. Her sisters had married in Bucaramanga, settled in the city, but not too far away. A new road had shortened the travel some. And didn't they know? A mutual acquaintance had gone on a stroll in the park alone, and nothing traumatic ensued. Perhaps a time of normalcy approached? Esther joked that Conservatives had begun acting like human beings.

They'll never be human beings, Doña Rosa said. *Conservatives are pigs and rapists.*

Esther waited for someone else to say something. No one did.

Anibal, ever one to defeat awkwardness, began to talk about a new bull he bought. Esther commented that Anibal got a good price on the bull, even though she had been involved in every step of the process.

Well, Anibal admitted, *Esther negotiated it.*

She should spend less time negotiating over bulls and more time grabbing them by the horns, Doña Rosa muttered.

Esther shot Anibal a look. He looked at his father, who whispered something to Doña Rosa. She shook her head at him and made a point of addressing the whole table.

We're all family, she said, *we can speak freely amongst ourselves. Or can't we?*

The table was quiet.

Doña Rosa barreled ahead. *And how are your outlaw brothers, Esther? Was the murderer pardoned in the new amnesty?*

It had been two years since Francisco and Trinito left for the coast. But Doña Rosa wasn't asking out of concern for them, Esther knew. So, Esther stood up from the table. *Excuse me*, she said and walked outside along the garden on the south end of the Rueda property for a few minutes, dragging her hand through the grass, a habit she'd cultivated as a child, gently causing the blades to sway, but never unrooting them.

I couldn't tell, she told me years later, *if Doña Rosa was testing me, if she truly just hated me, or if this was a misplaced affection.*

I understood my grandmother's sentiment. Doña Rosa was fond of testing the people she loved most. I've been at the end of her pointed scrutiny and could easily imagine how terrifying it would be for someone less secure in her love. I once asked one of my grandfather's sisters, my great-aunt Lígia, about this, and she spoke plainly, much like her mother.

Doña Rosa, even her daughter called her that, *always thought Anibal should have married a younger, less stubborn woman. We all loved Esther, even her, but Doña Rosa wanted Anibal's life to be less complicated. And Esther was never uncomplicated.*

Doña Rosa married when she was sixteen. Her father arranged it—and that was that. There was no room for love to determine their fates. She and Don José, eight years her elder, learned to love each other. *It's better to grow together*, she would say.

But that wasn't the case with Esther and Anibal. They fell in love. He was only a few months older than her, instead of years as Doña Rosa would have preferred. Esther had turned twenty-seven in July 1954, and no news was to be had about a baby. In no way did Esther conform to Doña Rosa's expectations of a daughter-in-law—she was not meek or ready to be absorbed into the fold. And so, family members claim, Doña Rosa did what she had to do to humble Esther.

Doña Rosa was always polite, even when she was vicious, and never raised her voice, always speaking in indirect attacks or unassailable truths—which made it hard to argue. Esther's brother *was* a murderer, technically, although Esther would always say it was manslaughter. He never intended to kill anyone. And sure, "grabbing the bull by the horns" could mean several things, but Esther had a blushing inkling as to what bull Doña Rosa referred. Still, Doña Rosa was infuriatingly *not wrong*.

Esther marched back to the house, willing herself to be meek, to be quiet.

As soon as Esther sat back down at the table, returning to what she supposed would be a cold meal, Doña Rosa had the girl bring her some hot soup. *Decency is not cowardice*, Esther thought to herself as she dug into the steaming bowl with a smile on her face.

Anibal squeezed her hand. *I thought you weren't going to return*, he whispered. He smiled as he said it. *I'm sorry*, he added. *She has quite the mood, and you look beautiful eating your soup.*

Esther smiled back. She breathed a little. There was Anibal, as always, loosening the knot.

When the soups were cleared, everyone breathed a sigh of relief. The ruyas had been dealt with, and this moment would be the furthest they'd be from having to eat the soup again next week. This was also the moment for coffee and dessert. A sweetness to follow all of Doña Rosa's salt.

The girl came out and served everyone tinto and an arequipe cake purchased from the bakery in Socorro that morning. Esther salivated over every slice she saw brought out from the kitchen. The cake looked divine, caramel dripping on the plates.

But after the last person had been served except for Esther, the girl did not return. No slice was placed before her, no coffee filled her eye-line. Esther furrowed her brow. She looked at Anibal. He looked at his father. His father shrugged.

Anibal turned his gaze on his mother. *She forgot to serve Esther. No, she didn't. I told her not to.*

Esther gasped. What new affront was this?

What reason is there to deny my wife a piece of cake? A tinto?

Doña Jacinta de la Garza told me that sugar and coffee can prevent pregnancy, and we're already fighting nature on this, don't you think?

Esther turned her head to the side. Anibal gave her a look, but Esther ignored it.

And what does that mean? Esther did her best to sound sweet and unbothered.

Only that I want my son to have his heir, Doña Rosa offered, *and I'm sure you wish for the same thing, don't you?*

Esther calmed herself. She tried to convince herself the woman meant well.

And you know, Doña Rosa added, *what they say about old cows.*

As the old woman continued describing the features of old cows, namely their low production, Anibal simply stared at his mother. He did nothing to defend Esther as Doña Rosa kept threading her jokes with more and more barbed wire. And so, Esther did what she had to do.

Everyone hates your soup.

Doña Rosa froze. Everyone stopped eating dessert. Anibal turned to Esther, only to see the red in her face. She was hot to the touch, and as much as he might have wanted to comfort her, Doña Rosa had still not reacted, and until he knew his mother's reaction, there was nothing to do but wait.

Doña Rosa stood from the table. *I think this meal is over.*

Everyone's cake was picked up, eaten or not. There would be no dominoes, no stitching circle, no listening to the radio. The rest of the evening was canceled—Doña Rosa had a headache named Esther.

Esther had said the one thing sure to injure Doña Rosa, and no one in the family forgot it. For decades. But Esther focused on what mattered to her, and what she cared about was Anibal. He chose his mother over his wife—he did not defend Esther. In his silence, she felt his betrayal. So in return, he had hers.

*   *   *

Esther finally spoke to Anibal. She came to him one afternoon, when he'd finished a particularly brutal day of branding and vaccinating. She came to him with her hair down and meticulously brushed, forever stubborn in its curl—just the way he liked it.

She walked to him and stood dangerously close, almost—almost—with affection.

She said that an old cow cannot be expected to produce much milk, Anibal.

He did not deny his mother's words. *She did, Esthercita.*

She hated when he did this, when he addressed her by a pet name in a sweet tone, when she was not in the mood for sweetness in any form.

I am no cow. She looked at him carefully.

You are no cow. He answered just as carefully.

She grabbed his hand, and every muscle in his body, every muscle he'd been contracting since their fight had begun finally relaxed. She squeezed his fingers against her own.

I did not enjoy our disagreement, he whispered. It was the closest thing to an apology that he could muster. She nodded.

He scooped her up, pressing her small frame into his large, barreled chest.

Shall we?

Esther nodded and let herself be swept away by this ocean of a man.

* * *

Esther never apologized to Doña Rosa. She simply showed up the next Sunday evening, as usual, and ate her soup without fuss or question.

Doña Rosa also said nothing to Esther, but there were no comments about cows, bulls, or any other creature. Just normal conversation about coups that Esther could tune out blissfully, enjoying her meal and getting through the visit as usual.

And when Esther finished her soup, Doña Rosa whispered to the girl and had another portion served. *For the skinny one*, was all she said, and Esther understood it for the compliment it was.

Doña Rosa and Esther found a compromise in silence, and as the weeks went by, they learned to enjoy each other's company. It was a delicate dance, but the two women learned the steps to keep harmony.

And when, in October 1954, Esther asked for a third portion of soup, after having already eaten her own and Anibal's, Doña Rosa raised an eyebrow. Her favorite son's skinny wife seemed less skinny suddenly. Esther had a glow in her cheeks. The woman looked positively radiant.

Anibal, Doña Rosa said, *you need to buy your wife a house in Socorro. And it's time to slaughter a steer. You need to throw a party next weekend and feed all the workers.*

Anibal looked at his mother, trying to understand her mandate. He looked at Esther, who smiled at him, nodding.

Yes, Esther said, *I suppose that is the custom.*

Doña Rosa laughed. But this time, with every peal, a tear streamed down her face.

Esther laughed too. *This old cow might have some milk in her yet.*

The National Front
(A GATHERING OF OLD GOSSIPS)

Bogotá, 1954-1958

In the town squares, the old men dissected the war, along with the wars of their fathers and grandfathers—picking apart the merits and obvious flaws of every engagement. The old men were angry as the past felt like a lie. *Wasn't war supposed to be heroic?* Instead, it felt like a prolonged exercise in futility—a generation of corpses piled up for reasons that were getting harder and harder to articulate.

Still, the old men gathered to play dominoes, drink, and discuss. *Did you hear?*—and they had all heard. Newspapers were written by party men and could therefore not be trusted—although all the old men read the newspapers and magazines diligently. They listened to the radio as well. But the best news, the news that needed repetition, the news that resembled the wind, that news came from other lips—rumors.

Never believe anything a Colombian tells you, I was once told by my half-Colombian father, *except for the part where it's all true.*

The old men chuckled at the new president's amnesty—amnesty is forgiveness, but it's not a magical pill that makes people forget. They would remember the wrongs, as old men did, and they knew what an absurd idea it was.

Amnesty. Sounds like an ugly woman's name.

The old men could laugh at history; it was a perk of surviving. Another round of drinks. Another conversation. Another game of bones.

*   *   *

In some parts of 1954 Colombia, people lived the same as they had in colonial times. Young people, especially young men, were trapped by poverty and wanted the lives they saw in the movies. They had their own conversations on street corners, angry cigarettes dangling from their lips. *When would they have cars and electricity? When would the wealth finally trickle down?*

Rivulets of young men stole away from their villages and towns for cities or the mountains—to find opportunity in work, crime or in the revolution—only to find themselves joining into a swell of discontent.

The Violence had not succeeded for anyone, especially the Conservative Party. Liberals had not left Conservative strongholds. The paramilitary had not remade the nation into one with Conservative values. Tens, or hundreds, of thousands of innocent people died for nothing. Within a year, it was clear the unelected president's early declaration of amnesty had also failed—too many Conservatives kept killing, too many Liberals defected to the guerrillas.

El Presidente was more dictator than president, but that certainly didn't stop him from calling himself a symbol of Colombia's progress and democracy. But reality could not be denied: Instead of just fighting the slightly-left-of-center Liberal Party, El Presidente's party was now fighting a socialist, laborer-driven guerrilla movement. There were dozens of new outfits, all ostensibly representing the people. Rojas knew that once the isolated cells started working together, he might have a real Communist threat on his hands. Internationally, Colombia looked exactly as unstable as it was. So, El Presidente made his case to the men of his country, old and young alike. He genuinely tried to improve people's lives.

When El Presidente pushed for agrarian reform, the people decided he was simply trying to appease the guerrilla—*it's all false promises so they'll put down the guns.* When El Presidente increased the armies to employ more people, it was called *a threat to democracy.* El Presidente brought state television to Colombia—*another person not to believe.* Telephones appeared in homes—*a conspiracy to stop us from gathering outside the telecom!* He pushed innovation: Airports (*for the rich*), women's suffrage (*for stacking household votes*), and a national campaign in forgetting (*as long as you have a gun to defend your memories*).

Rojas built highways and opened the National Observatory, and it was referred to as *dictatorial efficiency.* Dictators have a unique ability to accomplish great reforms, it's true. Perhaps President Rojas would have been a great democratically elected president. But he wasn't.

* * *

The Condor, monger of war and cheese, truly and verifiably died in 1956—and with him ended a certain era of violence. A commander without an army is only a man barking at the abyss. He died on the street, and the person who shot him was the son of one of his victims.

El Presidente wanted to refocus the story the people told. *Don't be like the Condor,* he encouraged the televised heads to say, *don't hate your neighbor, and instead hate the Communists—the guerrilleros, the bandits, the men in the hills. It's time to stop fighting one another, and to fight the real enemy of our country.*

After four years of running the country, Rojas unilaterally declared a new term for his "presidency." The people, across parties, gathered. They walked across the plazas to the government buildings wherever they lived, fists raised in the air, demands in their glares.

On May 10, 1957, eight years after the last election, and eleven years since the last free and fair election, the entire country of Colombia went on strike. The government, the economy, and the infrastructure (trains and all) came to a halt. Approximately ten million people protested in some form that day, entire families took to the streets carrying placards, infants and grandmothers alike in a country of roughly fifteen million. "A coup d'état of public opinion," scholars called it.

Conservative and Liberal, it didn't matter, the people stood, a temporary and organic amnesty achieved, all the in the name of overthrowing a dictator. El Presidente had brought them together after all. But what happened next is the real miracle.

A military junta, consisting of five generals, gradually began taking over the reins of government that very day, sending Rojas into exile. In July, other party leaders (including the ever-persistent Laureano Gómez on the Conservative side and one Alberto Lleras Camargo on the Liberal side) joined forces and created a power-sharing agreement called the National Front. The National Front was an experiment in political science; instead of fighting, the two parties would alternate the presidency, one term Liberal, another Conservative, allowing each equal access to power in four-year terms. Both parties agreed. Now it was up to the people.

* * *

In December 1957, a plebiscite was scheduled to ensure the people accepted the compromise. The referendum passed, and in 1958, elections took place for a new government. The parties were to share power from the top houses of government down to local municipalities—Liberals would only run against Liberals, Conservatives against Conservatives, with the knowledge that the next election belonged to the other party. Smaller parties allied themselves with existing parties, creating competitive factions.

The elections of 1958 proved successful. The Conservative Party, devastated by Gómez and his band of merry dictators, had a difficult time finding the right candidates, so the parties decreed Liberals would govern first. Alberto Lleras Camargo handily won the election against his Liberal cohort, agreeing to maintain the terms of the National Front and ensure its existence (instead of dissolving it as another would-be dictator). With time, the thinking went, the country would repair from the Violence and be ready to return to democracy.

Just like that, the Violence was over. Without walls or force, five men found a way to end a decade-long civil war. In a room without weapons, they reforged the path back to democracy.

*   *   *

Pedro Marín left the Cause, taking a second offer of amnesty by the Liberal regime. But after a brief stint as a highway inspector, the last legitimate job he would have for the rest of his life, he quit and returned to being a revolutionary.

The Cause still existed, still mattered. Cautious agrarian reforms improved the lives of a few workers, but feudal abuses continued. The death of a farmhand still meant little, and it was not lost on Marín that the owners of the land were more of European bloodlines, that the workers of the land were more indigenous. Marín argued that these were the same owners of the land who, hundreds of years ago, enslaved the native, brought the enslaved African to the coast, fought endless wars between themselves for endless power. Conservative, or Liberal, these owners of the land

and men in suits were the same thin-lipped men who had destroyed the world, who had taken what was never theirs.

The workers were the children of Bachué. They were the People of the Salt. Colombia belonged to them.

Marín and soldiers like him retreated into the terrain they knew best—the obscure and remote pockets of the eastern llanos. These southern lands were hot in the day while cold at night, prone to swamp-like flooding during wet season and desert in the dry. There's a reason they remain relatively empty to this day.

The retreat of Marín and other guerrillas into hiding proved a blessing for the small cities and towns in the mountains. Within a few years, Colombia began to look like other developing countries in the region.

The death tolls for La Violencia emerged in the late 1950s. Estimates declared that hundreds of thousands of people died during the nine-year conflict. The number doesn't account for the missing and should probably be closer to half a million. Most of the dead were the poor.

*   *   *

The old men still gathered in their small cafés with their friends and dominoes—and played on. And with time, the gossip began to change. Little was said about mass graves for the first time in years. A week would pass without a public murder. The people began to realize they'd been holding their breath for almost a decade. When they exhaled, they finally found themselves able to look at their neighbors in the eye.

Can we forgive? The old men weren't sure, even as they furtively glanced at the other old men, once their mortal enemies, playing dominoes at a café on the other side of the plaza. Heads shook as they have always shaken. *Maybe it's for our children to forgive?*

The Fracture
(A MIGRATION OF BONES)

Santander, 1955–1962

On April 28, 1955, Anibal and Esther welcomed Lourdes into the world, the first of their many blond-haired and brown-eyed children. She was named after the Virgin my grandmother prayed to the most as she tried to conceive.

In May of 1956, Esther gave birth to Alba, my mother. In June 1957, Jóse Alfredo—finally, a son—came along. In July 1958, she had Edgar Anibal. For a potentially barren woman, Esther suddenly had no problems conceiving. *My body remembered what it was supposed to do*, she is fond of saying, which is why the first time took so long—*there was nothing to remember just yet.*

In many ways, her body hadn't been hers for five years, and she realized how little she'd appreciated the time before children. She *had* become a cow (no insult to her), kept pregnant and milked. She was productive in other ways too. She learned to knit, embroider, and needlepoint. She became a maker of lace, of doilies, of tiny frocks worn for baptisms and then given away to the poor. She made clothes for orphans and her children. She ran two households, living and raising children between the finca in La Fuente and the city of Socorro, splitting her time between shopping for food and picking out which steer to slaughter. She enrolled the older children in an expensive school, and soon the finca became a place for weekends, or when the children had extended breaks from school.

She wasn't overseeing anything to do with the dairy operation anymore, but she knew enough about how things were going to not complain. Anibal bought another finca, parceling off a little more land. Canaán soon had a sister, Jerusalem. (Anibal never lost his affinity for naming his lands after places referenced in the Bible.) He and my grandmother dared to dream that they could live for a bit, raising their children in the lands that had raised their families for generations. They were foolish, of course, to assume that tragedy wouldn't find them.

* * *

For the first time in twelve years, in early 1960, there was a large funeral in Socorro. Funerals drew attention, demanded witnesses, which had been avoided during the Violence. But the parish priest had declared it time to face the world, to gather and grieve in public.

Doña Evangelina was utterly shocked. She said so at their weekly lunch, and Esther did her best to keep composure. Her sisters had all married and lived in other cities. Only Esther remained to play cards with Doña Eva.

I know he's your husband's kin, Esther, but it is an offense to God if the first large funeral we attend in over a decade is for a suicide.

Esther nodded, but even as her head moved up and down, her heart ached for Inés, wife of the deceased. Her sister-in-law was a good woman, and now, in the cruelest way, she was a childless widow.

They say that just before a meeting with a worker about a raise, Benito woke up after a quick nap, grabbed his revolver and shot himself through the mouth, dying instantly without a note or hint of motive. The five eyewitnesses to his suicide—his wife, his sister, a cook, and two farmworkers—all say he did it calmly, with a smile on his face. Fully sober and cheerful as he cocked the weapon.

The bad tongues around towns would say that his alcoholism made him crazy—that a man with that much aguardiente in his blood was unaccountable for his actions. That he knew Inés would never ask for divorce, that he wanted to set her free. Some say he was in debt. Others that he simply had nothing left to live for, had secrets that his death would keep sealed. No one blamed his wife.

After the funeral, at the gathering in Doña Rosa's home, Inés looked like a porcelain doll, her smile sad and painted on thinly. Esther hugged her tightly, and Inés re-entered reality for a brief moment. Esther had that effect on a lot of people.

You're going to have another baby, Inés said to her brother's wife. *I can feel it.*

Esther had been thinking about that all morning. Was her body done? A fifth child would only delay what she really wanted—to return to Anibal's side on the finca. Her fingers itched to touch blades of grass.

Instead of responding, Esther gave Inés a bundle of black fabric, tied together with string. Inés untied the knot and found that it was exactly as it appeared on the outside, black linen.

Inés nodded. It was customary to wear black for a year, more if the widow preferred. In those years, stores carried more black fabric than any other color. But Inés only had a few outfits for widowhood, as she hadn't attended a funeral in so long. Esther's gift was a kindness. Black fabric meant that Inés would have to sew the clothes herself, a distraction that was becoming of her new status. Esther hugged Inés and went to Anibal, who had watched the whole exchange, an idea emerging.

Esthercita, what if she came to live with us?
Esther assented and Inés moved in within the week.

*   *   *

A month later, the unthinkable happened. Don Trino collapsed in the inoculation pen, folding over a calf, syringe in his hand. He never stood up again.

Don Trino, who called Esther's daughters his doves, who taught them to count on heads of cattle in Mancarique. Don Trino who had given his children to fate, all of them far from his reach except Esther, and had seen them all prosper, all live. Don Trino, her father. She could not imagine him dead. But she had to.

The old women said that it was the crimes of his son that killed him. Doña Eva told a distant cousin that it was Esther marrying. His children all attended the funeral, delayed so a pregnant Hilda could arrive from Bucaramanga.

It was a grand affair. My grandmother told me over a thousand people came to pay their respects—even commodities traders and the head of the milk cooperative traveled from Bogotá. Old Conservative comandantes, used to fighting well-regarded Liberals, wore their uniforms out of admiration for the old man. An old German acquaintance of Don Trino's, a man with whom he had kept up correspondence, came from Florida.

Esther brought her two youngest, the babies strapped to her body on either side of her waist. Alba and Lourdes stayed at home, until they didn't. The four- and five-year-olds arrived in navy blue dresses, having escaped the finca, walked to a busy intersection, and taken the bus independently into Socorro, unaware of the frantic search for them that Inés carried on back home. When they arrived at the funeral mass, unsupervised, Esther sent word back to Inés and promptly sat the girls between her and Doña Eva, tiny mountains of grief and black linen.

It was a season of mourning that seemed somehow overdue. Few members of the family had perished in war—*we'd never be that dramatic*, my grandmother said to me once. *We die sensible deaths. Heart attacks. Old age.* Her father got the death he preferred, I've been told. He died on his land, doing exactly what he loved most—taking care of his cows. *We should all die so*, my grandmother told me.

When she got home later that evening, Esther considered a life without her father. He was just gone, like he'd only ever been a whisper in the first place. She conjured his voice, his smile, the inflections in his voice when he called her *Esthercita*.

She thought about her girls, taking the bus alone today, already not needing her. She had once been a girl like that, wanting to break free from the things she should have held on to the most.

She felt like a hand without an arm, grasping for anything, and finding nothing. There was no one to blame. Just his heart. And she could never blame that—that was the part of her father she loved most.

* * *

Inés's prediction proved to be true, and Esther told Anibal that she was pregnant again before she'd finished sewing her own black mourning garb. She expected her husband's joy, which was immediate, but she did not expect his second reaction.

I think it's time you stopped coming to the finca on weekends.

They were in their bedroom in the city, far from where he stayed on the finca, sitting on the edge of their bed, and she could not help but stare at the crucifix on the wall. He was suggesting the opposite of everything she wanted.

I can manage just fine, Anibal. Inés helps out a lot. And five will not be that different from four.

No, no, it's not just that. He had ambition to run for City Council, and then, in a year or two, for departmental senator representing Socorro. He needed her to be a visible part of the city's culture and social scene, as his wife. Esther was caught off guard.

I will be coming to the city more on the weekend now, Anibal explained. He had to reside in the city he planned to represent. And despite the finca being relatively close, at most an hour depending on the route, he couldn't live so far away if he planned to serve Socorro.

Esther thought about it. He had always expressed a desire to get involved with government when the risk lessened. And now that the Violence was over, and Liberal politicians weren't being killed indiscriminately, the time seemed right. He was tall, handsome, robust, and charismatic. She understood his appeal. She just wasn't sure she wanted to be a politician's wife. And she really wasn't sure about rarely seeing her cows.

Eventually, my grandmother talked herself into it. By the time Alberto was born in November of 1960, she was firmly ingrained in Socorro society, with events every weekend. My grandmother simply marched forward as she always had, doing what was expected of her as a wife and mother. The life she had envisioned, though, had slowly melted away into the life that Anibal envisioned. He visited the finca, bringing back reports that helped her feel connected, but it was a poor substitute. She told herself the situation was temporary. They were people of the land, *surely they'd return?*

But she was no longer a dairy farmer, she was a politician's wife. Of course he won.

* * *

Anibal would take his pickup truck to the many towns in the mountains and upon his arrival children would begin trailing the dust his tires kicked up. Shouts of "Don Anibal!" echoed behind him, and as he descended from the cab, he'd open his satchel to the children's delight and produce cheap sweets for their eager hands. The electorate not only knew his name, but had been long benefiting from his generosity.

My grandfather loved the people of rural Santander, and they loved him back. He won his first campaign in a landslide. And Councilman Rueda got to work.

When folks were hungry, Don Anibal got them jobs that paid up front. Don Anibal arranged marriages, solved trade disputes, and provided shelter when it was necessary. He was known to roll up his sleeves and work side by side with his laborers, spending hours installing fence posts only to then spend hours drinking rum with them.

He bought raw crafting materials for the women, procured radios and newly imported televisions for the people who lived on his lands, and gave a cut of his profits to his workers. Don Anibal was an exception in a country where few thought to treat the laboring classes well. He would never be one of them—he was still the boss and an owner of the land, but he tried to be better.

One day, in the early months after Alberto was born, my grandfather came home with a young girl. The young girl's father, who worked for Don José, asked Anibal to give her a job. Doña Rosa could not take on any more girls. So, the girl's father petitioned the boss's son, as a home for her in Don Anibal's house seemed better than the fields. My grandmother took one look at Melinda and remarked how much she resembled the Rueda stock.

My grandfather cleared his throat. The comment was never made again.

Don José's brothers, like so many of the other owners of the land, big and small, had their predilections. It was not unusual for a boss to visit their worker's wives. Or daughters. In Colombia, and especially during these times, everyone understood this to be so. Some working men encouraged their wives and daughters to seduce their bosses, to remain in good standing. Others promised their children's labor to the bosses' wives to retain favor.

The women and girls had little choice in the matter. Some participated willingly. Some resisted. The outcomes remained the same: a confusing and unacknowledged underclass of illegitimate children, without the status and access to privilege afforded the ones conceived in marriage.

One of Anibal's uncles had clearly fathered this girl. But it wasn't polite to talk about it, and it wasn't polite to keep her too close to the source. Just because it was written all over her face did not mean that the man who called himself her father knew. *Men are blind this way*, my mother tells me.

Melinda moved in and played the part of devoted nanny to the kids. Being under my grandmother's wing provided her with food, some education, and opportunity.

Inés also found a certain safety in the Rueda Angarita home. But as the councilman's widowed sister, she was granted a different status. Melinda slept on a cot behind the kitchen. Inés slept in a four-poster bed in a private room adjacent to a garden.

And Esther? Esther didn't sleep at all. She was the councilman's wife and had five children. Esther stayed up all night planning, making, and doing. She had her part to play as well.

*   *   *

Esther enjoyed the life of a politician's wife more than she anticipated. She sewed wounds, assisted in births, cooked elaborate meals. She taught people to read, organized fundraisers for the Church, and donated her time in myriad ways to the less fortunate, all with her children in tow.

The second time Anibal ran for office, in 1962, now for the departmental Senate, my grandmother left her children with her mother and joined my grandfather on the campaign trail, bringing only her youngest. My grandmother may have read as stern, but to the people of Santander, she never seemed arrogant or elitist—just honest. Many spoke of her generosity, of the way she quietly stuffed people's hands with dairy goods, making no fuss and demanding no thanks. My grandmother never considered herself above any task or chore—a humility born of being raised on the land, she claimed.

Over fifty years later, their names still brought out more smiles in small towns than I expected. *Don Anibal y su mujer!* One man told me how he'd been named for my grandfather, Sylvestre Anibal.

My father spoke of him often, Sylvestre Anibal told me. *Your grandfather was a good boss, a good politician too.*

*   *   *

One afternoon, all five Rueda Angarita children visited Doña Eva in Mancarique. Their mother had aged in her widowhood—deep creases lined Doña Eva's face, and her hands seemed encased in cloth rather than skin. Esther spent as much time as possible with her, worried about what losing Don Trino would do to her mother.

It was taffy-pulling season and Lourdes and Alba, the two eldest, were old enough to enjoy the fun of the melcocha with several visiting cousins. The sugarcane molasses taffy had to be pulled or it would harden. Anibal gathered a coiled rope of the taffy, pulled and pulled, slowly expanding and contracting the braided lengths of pure sugar and butter until, after he let it harden, he snapped it into seven pieces, one for each member of the family.

As soon as the melcocha touched their palms, the kids scattered to play.

Lourdes stayed to watch her father try to give her mother a piece of taffy, but Esther was having none of it. Anibal spotted Lourdes nearby and waved her over. Lourdes thanked her father after pocketing the taffy, and Esther took a turn slowly shaking her head.

That girl, she said, *is going to be fat, Anibal, and it will be your fault entirely.*

Anibal waited until he thought Lourdes left them, scampering off into the large corral to play with her siblings and the cows, before he responded.

There are worse things than having a little meat, Esther.

Not if you're a woman. Not in this world.

I would like you a little fatter, Esthercita.

She laughed a cruel laugh. *You might have to look for someone else then.*

Pregnancy had consumed the better part of a decade of her life. Her body felt like a cold and distant planet to her, which made intimacy with my grandfather complicated. Esther did what she could do: prayed, kept trust. Anibal would ride off for days, politicking and overseeing work on the land as she raised children. It took a certain amount of faith in him to keep the system working.

You can believe in me, my grandfather would say to her.

And she did. She believed in him as much as a person can. But no belief system could affect my grandmother's lack of humor about the matter. Or perhaps her sense of humor was more evolved than I'll ever understand. My grandfather eventually learned to stop mentioning anything that set off Esther's temper.

No, Esthercita. I only want more of you.

* * *

Lourdes sat on an overturned bucket in her nice dress, ruining the bottom with rust stains, pulling off pieces of taffy and stuffing them into her mouth as she ignored Alba's attempts to play a game. She worked the large pieces until they slowly disintegrated into her mouth, the sweetness of the melcocha a reward for the difficulty of eating.

Lourdes was a stubborn child and her father's favorite. She never felt the need to notice anyone that wasn't him, and that counted double for her younger sister.

When nap time came, Esther took her three young boys inside to her old bedroom and waited for them to fall asleep—Alberto on her lap, the other two lying next to her on her old bed. By this point, my grandfather Anibal had started a new game of dominoes with his brothers-in-law.

Lourdes doesn't remember the fall. All she remembers is that it began to rain outside as she sat on that bucket. She remembers the way the rain felt, how it refreshed her salty sweet tongue and soon made her realize how alone she was in the courtyard.

Alba watched from the barn, just too far to yell. She and Doña Eva stood beneath the red-roofed building and waved at Lourdes, trying to get her attention before she caught pneumonia from the downpour. Esther, along with the boys, remained asleep in the old bedroom, as Anibal played an increasingly drunken game of dominoes with his brothers-in-law. The rat-a-tat of the rain on the Spanish tile drowned any noise from outside—the loud romantic ballads on the radio indoors further ensured that no cries would be heard inside the building.

Why Lourdes decided to run in the rain, no one knows.

Her soft and treadless shoes stood no chance against the silky mud-covered tiles. Lourdes slipped, running toward the entrance to the house, and her legs split so wide that Alba and Doña Evangelina swore they heard her hips crack through the pouring rain. Doña

Evangelina raised the alarm and carefully snatched her granddaughter up and called for Anibal to fetch the doctor. There was no time. Lourdes had to be taken to the hospital. Anibal drove—drunk in his panic, sober in his fear.

*   *   *

About a half mile from the hospital in Socorro, at a makeshift checkpoint, a young man with a gun stopped the vehicle—it was unclear if he was a paramilitary, guerrilla, or someone who simply had decided to keep waging violence. He forced all the occupants out, including the howling little girl. After searching for guns and confiscating a small revolver, the man asked Anibal for a financial contribution, to help his fight.

I don't know what my grandfather could have been thinking. I know that he was not a man that paid bribes. He was not a man that ever supported a revolution. He was not a man that believed in the authority of some leftist bandits to even put up the checkpoint in the first place. He was a local politician, but that did no good in a situation like this.

In his desperation to get moving, Anibal paid the fine. What mattered more than anything was getting Lourdes to the hospital before any more damage could be done. But damage had been done.

The leg was fractured. The hip broken. Lourdes received the best medication and treatment possible. Doctors theorized that the ride down had worsened the leg break, and my grandfather, for the first time, thought about leaving Santander, the department he had defended, fought for, and served his entire life.

Esther had followed in a truck driven by one of her brothers, and within a few minutes of Anibal's arrival at the hospital, she'd been there to help. The rest of the children remained with Inés in Mancarique, waiting for news of Lourdes's injuries to reach them.

Anibal turned to Esther and declared, the way he did whenever he made up his mind about something, on a whim and with conviction and authority—it was time to sell everything to move to the coast. Esther urged caution and patience.

If Doña Evangelina lived in a city, Lourdes would have received treatment quicker, would have healed faster, would have hurt less. If Anibal hadn't been drinking and distracted by dominoes, he could have prevented the accident in the first place. If Alba had only played with her sister, Lourdes would not have been alone in the rain. If there hadn't been so much violence and so many revolutionaries in those mountains, they would not have had to stop on the way to the hospital. If they all lived in a city, there would not have been a checkpoint. An infinity of *ifs* circled in Anibal's mind as evening turned into night, but he decided to focus on the ones he could do something about.

* * *

In the first weeks after Lourdes fell, Anibal was ever-present, ever-attentive, ever-devoted. But gradually, as it became clear that she would be cast-bound for months, he began to disappear. First, he began attending political events alone. Then dinners at his mother's house. They still went on Sunday evenings, soup and all, but Anibal began attending Tuesday and Thursday dinners as well. He had excuses: They were closer to a certain place, or happened to be on the route, and he didn't want to bother Esther, she had so much on her hands.

Doña Evangelina took Alba and Edgar Anibal into her home, to help minimize Esther's burden. And between all the women in the house—Inés, Melinda, and my grandmother (along with the muchacha who worked in the kitchen)—they managed to deal with Lourdes. Her sons became afterthoughts to the saga of Lourdes and her injury.

The girl *was* in pain.

Some afternoons, Doña Eva would come visit with Alba and Edgar Anibal, and on one of those visits, she told Esther that maybe leaving Santander *was* a good idea. The situation in Santander was shifting into something else, something new that went beyond the Liberal/Conservative violence they understood. There were more and more checkpoints: some guerrilla, some paramilitary, some military. Violence and holdover grudges seemed to erupt occasionally, and Esther spent too much time alone for a woman with five small children. Even Doña Eva was considering a move to Bucaramanga, to live with her daughter Helena. As she said all this, Doña Eva looked for her son-in-law.

And where is Anibal? What is happening between you?

Esther did not know. But she knew that Don Trino's death had broken something in her. And Lourdes's fall had broken something in him. He was avoiding seeing his daughter in pain, and whenever he was home, it took every ounce of his being to fake happiness in her company. The girl loved him. *I want him*, she would say during her tantrums.

Sometimes Esther wanted to scream at her. At fate. At her dead father. At her husband. At everything that took her further and further from the things she loved. *I wanted Anibal too*, my grandmother told me.

* * *

The doctor in Socorro declared that Lourdes needed to go to the sea for physical therapy.

Otherwise, your daughter will probably never walk again. Even the sea is not a guarantee.

Anibal nodded. If Lourdes needed the sea, then to the sea they would go.

Initially my grandfather suggested that he go with Lourdes—just for a month or so, to see if it offered any solution. Esther knew that Anibal hadn't slept in weeks, that his greatest fears were realized when the doctors implied Lourdes might need a wheelchair for life.

Esther acknowledged that the sea wasn't a bad idea, but did not accept his offer of separation.

Fine, we'll all go to the coast, but not to visit. We're moving there. This is going to take more than a month.

Anibal did not argue. He had heard the rumors. He knew what was happening in those mountains. He could defend himself against violent Conservatives, he understood their ways. But the guerrilla was something new. Something ugly.

The coast offered safety. The coast offered opportunity. The coast would fix his baby.

Plus, Esther added, *I want to live closer to my brothers.*

The Hidden Republic
(A UTOPIA IN APOCALYPSE)

República de Marquetalia, 1964

Pedro Marín was thirty-six years old and the head of an impressive army. But what good was an army spread over the mountainside, divided into little camps and taxing local shopkeepers, butchers, and bakers for food. Marín wanted something more.

Over the years, Marín had learned to read. Cuban sympathizers would send books to him via visiting combatants, and Marín devoured both newspapers and philosophy with gusto.

Then, in early 1964, like a popular song on the radio those days, Marín decided to build a house in the clouds, except instead of a house, it was a new republic that centered the laborer and the soldier. He named it Marquetalia and placed it in a clearing high in the mountains of the department of Tolima. When he named Marquetalia a republic, he knew the power of that word. "Republic" conjured Roman senators and noble ideals. His experiment in governance would be different from Colombia's—and physically inaccessible to those who did not believe in his mission.

Inaccessible is exactly what it proved. The area, even today, can be reached only through various trails and roads that require at least three different forms of transportation, culminating in long paths that can only be trod by mules and horses. Even by foot, the winding way is perilous, ascending the Andes over small streams, loose stones, and ground prone to slide.

One could travel the path to Marquetalia for hours without encountering another soul. The cold of the higher mountains, combined with chilling winds, makes the trip uncomfortable on top of the inherent difficulty. A previous attempt by the Colombian military to enter the area years earlier, to provide aid to the people on the mountain's top, ended on a narrow pass, where only one man could slowly traverse at a time.

From the beginning of time, the region of Marquetalia belonged to the Páez, mountain people dwelling in the Andes. The topography guaranteed isolation, and whatever Spanish missionaries accessed the remote village eventually became a part of the community. Hundreds of years later, not much had changed. Isolation had its advantages, most visitors to Marquetalia became residents. It was easier than leaving and coming back.

The community grew to a thousand. Soldiers brought family, and those families began to farm. The campesinos began to work for themselves—using their skills for their own gain. Childcare, education, and minor works of infrastructure existed in Marquetalia. Marín had great plans for it. It was a utopia, a fantasy, and also a training ground for the next generation of fighters.

*   *   *

After Marín announced his intentions, the government never responded so quickly. The Conservatives controlling Congress passed a referendum declaring that autonomous republics would not be tolerated within Colombia and that the military had a sworn duty to combat Communist terrorism. Soon after the referendum was passed, U.S. president Lyndon B. Johnson authorized the sale of U.S. military equipment and helicopters to Colombia as a part of American Cold War initiatives.

By April 1964, the Colombian government's intentions became clear—guerrilla spies and scouts reported an invasion by the military within three weeks—with U.S. backup. The army planned to make an example of Pedro Marín.

Marín prepared for the war he knew was coming. And he knew the United States had helicopters. That April, his men dug caves into the mountainside as well as deep trenches and complex traps. He understood his advantages: the will and number of people—and more and more arrived every day, from around the country, ready to fight. He also had knowledge of the battleground and experience fighting on uneven terrain. The uninitiated faced great peril in approaching Marquetalia—the landscape could prove as deadly as any gun.

*   *   *

Marín tried to stop the impending attack. He, along with his top commanders, sent an open letter to the newest president, a Conservative named Guillermo León Valencia. In it, demands were made for roads to help commerce and trade, medical centers with doctors in rural areas, and schools. In exchange, the letter writers offered to put down their weapons and give up the fight. *Support our people, and we'll support your capitalism.*

By the time the letter publicly circulated, it was too late. The mail worked slowly; Marquetalia's lack of basic services had prompted the writing in the first place.

Years later, public memory of the event would state that the invasion of Marquetalia was a response to the letter. But it wasn't—even the letter's authorship proved questionable under scrutiny.

The public memory, while wrong, has value. The narrative was not unfamiliar to most Colombians: The working man demands basic rights, and the government responds with overwhelming physical force.

*   *   *

The attack began with smoke and metal birds. The morning of May 27, 1964, nine hundred and fifty soldiers marched on foot up the mountain, while hundreds more descended from helicopters. All under the command of the Colombian and U.S. military.

But Pedro Marín was ready.

In his memoir of the battle, Jacobo Arenas (also a guerrillero and second-in-command that day) describes the rockets and smoke bombs the military launched so its helicopters could land in a clearing. Within fifty-five minutes, dozens of helicopters dropped hundreds of men, at least eight hundred, in neat rows.

At the first sign of the Yankee-sponsored invasion, the one thousand civilians, mostly farmers, who lived in Marquetalia with the guerrillas, had gone into hiding. These agrarian workers were not the bandits and paramilitaries imagined by the Conservatives. They were men and women used to tilling the soil, some indigenous and some mestizo, interested in survival—not in picking up weapons for combat.

Marquetalia's greatest weapon was its location—and even against the helicopters, it remained true. The cold, the smoke, the natural echoes produced by mountain walls, and the dense mountain fog, as well as the quick evacuation of the people of Marquetalia, meant that for the first few hours, the military mostly fought itself.

Men stumbled blindly in the large clearing, shooting and stabbing whomever they encountered. It took far too long for the soldiers to realize that they'd only killed their own. And when they finally began to assess the self-damage inflicted, Marín and his men emerged from their tunnels and trenches to attack.

Marín charged into the smoke with his armed men, all forty-seven, in defense of the civilians. One can argue that if it weren't for Marín and his men, the civilians wouldn't have been in danger to begin with. If Marín hadn't established an autonomous republic, if he hadn't been extorting the local large landowners who then revealed his position, if he'd had more weapons, things could have turned out differently.

Marín was keenly aware of his comparative lack of military resources. During battle, he resorted to what he did best: hiding, sniping, and crafting elaborate booby traps. His methods proved effective. As women, children, and other civilians remained in the caves, Marín succeeded in keeping the army penned into the clearing where they landed.

When the military, and their American support troops, attempted to join the battle from various mountainous paths, Marín's men sniped the mules necessary to move their equipment forward, blocking crucial funnel points. Over eight hundred of the infantrymen who'd climbed up most of the mountain never joined the battle, stuck in a narrow pass overlooking the valleys of Tolima.

Marín ordered a strategic retreat. The people of Marquetalia—sure-footed on rocky terrain, well stocked with food set aside in anticipation, and grounded in their hatred toward the government—could last for weeks.

And they did.

* * *

The guerrillas waited. Then, little by little, they struck. Attacks by Marín's men became sporadic and surgical. One skirmish on May 30. Three fights on the third of June. Attacks and counterattacks filled the early days. The guerrilla did their best to thin out the military.

THE VIOLENCE

An awkward dance commenced. The guerrillas would strike a section of the military's camp and the military would retaliate. By mid-June, betrayals by double agents revealed the guerrillas' tunnel-and-cave system. Unable to fight back, the guerrillas did what they did best: They ran and hid again, regrouping to fight in shifting locations.

Days passed. The guerrillas remained in movement. Strike. Counterstrike.

Women in the caves, those mothers and wives and daughters, learned to clean, assemble, and fire guns. Those women joined the men eventually, taking on nicknames of their own (some of my favorites are "La Huella," which translates to "the fingerprint," and "La Marranita," which is "the little lady pig"). Training sessions reverently discussed the cultural enslavement of women, even as women did most of the Revolution's cooking, sewing, and cleaning.

Life found a pattern, even in a cave, even in battle. The guerrillas began the day at 3 a.m., on foot, so that they could attack their enemies by dawn. Small cells of guerrilla fighters were harder to find and harder to capture. The group did not move as a small army—instead it moved as independent assassins, turning the Colombian military's American organization and massive numbers into their biggest weakness.

* * *

That July, to the newspaper and foreign dignitaries, the Colombian government declared victory in Marquetalia—but fighting continued in the area well into October.

Although the numbers are difficult to confirm when it comes to Operation Marquetalia, U.S. and CIA counts say up to 2,000 Colombian troops battled 1,500 guerrilla combatants (of which 47 and Marín were armed). Colombian accounts have up to 15,000 domestic soldiers against 500 guerrilla (oddly enough, the fact that only 47 and Marín were armed remains consistent). Who or what counts as a guerrilla is not consistent at all.

Death tolls for the months-long operation (although some accounts place it anywhere from twenty days to five months) range from 15 guerrillas to 500, up to 1,000 Colombian soldiers, and either seven American soldiers dead or about 50 buried in a mass grave.

* * *

Marín and his surviving soldiers met in a secluded ranch in Tolima that October and talked things out. The United States government's involvement in the destruction of his republic (that's how he saw it) did not sit well. He'd just finished reading Marx and had exchanged several letters with Fidel Castro.

The official Communist Party in Colombia and Cuba offered Marín their support. And now he began earnest discussions with Jacobo Arenas, who established himself as the official liaison to the Communist Party in Cuba. *What kind of funding could the Party offer, what kind of weapons, what kind of supplies?*

He'd resisted Castro's entreaties until then, hoping to avoid proving the government right. He didn't fight for a party or a group of intellectuals—he fought for the people. But the people didn't have the guns that the Communists did. And Marín now had a larger mission—the complete overthrow of the Colombian government and resistance to North American imperialism.

The guerrilla fighter is the Revolution incarnate.

Marín now believed in revolutionary socialism. He believed in the taking of property without consequences. He believed in the right of one man to kill another in the name of something bigger. Before, he'd wanted more—more rights, more access, more assets—for the campesinos, but now, he wanted to take it all.

*   *   *

His men took on a new name, Bloque Sur, the Southern Bloc—which by 1966 would be renamed the FARC, Fuerzas Armadas Revolucionarias de Colombia (the Revolutionary Armed Forces of Colombia). Eventually, tens of thousands of combatants would join his cause. But people just called them the guerrilla. There were other revolutionary armies in Colombia, but the FARC was the first that promised to wage a forever war.

Marín's war had been given a new ideology, Communism, a new purpose, and, most importantly, it had a new name.

The Land of Salt
(A WHISPER OF MARSH)

Barranquilla, 1963-1968

The house in Barranquilla—Colombia's door to the Caribbean, mouth of the Magdalena and the golden port of the Atlantic—had five bedrooms, a yard full of fruit trees, and a living room that boasted a long planter beneath a skylight along the northern wall. Its blue-gray concrete walls seemed solid, bulletproof. Not that it mattered.

In Barranquilla, the smell of the previous night's rum glistened on skin at church on Sunday morning, and Anibal appreciated the honesty in the Caribbean breezes that whipped through the city. It had taken them a few years to settle, with moves to Santa Marta, Ciénaga, and Fundación, towns in the Magdalena River Valley, but nothing felt right until Barranquilla. When they bought the house, Esther liked it. With time, she learned to love it—and the city.

*   *   *

Twice a week, no matter where they were, Anibal bundled Lourdes up in his Jeep Willys and drove her to the beach. He'd talk as they drove across the sand along the water's edge until finding the right spot. Little by little, Anibal retaught Lourdes how to walk.

He began by digging a hole. My grandfather then lowered his weight onto his knees, and used his large hands to move the sand into a steady pile. He'd grab a small spade he'd brought along and continue enlarging the hole. He'd always choose a spot too far for the tide to fill the hole with water, but close enough to see and smell everything. When the hole was the right size, Anibal picked up Lourdes, the small child encased in her cast and buried her in the sand. She didn't say much, plastered from the waist down, with a few strategic holes for life's functions. She'd been in pain and in a series of casts for the better part of a year, waiting for her hips and legs to heal after the accident.

He pulled a mango wrapped in the day's newspaper from his pocket. After carefully peeling, he gave Lourdes the fruit and plopped down next to her. The sand warmed under the day's sun, and he swore that the color would return to her legs once they removed the plaster. Lourdes ate the fruit joyfully and believed that her father would cure her, that the heat therapy would work.

Anibal told her about the new cows in the finca, about the land his own father had bought near Fundación. How much each cow weighed and what the different grasses did for its fat ratios. Lourdes tried to wiggle, forever attempting to resolve the itch of her lower limbs. But her father's voice proved salve, and at times she'd forget her circumstance wandering through his baritone lullaby underscored by the sweetness of fruit and the steady pull of tide.

As the sun climbed through the morning, Lourdes felt the heat baking her legs. When it grew too hot, Anibal would remove her and cool her off in the breeze. Then, when she felt normal again, the whole routine commenced anew.

When her cast was removed, Lourdes could not walk. Her muscles had partially atrophied and although her hip and leg had set correctly, movement proved difficult. She'd cry for hours, watching her sister and brothers play, running around the house as she was confined to a chair.

Still, she was taken to the ocean. Without the cast, her legs felt the sand's impact directly. And in the water, tentatively and with Anibal's help, Lourdes would move her unsteady legs. Months passed, and her ability to walk seemed as far away as ever. Anibal's faith did not waver, and the therapy was never abandoned.

Waist-deep in the ocean, Lourdes learned to lean and eventually to steady herself on her father's capable arms. She learned to tentatively move her legs beneath her. With time, she could slowly shift her movement from one side to the other. Near the end of summer, Lourdes timidly stood—her father the only witness to the first of her little miracles.

And all the while, Anibal Rueda told Lourdes stories—the women he'd composed songs for, the beers he preferred, the accordion ballads that rang truest, the fashionable dances he'd loved as a teenager.

And one day, almost a year and a half after the accident, Lourdes Rueda took a step, and Anibal Rueda became undone.

*   *   *

I'm happy in memories, my grandmother once told me. *I don't always know I'm happy in the present, but I remember myself as happy as I know I was.*

Anibal and Esther had struggled to leave Santander, selling the land Don Trino had gifted them. Their people had resided in those mountains for hundreds of years, but he knew that the coastal plains offered more opportunities for their family to thrive. And they did, primarily because Anibal had a good eye for cattle. The cows and bulls he bought produced generations of high-yielding milk cows and steers for slaughter. Soon, his herd became the envy of other ranchers—and Anibal began buying more land. He spent afternoons consulting with neighbors about quality haunches and excellent feed.

No one could deny his expertise. Esther loved this about Anibal. His desire to provide for his children, and by extension, to secure his legacy. It was the same impulse that drove him to local politics.

In her photo albums, there is a photograph of them at a wedding around this time. She is straight-lipped and defiant, her hair forever curling at the edges. His hand is resting on hers. He is in a suit, sweating and elegant at the same time, a smile on the edge of his lips, a whiskey glass within reach.

He got me to dance that night, she told me. *He stepped on me. I didn't want to tell him, though. I just let him destroy my feet.* Her eyes teared up. *He was very fat, your grandfather.*

I nodded. My grandfather's size is constantly referenced, as though he were some character from Greek lore: Anibal the Great. Named after a general who crossed the Alps with elephants. Named for a man who dreamed bigger than those who came before him.

She told me how they stayed late at the wedding. How she felt terrible for Inés, who had offered to stay with the kids that night, including the not-sleep-trained baby. But she also mentioned how my grandfather kept humming the songs they'd danced to after they got home. She described the care with which he tucked in his children. He prayed over Lourdes. He moved Alba from Alberto's crib back to her own bed. He grabbed a book from Edgar Anibal's bedside and reshelved it.

He took his wife into his arms and buried his head in her neck. My grandmother closed her eyes and closed the album.

When he wanted to be, he was the perfect man.

* * *

She asked him, politely, that Christmas, well after the birth of Nidia how he felt about her taking precautions. Precautions like birth control. He disagreed. A large family was a good one, what God wanted, and he could provide. Six children, my grandmother knew, were enough. She was exhausted. She needed a break.

We'll talk about it. That was all my grandfather would say. *God has a plan for us.*

She was pious enough to agree. Yet, this wasn't their first or their last word about the matter. Not that anyone ever heard them raise their voices or speak in any way that was not courteous. In fact, when they were angry, the silence and formality increased. *Mr. Rueda, will you please do me the honor of attending upon me* was not an unusual phrase. She often went two or three days without uttering a word.

* * *

Barranquilla is forever hot. The city has two seasons: Nine months of dry heat they call summer, and three months of warm rains they call winter. In Santander, the climate was temperate, and the tempers were hot. The coastal plains were its opposite in every way.

Esther missed the mountains. She missed the early morning fog—the way flowers needed to reach an exact dew point to open. She missed having to wrap up in a blanket on the rocking chair in the evenings. She missed the incline in her step every day, even as she grew accustomed to the level.

We're mountain people, she's fond of saying, smacking her thighs. *It's why Angaritas have such good legs.*

Often, she would close the door to her bedroom, open the windows on either side of the bed, lie down, and just let the breeze blow over her sensible linen dresses. If she lay still enough, Esther became a rock. A rock that felt nothing but the cooling winds.

But life on the coast wasn't even easy for the rocks—erosion threatened them constantly. There's only so much that any of God's creations can take. At some point, even the rocks don't recognize themselves.

Esther thought often about the life she had imagined for herself as a girl. And as the voices from downstairs called for her, forever in need of her assistance, she considered the beautiful silence of disintegration.

*   *   *

Barranquilla borders the western end of the Ciénaga Grande de Santa Marta, the largest marsh and lagoon system in Colombia. On a good day, it takes four hours to get from Barranquilla to Fundación, the town closest to the Rueda Angarita fincas.

A narrow toll road connected Barranquilla due east directly to the city of Ciénaga, creating a barrier against the sea as well as a conduit for quick and safe passage. On the left, the Caribbean Sea and Atlantic Ocean are but a few feet away, and to the right, a large expanse of interconnected lagoons and marshes host an endless array of hollowed, gray trees—mangroves poking through like lonely, silver arms in the dark waters of the swamp.

My grandfather drove on this road at least twice a week. He had a name for every segment of the drive, and he knew when a gray tree stump had finally collapsed into itself. He knew when a new shack sprang up on the embankments. He knew the names of the old men selling tinto out of thermoses next to the toll booths. He knew every bend, he knew the name of every finca bordering the road, he knew the indigenous words for the wild grasses that dotted the horizon.

Anibal had no trouble leaving Santander, forever adaptable—*a chameleon*, my grandmother called him. No matter where God took him, Anibal easily adjusted to the new way. His motto was "a la tierra que fueres, hacer lo que vieres," the Spanish equivalent of "when in Rome, do as the Romans do." He resigned his post as senator, citing his daughter's need for a new treatment. The people understood.

Like all things, the marsh eventually ends. After going through the city of Ciénaga, my grandfather would make a quick turn to the right and watch the landscape negotiate the intersection of mountains and coastal plains. The trip has no elevation, but just out the window, the northern sierras loom, tangible and rising colder than the valley below. There is something wonderful about the Magdalena River Valley as it meets the coast. The Spanish first landed here, at the intersection of the xeric and tropical—a place constantly embracing its own contradictions.

His children remember how much Anibal loved this drive. How he would whistle along to the songs on the radio, window down and arm out, a revolver still hidden underneath his seat, Santander's habits forever in him. After passing Aracataca, the land of García Márquez, he would take the turn for Fundacíon. *The most beautiful ugly city in the world*, my grandmother calls it.

Fundacíon is a cattleman's town. Every rancher in the region had reason to be there. The milk co-op's office was in Fundacíon. So was the bank and the cattle supply stores.

The farmworkers hired by the owners of the land usually lived on the fincas. Some owners would stay in the houses that remained on the ranches, weapons by their side, but most retreated into places like Fundacíon, or made the same drive my grandfather did from cities and towns that grew to meet the demand. There were hotels in places like Fundacíon. Restaurants, brothels, and bars too.

My grandmother often points out the church in Fundacíon. It was built in the late 1800s, to replace another church down the valley that crumbled after three hundred years. *The faithful were here first*, my grandmother reminds me.

* * *

The stability of life on the coast in the mid- to late 1960s allowed my grandparents to develop a routine.

When the cows needed him, Anibal tended to them, spending a few days on the land and the rest in Barranquilla with his family. He trusted his workers, but it was important he be there for anything that affected the accounting. Esther taught him well. Sometimes, the overseer needed to be overseen.

When Anibal had enough money to invest, more neighboring fincas in the Magdalena River Valley were slowly acquired. They required more work, and by 1965, Anibal had a house built in Galilea, the largest of the Rueda Angarita fincas. Eventually, he'd sleep there four nights a week, alone under a creaky fan, often with a bottle of whiskey and his revolver as his only company.

Esther offered to stay with him—to leave the children with Inés and Melinda. But the cafés buzzed with rumors of guerrilla moving down the mountains into the valleys and plains of northern Colombia. As Anibal presented it, the loneliness was quieter than the uncertainty.

I couldn't live with myself if something happened to you, he told her.

* * *

Francisco Angarita Sarmiento, runaway criminal brother forgiven by amnesty and memory alike, had been living in Cartagena, about eighty miles west along the coast from Barranquilla, since he fled Santander. Soon after Esther set up her house in Barranquilla, he decided to make the move himself, packing his few belongings into a pickup truck and making the hour-and-a-half drive from the colonial city to his sister.

A few weeks after showing up at their house, Francisco asked to speak with Anibal. Within an hour, the two men emerged, big smiles on their faces. Esther looked to her husband and her brother—she did not like this new friendship, not one bit.

But Anibal laughed and shook her gently into his arms, crushing her in a hug of pure joy.

It seems that your brother wishes to marry my sister.

Inés? Esther could not believe it. *Francisco?*

Francisco laughed. It was true. They had a certain understanding.

You'll have to get new paperwork, Anibal suggested quietly.

Why is that, Anibal? Esther did not understand what paperwork had to do with this startling news.

Well, she can't marry the same man twice, can she?

Even though amnesty had been formalized ten years earlier, Francisco had hesitated to establish himself under his legal name on the coast. He'd continued using the papers of one Benito Rueda, dead husband of Inés Rueda—the very woman he planned to marry. So, yes, paperwork was of the essence.

It seems cruel to the memory of Benito, Esther noted before crossing herself.

Francisco and Inés married quietly at the justice's offices downtown, under their own names, and again in a small church near Anibal and Esther's home. They bought a house down the road.

* * *

Francisco and Anibal drank together often, and in those evenings back in 1966, they began to hatch plans to move their families from Santander to the coast.

Doña Eva declined, preferring to stay in Santander. But within a few months, after many phone calls and logistical work by Anibal, Don José and Doña Rosa moved to the coast, with eight of Anibal's siblings and their families too—along with a formal invitation to soup dinner on Sunday evenings.

My grandmother held this against her brother for years.

The Guerrilla Priest
(A MURDER OF REVOLUTIONS)

Bogotá, 1970

The Church *parted ways* with Father Álvaro for having Communist sympathies in 1970. But, despite being defrocked, the people under his ministry still called him Father Álvaro. *I was still a priest but without a church*, he told me. *Some habits are impossible to shake.*

Father Álvaro was *almost exactly* five feet tall, with eyes as wide as espresso cups. In 1970, he looked like a tiny, 1920s movie star, all toothy in his smile and sincere in his pomade and Catholicism, despite his breakup with the Church. He joined the ELN, Ejército de Liberación Nacional (the National Liberation Army), another group of guerrillas, separate from and occasionally hostile to Marín and his FARC.

It took me a few months to get started, but I went from exemplar priest to persona non grata faster than you can say "Liberation Theology." I became a guerrilla after I met Camilo Torres. Excuse me, Father Camilo Torres. And you know, I was there when he said it: "If Jesus were alive today, He would be a guerrillero." That's what the priest said, but he was no ordinary priest. And after he was martyred in 1966, pues*, I had to go off into the mountain jungles in my best boots.*

After the priest, professor, popular thinker, and beloved orator Father Camilo Torres died during his first operation as a guerrilla, in an unexpected standoff against the National Police, the guerrilla took advantage to create a martyr, painting his face on bare walls and popularizing his story.

One priest's death radicalized others, especially Liberal members of the clergy, who never condoned the Colombian Church's influence and support of the Conservatives and their Violence.

Father Álvaro remembered Torres as humble, kind, and incredibly intelligent. He was a man to advocate for the poor, who believed that the Church was accountable for her gilded ceilings.

He was right, Father Álvaro knew it in his bones. "Tenia razon," translates literally to "he had reason," and Father Álvaro felt this to be true as well. Father Torres died for something bigger than himself. That was more Christlike in his estimation than living in the decadence of the Vatican.

Maybe I deserved it when the Church left me, he said. *I left her first, I just didn't know it.*

* * *

In late 1970, after learning to be a guerrilla in the jungle for the better part of a year, Father Álvaro returned to Medellín for his sister's funeral. She'd been killed in crossfire, an innocent casualty of a new conflict cause by a new kind of bandit, the drug dealer.

American habits paid well, and coca grew in the Andes—a gift from Chiminigagua, god of light and land. What was sacred to the Muisca people had now become a party favor for the decadent Yankees, and a hungry people cannot be blamed for profiting from the black market. At least that's how Father Álvaro saw it.

He started working to help the poor in his sister's former neighborhood. Father Álvaro opened a soup kitchen, attended to the dying and sick, and did his best to live up to the ideals martyred priests had taught him. He still gave mass, a relic of being a priest himself, and he carried a gun, a function of his time in the jungle. His new parishioners without a church called him "el curita guerrillero," the little guerrilla priest. He enjoyed the moniker. *More habits.*

The National Liberation Army used Castro's Cuba as their example of what was possible in Colombia. Even better, Colombia had enough food and natural resources, enough emerald, orchid, gold, and fruit to keep her people happy without the outside world. *Good luck blockading us!* the cry went among the dreaming hopefuls, imagining a Colombia free of imperialists and governed by the poor, a utopia of social justice.

But Father Álvaro saw what was happening in the cities too. Poverty forced creativity, and nothing paid like cocaine did. Most Colombians don't consume cocaine recreationally for a reason: It's more profitable to sell it. The addiction was to American dollars—and it was impossible to curb.

I left the guerrilla, Father Álvaro sighed, *in 1970, to fight the War on Drugs before it was the War on Drugs. There were too many people who fled because of the Violence, and the cities grew too quickly.*

The poor of Medellín, as well as the poor of Cali, were being recruited into a different kind of war. Father Álvaro saw it: The chaos of one war opened the door to another. There was no guerrilla group who cared about the children on the street, about their futures and dreams.

Children were becoming assassins for the narcos, unsuspected and small enough to disappear into a crowd, while poor enough to want more for themselves and their families. *The children,* he said, shaking his head, *we turned them into monsters.*

He dedicated the next twenty years of his life to working with those children, the poor ones in the "communes," the poverty-stricken hillside developments of tightly packed corrugated metal and cardboard houses that surrounded the main city of Medellín.

If I had a magic wand? he told me, *I would travel back to 1970 and kill all the narcos and maybe even some of the guerrilla.* He paused, recollecting that he had been a guerrillero once. *They all lost their ideals. They all became drug dealers. They are all responsible for what happened to those children.*

We lost a generation of poor youth, he said. *We let them become murderers and cocaine mules. We took little ones who, a generation ago, would have grown up in farms and instead raised them in slums.*

And we students of history, we men of God and revolution, all saw it coming, but we were called radicals and expelled from our pulpits. Father Camilo Torres had a quote for this, he said, unable to help himself in quoting the original guerrilla priest:

"No sé si el alma es mortal, lo que sí sé es que el hambre mata," which translates to, *I do not know if the soul is mortal, what I do know is that hunger kills.*

The Frozen Melt
(A BOLERO IN ABSENTIA)

Barranquilla, 1970

Anibal took Esther out to dinner in Barranquilla in April 1970. She was in the middle of planning Lourdes's fifteenth birthday, when Anibal surprised her with a meal at the best hotel in the city: the Hotel del Prado. She loved their napkins and tablecloths, the pattern on their cutlery—and he knew this. So when he'd suggested the place, she was both immediately suspicious and unable to resist. The glassware was divine.

As they sat under a particularly beguiling chandelier, Anibal began his case.

It's been six years since Nidia was born.

She corrected him, five and half. Her birthday was in November.

Esthercita, it's been a long time since we've had a baby in the house. Are you sure you're done?

She was not sure—that was part of the problem. Esther had mixed feelings about having another child. She had been so busy trying to survive civil wars, regional politics, and her children's various maladies and ailments, that she'd never really gotten to just enjoy her children's babyhoods. Maybe she could have one last child, one that wouldn't be born under a cloud of violence or uncertainty. But at forty-two, almost forty-three, she felt done. Six pregnancies had alienated her from parts of her body that were only now beginning to recover. Another pregnancy at this age felt vulgar, bordering on obscene. What kind of gentlewoman farmer lets herself get pregnant in her early forties? The rhythm method had been working just fine. She hadn't been pregnant in almost six years.

I don't think we should have another child, Anibal.

He took a long sip of his whiskey, before he responded.

Well, if the sergeant says we're not having another baby, then I suppose we are not having another baby.

She did not dignify that with a response. Normally, when he called her "the sergeant," she found it pleasant, playful. But when he deployed it during a fight, because yes, this had somehow become a fight, she bristled under its intimacy, under the hold the word had on her.

He'd straighten his posture when he said the word—evoking his military service even as he granted her a fake rank, superior to his own.

She sipped her wine.

My family thinks I should run for Council in Fundación, or maybe for departmental Senate? If you don't want to have another child . . .

She looked at him, cocking her head sideways, almost whispering what she had to say. *In what way does having a seventh child prevent you from leaving your family? Who in your family thinks you should leave me for politics? Who in your family does not want you at home, with your wife and children?*

Anibal did not say a word. This was the same fight: Anibal was never home enough.

*   *   *

The children did not realize it, but they often benefited from their parents' quarrels. Esther would retreat into her bedroom, barricading herself behind a lock and underneath a noisy fan, a cross-stitching or embroidery project calling her deeper into her silences—and Anibal took the kids out for ice cream.

The Heladería Americana, by the old soccer stadium, was a Barranquilla institution. The ice cream shop had been founded by Greek immigrants in the 1930s. They were famous for the Frozo-Malt, a delightful combination of ice-cold, chocolate-flavored Mediterranean custard, and hot, melted chocolate and caramel syrup, with a crisp sugar cookie on top. Anibal loved Frozo-Malts. As did the kids.

As do I. The ice cream shop and its historic menu still exist, and I've experienced the glory of the Frozo-Malt myself. Even the name, I can never stop saying it—"Frozo-Malt"—the interpretation of two English words from a Greek man who came to Colombia via New York. Frozen and Melted, now pronounced "Frozo" y "Malt," utterly Colombian and global at the same time.

I was taken there by my Aunt Lourdes. She described those afternoons with my grandfather. He'd come downstairs, after some quiet discussion with her mother, and announce to everyone that they were going to the Heladería Americana. They would cheer and pile into his truck, the oldest kids riding up front.

When they arrived, he'd flip a coin to a man standing in front of the shop, who would watch the car, and they'd walk in, ready to order six Frozo-Malts. To this day, my Aunt Lourdes will not order anything else from the menu. Eleven-year-old Lourdes would not have been able to order anything else either.

After years of physical therapy, Lourdes insisted on her independent mobility—often exploring hidden parts of the city. She flourished in school, and she loved her walks there and back home, grateful for her recovery. She wasn't an athlete, but she danced well enough and could run away if needed. Her previously broken body felt like a dream, something she knew she'd lived through, but somewhat vague in her memories.

Anibal never quite let go. He constantly checked on her and worried about her. She hadn't really grown for a year, and it seemed like she might be child-sized forever. She didn't mind. She could walk. He minded, though. He wanted the world for his daughter, for all his children.

In Barranquilla, there were carnivals, live musicians on every corner, and ice cream shops. In Barranquilla, he could dream for his children, as long as the land provided. They could be anything.

For all the indifference to politics on the coast, the talk of the day was the drug lords of Medellín and Cali, far in the interior of the country. The people also spoke of the guerrilla, mostly the FARC, slowly infiltrating mountain and plain alike, increasing the numbers of young men recruited into the newest civil war. New recruits, to both the cartels and guerrilla, required new uniforms, housing, and weapons—and money. Kidnappings began to fund their efforts, and the people of Barranquilla could only watch the televised news from afar.

For so long in Santander, the Violence had made even the most simple pleasures impossible. Anibal wanted his children to always love escaping Barranquilla's heat with a frozen treat. Even as the dessert succumbed into a sticky mess, Anibal never worried—the point of the Frozo-Malt was the melt. It's why you save the cookie for last—to scoop up the soup of melted sugar that remained.

* * *

After the argument about a last baby or his political run, Anibal took the children to the Heladería Americana. After grabbing their desserts, the man and his children stood outside, eating and slurping, their hands gooey with caramel. After washing their hands, they rode home, expecting to find Esther fussing over something in the kitchen or sewing something, happy to see them all—the storm of her anger over, the sweetness of embrace returned.

Except this time, she wasn't in the kitchen. This time, the morning after their disastrous dinner, she refused to leave her room.

The sergeant is not feeling well, Anibal explained to Lourdes, Alba, Jóse Alfredo, Edgar Anibal, Alberto, and Nidia.

Esther did not come out for breakfast the next morning either, instead Anibal instructed Melinda to bring her some aromatic teas, to raise her spirits. When Esther emerged, ready to talk, ready to confront Anibal with a look of both forgiveness and penitence on her face, he was gone, along with all the children. Ice cream two days in a row. This was unheard of.

She took the time to clean up, to work on her embroidery, to go over the ledger, double-checking figures on the dining room table. She took to her bed, opening the windows, and letting the breeze turn her into stone.

She stood in front of the electric fan, and she turned it to its maximum setting, as she had often seen the children do, and she let it hurricane over her, transforming her from stone into a mountain.

Esther was rock and mother, a person of salt and iron, caressed and calmed by the wind.

By the time Anibal and the kids returned, she had found serenity—she needed control over her domain like her husband needed the ice cream. Anibal had this way of wearing her down, an ocean to her mountain, a relentless tide of persuasion masquerading as innocent conversation.

She didn't want to stop his dreams. She just wanted him home. Part of her assumed that the move to the city was temporary, that the city would eventually yield to the cattle that sustained them. She wanted to move to the land, to the finca—even if they never returned to Santander, she'd wanted to return to her cows, wherever they were. Or at least, maybe to Fundacíon, as much as she hated that hideous town. Lourdes was well. They didn't need the ocean. They needed to all be together.

But on this Anibal was immovable. He did not want his daughters on the finca. The Violence might be over, but the guerrillas were not a figment of the government's imagination. Neither were the narcos. Had the Violence taught her nothing? The city was safer.

We will never live on the land again, Esthercita.
What's wrong with the land, Anibal? The land has given us so much.
Yes, but we need to give our children more.
She couldn't argue with that.

* * *

On the question of another child, Esther felt adamant. The more she considered it, the more she found all the arguments for having a baby to be selfish. Six children were enough. But she had to relent on something. She prayed on him going back into politics, hoping God would give her an answer that went against her own heart. She'd relented on so many things already. She relented on little things, like ice cream for the kids even though they hadn't eaten a good lunch. She relented on big things, like buying more fincas, like taking more financial risks, like supporting the relocation of her in-laws. Over the years, she'd followed Anibal wherever he wanted.

Relenting is like that, she tells me. *You just give in, little by little, until you don't know who you are.*

* * *

She decided to stop *counting her days* (the expression she used for tracking her cycle) in August, no longer making marks on a small calendar she kept next to her ledger. If God wanted her to have a child, she'd have a child. If His Judgment was otherwise, she'd let Anibal run for office. It felt good to her, to leave the decision to fate, to God's plan.

By Christmas, her womb was still empty, so she gave in to politics. There were worse things than local governance, and Magdalena departmental politics seemed tame. At least, Esther thought, this would get him away from the Ruedas.

When he began to campaign, she said, *I will go with you. The older children and Melinda can get the younger ones to school.*

Anibal agreed. It's always good to have the wife on the campaign trail.

*   *   *

At the end of the summer of 1970, Esther and Anibal finished campaigning. She never wanted to shake another hand again. *Too many sweaty palms*, she'll tell me, evoking a nightmare of infinite wet hands grabbing for my own.

On the ride back home to Barranquilla from Fundacíon, my grandmother remembers holding my grandfather's shoulder as he drove. He looked at her, and she smiled back at him, all teeth and no irony.

They'd spent three months together without children or family, just cows and cattlemen, small towns and even smaller settlements. They had met people and stayed under a variety of roofs, from thatched to cinder block to the ubiquitous terra-cotta tile of Spanish imposition. Three nights they'd spent in hammocks under the stars. But they had been together, Esther and Anibal, without interruption. It was a gift. She beamed. The campaign had been the answer to her prayer all along.

Esther grew to love the drive between the town of Ciénaga and Barranquilla, the nothingness of the ocean confronting the bog. The marsh and the sea underscored how precious the land was—anything can wash away.

As they approached the outskirts of Barranquilla, Anibal pointed at the construction of the new bridge over the Magdalena River. Rather than open to allow boats passage, the new bridge would be high enough for even the tallest shipping vessels. It was a sign of recovery—a nation invested in modern infrastructure was not a nation at war. Anibal had been waiting all summer to show Esther progress on the bridge.

She looked over. It was impressive, a large-scale engineering project in cement and cable. Bridges existed in Santander, but nothing of this size. Both my grandparents were born in 1927 in the rural mountains of Santander. Barranquilla in 1970—cosmopolitan high-rises dotting the horizon—could have been another universe.

You'll never guess the name of the bridge, Esthercita.

She looked at him, confused. Who cared about the name of a bridge?

Anibal started laughing as he spat out the answer, "Puente Laureano Gómez," for the former Conservative president and political agitator.

I really hated that guy, my grandmother said.

I know, my love. It's one of the things I love most about you.

At this, she smiled.

*   *   *

They pulled up to the house and as they parked along the street, the door opened. The kids rushed out, all six made of arms and legs and energy. Anibal picked up Lourdes, spun her around for good measure, and then began hugging the others. They'd all grown in the weeks they'd been apart. Esther did not like that—she was so accustomed to witnessing the subtle changes in their development. To be confronted with the shock of difference felt like something reserved for a more distant relative. A mother should know how tall her sons are, after all.

Francisco and Inés emerged from the doorway, and before Esther even got a good look, Anibal began to whistle. Inés had grown too.

And they said you would never get pregnant, sister!

Inés blushed, unable to hide her embarrassment or her pregnancy.

Esther remembered what all the bad tongues of Santander had said about Inés. How they'd blamed her for never having children with Benito. And here she was, married to Francisco, and pregnant. Well into her forties! *How delightful and obscene it all was*, Esther remembers. She laughed and hugged her brother. Francisco coughed a little, but soon returned the hug. Inés grew shyer when Esther approached.

I wasn't sure when to tell you, Esther.

Inés, more than anyone, knew how much Esther both wanted and did not want to have another child. She knew all my grandmother's doubts and all her hopes. She had assumed that the old wives back home had been right, so Inés never really considered herself likely to get pregnant. But now that she was here, she couldn't help but beam her joy and certainty.

For a second, for a brief second, my grandmother was jealous.

*   *   *

Anibal won the election onto the Council. *Of course he won*, my grandmother will say. My aunts and uncles, his children, will remember his absence, a season without ice cream. He still arrived most weekends, but three days home turned into two with Council work, and the demands of the children's lives soon made it incredibly difficult for Esther to escape.

Anibal took the kids to the Heladería Americana in late May 1971. Alba remembers, because it was almost her fifteenth birthday.

Esther and Anibal had been fighting for a few weeks. The kids knew because of the silence, and because Anibal had not left for the finca or Fundacíon in almost a month. Esther had thrown away her calendar that morning, breaking her awkward quiet by bemoaning its uselessness and petty revenge.

That evening, my grandfather had brought an accordion band to serenade my grandmother, standing below her window as he belted love songs into the abyss. Something was happening and the kids had been on edge for days, waiting for perhaps another trip to the heladería.

When the day finally arrived, the kids got off at the ice cream shop and my grandfather threw a coin to the man up front. Lourdes remembers how normal it all felt, how excited she was about the Frozo-Malt.

But this time, something was different. Anibal did not go inside the ice cream shop, instead he waited.

A few minutes passed, and then another car parked next to his truck. Francisco, Inés (with baby Beatriz), and Esther emerged. My grandfather ran to his wife, linking his arm with hers.

My grandmother was almost forty-four years old, with six children, the youngest of whom was eight. She thought she was done with this part of her life. But here she was, about to sit down at an ice cream parlor with her children to tell them that she was pregnant. Anibal ordered for everyone.

Aren't you too old? Lourdes asked after hearing the news.

My grandmother wanted to slap her, but instead she ate the sugar cookie on her Frozo-Malt.

Anibal shushed Lourdes and turned to his wife, sweating even inside the cooled ice cream shop.

It's going to be all right, Esthercita. I'm not going anywhere.

But she also knew that she could not keep him either. She was pregnant with a husband in politics. She was stuck at home, with child, surrounded by children, and unable to travel even to the finca. In Esther's estimation, there was nothing worse.

Pablito
(A BAPTISM OF FIRE)

Medellín, 1971

The Violence revealed that the Conservatives only wanted more power. The paramilitary revealed that the powerful could kill without consequences. The guerrilla revealed that the poor could begin to fight back. But the gangsters? The gangsters just wanted to take. So they took. It was that simple.

It's always one thing after another, after another, after another.

El Jabón laughed. *Without the Violence, without the FARC, without our stupid government, there's no Pablo Escobar. It's all an interconnected chain. Without 1948, there's no 1969.*

That's when Don Pablo decided his life. He left school—he was studying in Medellín. Between '66 and '69, he formally leaves study and decides to become a gangster. *But that decision didn't happen overnight. That decision began the night he was born, in 1949. See, one thing causes another, and another, and another, and another.*

No Gaitán means no Birds means no Marín means no guerrilla means no Pablo Escobar.

Everything is a chain. Without 1969, there's no 1971. And in 1971, I started working for Don Pablito.

*   *   *

Over the years, El Jabón had many nicknames. (*Let's use this one, I use it in my old age, now that I'm preoccupied with my soul.*) He also had many jobs. Most of them were working under Pablo Escobar back in Medellín. He started as a kid and over the years was a runner, a distributor, an enforcer, a logistics manager, and a bookkeeper.

I was ambitious, but I knew that the closer to the boss, the more likely you were to be killed. By the government. Or a rival gang. Or the man himself. And, "bueno, aquí estoy."

He did enjoy having dinner with Don Pablo, though, which happened often enough for El Jabón to consider El Patrón friendly. Mythmaking mattered to Pablo Escobar, and according to El Jabón, he never shied from retelling his own story.

Don Pablo would often say that he was baptized in fire. That his destiny established itself the year of his birth, when the Conservatives burned Rionegro.

*   *   *

On November 15, 1949, two weeks before the birth of Escobar, the Conservatives lit the center of the village of Rionegro, Antioquia, on fire. Rionegro was a mostly Liberal town; in rode a Conservative-backed posse, set on burning out the most prominent Liberal family in town. But, through an error of cardinal directions, the bandits ended up burning down a Conservative home instead.

Fire doesn't listen to orders. As the wind picked up and the main plaza began to burn in its entirety, the town evacuated. Within three minutes, most of the women and children ran up the mountains for protection.

THE VIOLENCE

The closest fire trucks were an hour away in Medellín. The men filtered back into town and began a water chain, doing their best to slow the fire's progress. Containment is sometimes the only strategy.

Don Pablo, asserted El Jabón, *said he felt the flames of Rionegro inside his mother's womb.*

Hermilda Gaviria de Escobar, Don Pablo's mother, gave no interviews about that day. But the Escobar Gaviria family was firmly middle-class and Conservative. Living in a Liberal town during the Violence surely created worry.

Her own people had been complicit in the destruction of half her hometown—a second cousin of hers had lit the torch. Two weeks before giving birth, hiking out on a mountainside, driven there by her family's own party—it cannot have been easily forgotten.

Hermilda remembered, that much can be ascertained. El Jabón confirmed.

His entire childhood, his mother told him this story. And Don Pablo learned that the only good actors in the story were the ones who came to fight the flames. He also learned that the only ones with power in the story were the men who wielded fire. Terror and fire.

A good lesson.

* * *

El Jabón tells me about his own father, a construction worker named Lisandro.

When my father was seventeen, he ran away after he found out he'd been kidnapped by the people he thought were his parents. He joined the guerrilla in the early 1950s. He didn't like holding a gun. He didn't like sleeping on the ground. He left for Medellín. I was born a month later, when he was nineteen. He told me to stay away from the jungle, so I hung out in the comunas. And then I met Pablito.

El Jabón looked wistful.

He stole cars, and ran a few rackets. He told people their cars were junk when they were fine. Sold parts in the black market. He was cool, always wore nice jackets. Not expensive, just fit well.

* * *

The comunas in Medellín are the love child of a favela and a maze—human density at its limits, a hillside of cement, plastic sheets, and corrugated metal. The people who live there know its pathways, its shortcuts, its secret staircases, slides, and ramps. The uninitiated are chumps, stuck at the bottom or top, barely able to consume the sight.

El Jabón grew up nine houses, as the condor flies, from one of Escobar's safe houses.

He was six years older than me. We all knew him. He was our hero. If your hero asks you to hold on to a thing or two for a week or so, you do it. We were poor. He paid cash up front. How could we not love him?

* * *

Escobar didn't want to be Pedro Marín. *I'd be screwed fighting in the jungle*, said Escobar in an interview much later in life.

In the years after Marquetalia, the FARC grew exponentially. But new members caused new problems, mostly on the logistics side. Relying on an already trod-upon peasant class to harbor and feed a growing army only worked for so long. As people continued to flee to the cities, the FARC needed to adjust and make money. Cattle rearing and traditional cash crops took time and required a large up-front investment—feed, large pastures, vaccines, fertilizers, pesticides, and other structural costs.

Coca, on the other hand, required very little. It grew in impossible spaces. With his back against the wall, Marín searched for a solution. Eventually, he remembered his own words: *The newest techniques are also the oldest.* So he turned to the oldest, and most potent cash crop in Colombia.

The indigenous of the Colombian Andes had been using the coca plant for centuries. It figured prominently in medicine, recreation, and religion. Consuming the crushed leaves with powdered lime (usually ashes, teeth, bones, or seashells) accomplished a bit of chemistry—namely the alkalization of the coca leaves, aka primitive cocaine. A ceremony (tracing back hundreds, if not thousands of years) marked a young person's transition into adulthood with the consumption of alkalized coca leaves prepared by the mother (sometimes in her mouth).

By the time the FARC decided to monetize the coca plant for its own causes, a ready market existed—in the late 1960s and 1970s cocaine consumption had boomed worldwide. Traffickers existed—all the peasants had to do was grow the crop. And all the FARC had to do was protect their deliveries in exchange for a cut of the profits.

Sociologist James Brittain noted that "the FARC's leadership, support base, and membership come from the very soil from which it provides its subsistence, for the insurgents largely consist of peasants from rural Colombia, who account for approximately 65 percent of its members."

From the beginning, the FARC included the indigenous, Afro-Colombians, Bogotá intellectuals, and women—over 45 percent of comandantes were women. This was not just a coalition of the disenfranchised and exploited—by the early 1970s the FARC became a force to be reckoned with—and, with the exception of Cuba, one of the most successful revolutionary guerrilla organizations in the Americas.

To the middle class, though, the FARC became an enemy. They were an enemy of the state, an enemy of peace, and, most importantly, enemies of forgetting. As people in Colombia tried to move away from the Violence, tried to forgive and stomach amnesty, the guerrillas existed as a reminder of unpaid consequences. It was easy for the middle class to move on—they didn't make up the bulk of the dead, they didn't lose land, and they didn't face the same violence.

For middle-class Colombians, the late 1960s and early 1970s were a time of calm and booming industry. With the National Front in full swing (the system of shared power would last until 1974), progress came in fits and starts. Often any measures enacted during one party's time of national control were undone by the next administration. Third parties were completely excluded from the process. But alternating power did quell party-motivated violence, which allowed the rich from both parties to prosper.

Cocaine offered the guerrillas and the campesinos access to some of that prosperity. It also offered the state access to U.S. dollars. The Colombian government officially characterized guerrillas as "narco-terrorists," and in doing so appealed to the United States for financial and equipment resources to better fight the political, economic, and violent threat the guerrillas posed.

But Americans were on both sides of the operation. The chemicals necessary to turn coca plants into cocaine, the vats of sulfuric acid and sodium carbonate, came from mostly companies in the United States. Complex distribution systems were set up and, somehow, bulk chemicals ended up making the trip from warehouses in Miami to the jungles of rural Colombia, only to be replaced with processed cocaine, ready for distribution up north.

Everyone tried to get a cut of the pie. Paramilitary groups and guerrillas fought over territory. Competing factions would hijack shipments as they were delivered to state-run facilities, sometimes under the protection of the military. It was not unusual for paramilitaries to protect deliveries from chemical processors to packagers, even as the guerrilla had protected the same leaves from the finca to the chemists. War didn't matter as much as profit did.

Different industries sprouted to handle all other facets of the trade. One group of men performed the necessary chemistry to produce the powder, another packaged and warehoused it, while another took care of sales and shipping logistics. Cocaine became an industry with players from the rural lowlands all the way to the big cities.

The guerrilla used their money to fund their war against the government. The paramilitary, the private armies still in existence, used their money to fund their side of the war against the guerrilla. Above all these soldiers on the ground were the traffickers, the men who kept their hands clean of leaf, but covered in blood. Men like Pablo Escobar, who didn't care about revolution, who wanted power and money.

By 1969, the myth of Escobar had been established throughout Medellín—hundreds of deaths had been attributed to his orders. He was a local gangster ready to scale up. That's the beauty of giving orders, Condor-style, something learned by politicians and outlaws alike: To kill without getting your hands dirty, to violate the sanctity of life without ever violating personal principles. Escobar knew it was harder to get caught without a direct link to the crime. He craved the respect that came with being the boss, but balanced it with his need to remain free.

Pablo Escobar loved that his name had become synonymous with a certain brand of fear.

Don Pablo cared about how his children remembered him. It was important to him, his legacy, said El Jabón.

You know Escobar was a failed race-car driver. There's no shame in it. If Pablo Escobar had been better on the steering wheel, the world would be a different place.

Or someone else would have converted into a type of Pablo Escobar. Pablo Escobar was inevitable.

* * *

El Jabón was born in the comunas to a girl whose family had fled violence in Santander. His father had been kidnapped as a baby and then disappointed as a guerrilla.

I try to imagine a fifteen-year-old kid committing his life to a gangster—a gangster who paid up front, in cash. But from the beginning, Don Pablo demanded everything from El Jabón, including his life. El Jabón became a henchman to a villain. He became *that guy*—spear holder number nine, a supernumerary in his own story. El Jabón is the blurry face in the back row, the man whose face is turned as he opens a car door, the man in charge of leading guests from one room to another.

I'm not the important part of the story. Don Pablo is the story, he was always the story.

PART IV

*

Heaven and happiness do not exist. These are stories told by your fathers to justify the crime of having brought you into this world. What exists is reality, brutal reality: this slaughterhouse where we came to die, if not to kill . . .

—Fernando Vallejo

The Marlboro Kid
(AN ADOLESCENCE IN DOLLARS)

Medellín, 1971

I once saw a mug shot of a young Escobar, convicted for attempted kidnapping right around 1971. He's baby-faced and more attractive than I care to admit. His other accomplices look tough, but Escobar is smirking. It was always a deadly game for him.

The man El Jabón called a failed race-car driver stole cars to fix them to sell them to then steal them back again. *He often sold people back their own stolen cars, which really was more like kidnapping vehicles, not as good as kidnapping people, a field he moved into after realizing that it was easier to transport a stolen person than a stolen car.*

El Jabón thought he was a genius.

We were broke. The whole country was broke. This was right before cocaine exploded. We were just a bunch of broke kids stealing to make some money. Pablo was the best at it.

Kidnapping was lucrative and easy. Escobar began working on "Sequestros Express," which involved same-day returns. A relative would be kidnapped on their way to work, and with some quick banking maneuvers, he could be back by dinner.

You picked someone up. You yelled at them a little. You took them to an apartment and waited for a phone call. You dropped them off. It wasn't hard. Don Pablo liked to make the calls himself.

The failed race-car driver was a talker.

*   *   *

No man is either perfectly good or perfectly evil. Take Diego Echavarría. He owned a textile mill, inherited from his father, as well as a large finca. Historically speaking, he was not known for treating his workers well. Members of the community grumbled as strikes were broken up, scabs were brought in to discourage attempts at unionization, and the police were often weaponized to fight any organization.

Contrast that with the man who opened schools in his communities, invested greatly in his small town, just outside Medellín. But the very same Echavarría invested in medical facilities, job training, and community literacy. He was a bad man to some, a hero to another.

In late summer 1971, seventy-five-year-old Diego Echavarría was kidnapped outside his home. A group of men in a red and white Jeep pulled up next to Echavarría's limousine, removed the driver, and absconded with Echavarría.

A ransom note soon appeared, asking for the equivalent of $50,000. Reports differ as to whether the family paid. Some say that pride prevented them from giving any money to the villains who kidnapped the patriarch. Others report that the family paid in its entirety, two prominent businessmen having been freed from the same group after the kidnappers received payment.

Six weeks after he was taken, the corpse of Diego Echavarría surfaced in a neighborhood named for his father, blocks away from Escobar's childhood home in Rionegro.

THE VIOLENCE

Word on the street spread. *This was the work of that terrifying young man*, the people whispered, this was a new era of insecurity, this was the time of Escobar.

*   *   *

"Pendejadas de gringos," said El Jabón. *Don Pablo at that time worked for the Marlboro Man*, an older mafioso-type who was better known than Escobar and offered to mentor the younger gangster in the way of high-profile kidnappings.

The Marlboro Man had begun the Marlboro Wars in Medellín. He had enough money to buy out the city's supply of American cigarettes, creating a black market with demand-driven inflation driving up tobacco prices astronomically.

You know who else worked for the Marlboro Man? El Mono Trejos.

El Mono Trejos (nom de guerre of one Néstor Trejos) claimed the murder of Diego Echavarría a couple of years later. Newspapers of the time record him as the perpetrator. There is, in fact, little to no mention of Escobar.

Escobar was a twenty-one-year-old kid in early 1971. If anything, he was the guy that shoved Don Diego Echavarría in the car. El Mono Trejos was in charge of the operation, and El Mono Trejos is the one that went to jail for it. That didn't stop Don Pablo from taking credit. He took credit for the Marlboro Wars too.

Years later, Escobar used the nickname "Doctor Echavarría." Many thought this was Escobar clearly linking himself to the infamous kidnapping. Two major biographers consider Escobar's involvement a fact. By killing an industrialist that owned Coltejer, the largest textile mill in the country, Escobar would have elevated his celebrity nationally. Of course he claimed the kidnapping. In 1971, there was no bigger crime to claim.

Echavarría had angered no mobster, had not been involved in any shady dealings. At the time, the biggest preoccupation of Diego Echavarría was building the skyscraper that would come to define Medellín's skyline.

His kidnapping was supposedly an act of principle by the gangsters—a sign from them that no one was above the people's justice. No one was beyond the reach of a bullet. The rich, now afraid of any poor person that eyed them too long, retreated into their estates. Walls came up, guard booths were installed, and night patrols made sure no one came close.

The Echavarría kidnapping also signaled the beginning of a new era. Gangsters like Pablo Escobar widened the gap between rich and poor, changing the landscape, preventing the two classes from even interacting, except as one served the other. *Security* had become a part of the Colombian lexicon, in the city as much as in the country. To be poor no longer signified tragedy, to be poor was also to be dangerous. Anyone could be an agent of a gangster, a cartel, a guerrilla group. That Escobar took credit makes sense—his mastery of terror was never in question.

*   *   *

In late 1972, Pablo Escobar took twenty neighborhood kids, including El Jabón's brother, to the movies. They went to see *The Godfather*.

He wanted to be Don Corleone—big. He wanted to be the capo di capos. My brother spent three weeks after that learning Italian from a book a priest gave him. We all wanted to be gangsters. Even those of us who were already gangsters.

They were living their own biopics, he told me. They wanted their lives to feel like the movies. But what they wanted most of all was everything.

How did Pablo Escobar become the biggest gangster in Medellín? By saying he was—until it became true.

We are who we pretend to be, after all. So, Escobar ran with his stories. It didn't matter if he took credit for a murder years later, it didn't matter if someone else had obviously done it. Any murder he wanted to claim became a part of his story—here was the cruelest outlaw, the one to be feared the most.

And didn't it all come true, anyway? Along with the Medellín Cartel he founded, Escobar grew to be everything he promised and more. Escobar was a smuggler of contraband, any contraband, all contraband—it just so happened that the most profitable contraband was cocaine. When he was caught, he bribed, intimidated, and killed his way out of the conflict, which only increased his power.

Escobar certainly incited violence. He took over smaller smuggling operations until he became one of the richest men alive. The myths about him outnumber the facts—as is true of every person who courted his type of infamy. But I'm fascinated by the stories he told about himself—the mythology he ascribed to his youth. In Pablo Escobar's mind, even before he built up the cartels in Medellín, even before any of the stories became true, he had always been the biggest, the stuff of legends. He was the Godfather before he ever saw *The Godfather*.

Pablo Escobar was baptized in fire. It didn't matter that the fire happened before he was born, and it didn't matter that he'd been baptized in a church normally and without consequence. *He was baptized in fire* would always sound better. More badass. More gangster. The kind of thing that appealed to kids in the comunas.

In 1972, the legend was just starting to get built.

The Impossible

(A REQUIEM OF BETRAYAL)

Barranquilla, 1973

He couldn't be saved.
   That's what Esther had been told. *Anibal couldn't be saved.*

Esther looked at her seven children, all gathered around her in the living room of this fancy city house. She knew she had to go through the motions of saving him—run to his bed, pray by his side. She couldn't just wait for his death to reach her—she had to find it, and in doing so, confirm that the voice on the phone wasn't just a lie.

She considered all the versions of this impossibility—how could a man with so much life be dead? But each time she contemplated the details, instead of making his death a reality, it all seemed to take her further away. How could mere words signal the end of what she'd known? How can a phone call take away over twenty years of familiarity and make everything strange and new? Surely this was all a terrible nightmare or a test from a Higher Power.

But she knew.

There are truths that are absolute.

His heart had stopped beating. An infarction, embolism, heart attack.

Anibal survived his country's madness only to be killed by his own heart.

He couldn't be saved.

In Colombia, not everyone dies in an easy way. Some bodies disappear, never to be found. *Presumed dead.*

Someone always finds the corpse, of course. Eventually, a stranger will stumble upon the shell that was once a person. Sometimes it takes days, years, decades. Some hands will, at last, cradle these bones and some will try to find the story contained within—try to reunite family with body lost.

There are the priests that anoint the body. The morticians who work with death, who make their living by guiding the bodies to rest. Here are the hands that shape the end of so many lives. There is an art to it, of course. A certain patience and a certain empathy grounds the custodians of our passage.

There are the phone calls to be made. Before that and still after, the letters to be written. The forms to be filled out, certificates generated for official counts and bureaucratic fulfillments.

What does a forty-five-year-old farmer and regional politician mean to his country? Does he mean as much to his nation as he does to his wife?

My grandfather's death was not anonymous. There would be questions asked. There would be explanations given—a luxury really.

But in a style characteristic of his country, my grandfather's death would remain a secret for us all to unearth. A story that never quite added up, no matter how many times it was told.

In this way, my grandfather's death is quite Colombian. What matters is that he never returned. That he couldn't be saved. That Esther was now alone, with seven children.

* * *

My mother, Alba, said that only she and Lourdes went with my grandmother in the car to Fundación. But Alberto remembered all eight piling in, seventeen-year-old Alba at the wheel as my grandmother sat stern on the passenger side, holding the baby. All my grandmother's children have different stories about this day. Not to mention the extended family.

In my great-uncle Francisco's story, my grandmother made arrangements for her children. Esther got a cousin to watch them until she could send for them the next day.

In his version, told to me when I was a child, it is Francisco and a weeping Inés who picked up Esther from her house to begin the drive to Fundación. In his memory, Esther commented on how lucky they were to have the phone in the house. How quickly she got the news. That's all. Then silence.

In my mother's and Alberto's stories, the facts aren't so different. Her silence, as she gathered her thoughts and did her best to make sense of the information, remains consistent, in every telling.

I imagine that the drive felt eternal. That Esther stared out the window—like she still does. That my grandmother counted every mile as she approached Fundación like a clock winding down her life. Her heart was in her throat, and her throat sealed shut by the weight of her heart. I imagine she tried to pretend it was all a misunderstanding. I can imagine the responsibility of seven children pressing upon her.

The way Alberto told the story, one could imagine my grandmother becoming the Widow Rueda as the car rounded each bend on the road. The wrinkles around her eyes settled. The frown on her face deepened as the trees grew thicker and greener. The worry in her permanently nestled beneath the performance of calm. This is the story Alberto told.

A story where she sat for over three hours in silence. A story in which he watched his mother enter the hospital and waited for her return. A story where he readied himself for an eventual confrontation with his mother's grief—but instead, all he ever felt was Esther's muted ire.

* * *

In all versions of the story, my grandmother walked into the hospital alone. In all versions of the story, my grandmother did not request an autopsy. In all versions of the story, my grandmother chose to see his body one last time. In all versions of the story, she gathered her children at some point that day and told them their father was dead, like so many other fathers were. She told them to remember him, as few get to remember their fathers. And she set herself to that task as well.

* * *

She will remember his smile. She will find it in the thirteen grandchildren God would grant her. The guileless way the corners of our mouths gather and pull. The way our cheekbones stretch against our good humor.

His handwriting she kept alive easily. The little notes and love letters he'd written. *I'll love you forever.* Some lyrics to a song he loved on a scrap piece of paper, glued into a notebook only an arm's reach away.

She'd see his eyes again in the grandson named for him. His belly and stature in the grandson with the eyes least like his—small and brown, unlike Anibal's bloodshot blues. His brown hair with blond roots graced a granddaughter's crown. His laugh emerged from the mouth of another. Together we make his memory real enough.

His love of song and dance we all share, but only I can hold a tune (something I get from my own father). The descendants of Anibal Rueda were not very musical in voice or instrument, but all of us can dance.

And we dance to the same songs our country always has—the rhythms ingrained in our steps. Our love of songs and ballads of vengeance and cumbias of loneliness guide our feet as they always have. The one about the love-scorned drunk. The one about the man who collapsed in his mistress's arms. The one about murder in the countryside over something petty. The boy caught by a stray bullet intended for someone else. The woman raising a child that looks nothing like his father. The justice of a revolver. The smile of indiscretion. The heat of the day like a madness.

The one about the man who died, leaving a widow with seven children in an uncertain country.

The same lyrics transposed onto new beats, or the same stories told with new words, but we dance on, the familiarity of the story preventing us from hearing it anymore, until sound and beat and rhythm and heart and body and soul are one. Here are our stories. Here is our inheritance, our legacy, our family's pride. Here we are, after all. Still moving. Still singing the songs.

Our rhythm we got from our grandfather. Our ability to survive is all her.

*   *   *

The only thing my grandmother will tell me about the day my grandfather died is that she knew. She knew my grandfather was dead as soon as she picked up the receiver. She knew before she heard a word from the man on the line, something in her body told her that her life as she knew it was over. And she knew, even that day, that she'd never love another man again. She accepted that reality instantly and on a profound level. As usual, Esther wasn't wrong.

* * *

She won't tell me that he died of a heart attack in another woman's arms. She won't tell me that the woman called for help naked, wrapped in a sheet—that it had been a young woman, the daughter of an old farmworker.

She won't tell me that it was sudden—the way everything she knew collapsed. She will not tell me she has yet to recover from the shock. She will not tell me how she wished she'd gotten to talk to him, one last time. She will not tell me how her heart has broken in his absence.

She will shed quiet tears when she thinks of him too long. She will show me his love letters. She will anger when infidelity is discussed. She will never mention to her grandchildren how their grandfather died.

Everyone remembers a stoic woman, discovering on her husband's death that he'd been unfaithful. Everyone knows the sob she choked back. The wrath she held inside her chest.

She hugged her children. She told them to love their father. She clumsily sewed up every wound in her heart, because she had to. And she vowed to never speak ill of the dead.

* * *

The truth is whispered to me by older cousins, by a drunk uncle, by my mother when I finally summon the courage to ask. There is no more discussion to be had. There is only the cruelty of every pause when my grandmother talks about him, in everything unsaid, in the waterfall of grief and shame and anger that coexists next to the mountain of her love.

*   *   *

Even when my grandmother does talk freely, her stories rarely add up. My grandmother preaches memory but does nothing to record it. She tears up any pages where she might scribble a note, refusing to give her life permanence.

Some stories are alive and well. She talks about her childhood, what it was like running her father's finca with him, about her sisters, all of whom she misses dearly. She'll point and laugh at a picture of them as young ladies, as if she can't imagine those women as anything but old, herself included. She'll talk about her cows. She'll tell me how she never heard from her childhood crush, the doctor Carlos, again.

But when it comes to the darker edge of things, or anything that could be disrespectful to her or her husband's memory, she quiets. Details about the Violence usually devolve into a discussion of President Laureano Gómez's unpopular politics. There are simply matters I should probably let go. And, of course, those are exactly the ones that drive my curiosity.

After all, this is my homeland. Or half of it. I speak the language fluently, I know the food, I cheer for the soccer team. I feel connected and disconnected at the same time, as I am the farthest from Colombia. Learning the family history grounds me—here are the people whose blood I share. I am a product of their lives. It's easier to focus on that than on how far away Texas, and eventually Pittsburgh, are from Barranquilla.

My other cousins don't have these feelings—*why dwell on the past*, they ask? There is no time for the past, don't I know that the cows have needs? They aren't going to milk themselves.

THE VIOLENCE

My grandmother never remarried, never went on another date, never did anything but devote herself to her children and the land. Both grew and thrived. The Magdalena River Valley is stocked with banana and palm trees, flat for the cattle, flush with life; the soil bears guayaba, lulo, and maracuyá. Our family gave up the coffee and tobacco of Santander for coconuts and salt when we fled. We left Socorro with our money sewn into our hems, with new soil to clear—reborn in our work.

* * *

After my grandfather died, a notice was placed in the newspaper announcing his death. Any claimants to his estate needed to appear at the funeral a week later, by law, to stake said claim. A formality of Colombian law, usually, but a necessary formality, nonetheless.

My grandfather was buried on a slight hill in Jardines del Recuerdo, a large cemetery just outside Barranquilla. Lourdes, only seventeen, handled the arrangements. She picked a spot on a hill, overlooking the big avenue below. She liked the idea of being able to wave to her father when she drove by. My grandmother remained indifferent. All graves were the same to the dead.

Lourdes had done her best. She'd hired a good accordionist. She made sure the mass before the funeral was exactly as Anibal would have wanted it. She invited all the Ruedas and the Angaritas, the local politicians and the local workers. My mother claims that hundreds came to the church and even more showed up at the burial.

And then the women arrived. They didn't arrive in a group, but slowly, as Esther scanned the crowd, she saw them: strange women too sad and too unknown to her. She asked Lourdes if she knew those women. Lourdes shook her head. What struck Lourdes, though, was that most of those women had brought their children, and those children looked uncannily like her dead father.

The claimants had arrived.

Francisco and Trinito did their best to corral the grieving women, to keep them from Esther. But when the service was over, the women stood and asked for what was theirs, for what belonged to their children. And Esther had no choice but to give.

* * *

To have just been widowed, with seven children, to have to confront the monument that is grief without preparation or warning, to encounter deception and betrayal, to rethink your entire relationship with the person as well as your own grief at their loss, to be angry at them for dying as much as for cheating, to keep it together, regardless, to go through with the burial and hold your head high.

To be humiliated, because he'd humiliated her—his sins were in plain sight. And then, to confront the extent of your husband's crime against you, to see with your eyes the offspring of his betrayal. To know how far these children traveled on buses and carts and horseback and cars and trains, how worn their feet and shoes were, to see them and to know they ranged from small babies to strapping young adults. To now suspect every absence, every late night, every long day in twenty years of her own memories. To know that the marriage she knew was a sham. To never be able to hold him again. To never get to yell at him and let all this hurt out of her body—to never get the chance to undrown. To come home to a bed that will never have him again. To spend the rest of your life making yourself small in order to accommodate a largeness that remains absent.

* * *

I have never heard her mention the circumstances of his death. Not to me. Maybe to others she was more forthcoming. I always imagined that because my mom had left Colombia, and because I'd grown up on another continent, that it was somehow my fault I didn't know.

She only referred to his death as a marker in her life. Before Anibal died and after Anibal died. But the moment of death itself, that moment was unspeakable, and I'd never thought to question why.

My mother, aunts, and uncles tell me that my grandfather was a good man, with so much life and love to give. That my grandmother was cold, harsh. That perhaps they weren't right for each other. That he was gregarious and larger than life. That she somehow deserved it.

* * *

Five mistresses and eight children revealed themselves to the family, the oldest older and the youngest younger than his legitimate children. None of my half-aunts and uncles are welcome in the family. I know none of their names. When I tried to get in touch with them, my mother threatened excommunication.

They took half of our inheritance.

They were entitled. They were his kids. I knew it was useless to argue, but I tried.

No, they weren't. He had only seven legitimate children.

They are still your half-siblings, he was still their biological father, I offered.

Never. My mother insisted. *I do not acknowledge that. I do not acknowledge them. I would never do that to your grandmother.*

My mother and her siblings love their Esther, even though they think his infidelity was her fault. They blame her for not knowing. For not dancing enough. For not smiling enough. For being pregnant or nursing for almost half their marriage. For never kissing him in public.

The mythology of my grandfather remains intact. Because they loved him, because he was good and kind and fun, because the dead achieve perfection in a way the living can never attempt. Because my grandmother didn't give them enough hugs or ice cream when they were young, because my grandmother was too busy doing everything she could to keep them safe and well.

*   *   *

She treated the women as fairly as she could. They did take half of Anibal's estate, mostly in cows, and a large payout, divided among the tiny humans she refused to call his children. She did not speak as she signed over the necessary documents, a lawyer handling the unpleasantries.

My aunts tell me that my grandmother terrified these women. She was ruler-straight, her mouth set into a hard line. There was no empathy, no sisterhood. My grandmother hated these women, not for who they were, but for what they represented. Anibal had never been the man she thought he was, even though he was exactly the man she thought him to be. Nothing and everything added up, only her lack of guile, her idiotic lack of suspicion.

Had there been a moment when she considered infidelity? Of course. But Anibal had always promised to be more, to be different. He mocked his brothers and uncles, the men who did such ignoble things, he had always laughed with her at how easily men betray. He was suddenly no different, but she could not square that with the man she knew.

When it was over, my grandmother appraised her life. She had seven children, including a fifteen-month-old and an almost-eighteen-year-old. She had six fincas, mostly close to one another, and another twenty mouths to feed there, not to mention the people who worked for her in the city. She was a woman of means—but not wealthy enough that she didn't have to work.

She was lucky in one regard: Anibal had honored his word and put the main finca, Galilea, in her name.

It's yours, he'd said, as she signed the paperwork. Because of that, his bastards couldn't even step foot on it.

For a long time, according to my mother, this is the only thought that made Esther smile.

Her finca was hers. Her cows were hers. And no one was going to take them.

El Encanto

(A CONFERENCE ON FORESTRY)

Amazonas, 1974

One of my favorite aphorisms in Spanish is "tanto va el cántaro al agua hasta que por fin se rompe," which translates roughly to "a pitcher of water can only take so much water before it finally breaks." It means more than simply pointing out the lifespan of an object, it's closer in meaning to "one can only take so much." The English cliché would be "before the dam bursts." Inevitably, and without care, everything can fall apart.

*   *   *

There were too many guerrillas. The FARC, the ELN, the EPL (Pelusos), the M-19, the MOEC, the ERC, the ERG, the PRT. Keeping all their names and causes straight required a small encyclopedia of ideologies, demands, acronyms, and philosophical underpinnings—all were leftists, all ostensibly fought for the workers, all disagreed with one another. Most funded themselves through kidnapping, protection fees, and cocaine trafficking, funneling American dollars into their war chests.

Soon the guerrillas were no longer just in the mountains. They infiltrated the llanos, the coastal plains, and even the southernmost reaches of Colombia, deep into the Amazon.

*   *   *

Lorena grew up in a different Colombia. She knew this even when she was a girl. No one had to tell her. The books that the priest brought to El Encanto showed her as much. Their drawings had homes with only one family living inside, with bedrooms, with beds instead of hammocks.

The maloca where she lived housed six families in an open area, hammocks on one end, and the floor mats for the mambe ceremony on the other. This is how the maloca had been laid out for a thousand years.

She liked El Encanto, the nearest city to her tribe. She liked her people, the Uioto. They lived in the Amazon as they had lived always, with some minor exceptions: She spent her mornings learning Spanish in the church school and her evenings working on the land, a role usually reserved for men.

But everything changed in August 1974.

That was the summer of guns. First the guerrillas. Then the cartels. They came through the snakewood trees.

The guerrillas made a request of the Uioto at gunpoint: We will tax what you make from the cartels. The elders made nothing from the cartels. The request seemed frivolous. Then the cartels arrived and made a request at gunpoint: Grow coca leaf or die.

Lorena, only ten, spoke the best Spanish of her group. So she did the talking for the six elders of her maloca, her family group and home, listening as they debated and only repeating back to the cartels what she thought prudent and diplomatic.

The coca leaf is sacred. It is for mambe. It is not to sell.

One of them asked her if all the elders of her tribe felt this way. She said they did. He shot two of them, in front of Lorena, and asked if anyone wanted to reconsider.

The remaining elders asked for time.

That evening, the four living elders began the ceremony they called mambe. They combined ground coca leaves with the ashes from burned snakewood leaves and ground it into a paste they then pressed into their mouths, while chanting and singing supplications.

The gods spoke to them through the night.

The next morning, the elders wept.

The children—Lorena included—were sent away, up the Putumayo River to the city of Pasto.

I could not argue, she told me. *It would be arguing with God.*

* * *

Her family's maloca no longer exists. Parts of it have become a storage shed, others were stripped and repurposed to make a chute system that helped transport the leaves from one cement tank to another.

Her father died at the hands of the FARC after arguing about protection rates. Or so she was told. Two of the young men she knew growing up joined a different guerrilla group. Another joined the cartels. Two of her sisters married men who process cocaine out of the leaves grown on her family's land. No one lives in malocas anymore. None of them strung up their hammocks anymore. None of them practiced mambe.

Their children no longer speak Uioto. Lorena does not visit El Encanto anymore.

I was gone for so long, and I have so many memories of what it was, she told me. *Why go visit what is not?*

She sang me a song that belonged to her people. It was a song about finding the stars in the bounty of the rainforest. She stopped singing suddenly, angry and crying at the same time.

The drug dealers, traffickers, and protection agents, guerrillas and cartels, they all treated the people the same. They had all promised to take care of the most vulnerable, and at first, they all had—the priests, the Condor-types, the guerrillas, the narcos, the presidents, the elders of her tribe. But eventually they all succumbed to the violence of it all. Because here she was, ripped from her homeland, ancient blood on new soil—and her people, and the ancient ways, were dying.

This was wrong. The gods would have never wanted this.

They were all thugs in the end. The cartels took our entire way of life. And then we had to pay the last of what we had to the guerrillas to protect us from the cartels that already took.

Ideals? None of them ever had ideals. They were all just thugs.

The Widow

(AN EXPERIMENT IN MATTER)

Magdalena River Valley, 1975

Esther learned the names of all the widows on her block. She learned every cause of death. She learned how long they wore black. She wore it longer. She learned the names of their children. She sent them small gifts for their First Communion.

The Widow Cárdenas lost her husband on a Sunday afternoon. He went out to buy some barbed wire and never returned, his corpse discovered a week later in a mass grave.

The Widow Sancho lost her husband on a Friday. He was killed by the FARC.

The Widow Longoria lost her husband, he was killed by the M-19. The Widow Chávez lost her husband, he was killed by the ELN. The Widow Treviño lost her husband, he was killed by the AUC. The Widow Pulido lost her husband, he was killed by the EPL.

The Widow Garza's husband was killed by the cartels. The Widow de la Garza: Depression. Suicide. The Widow Raúl: Natural causes. The Widow Restrepo: Machete. The Widow Cantú: The guerrillas. The Widow de la Cruz: An assassin. The Widow Martír: Heart failure. The Widow Fernández: Convulsions.

Widow. To be empty. To be without. Destitute. Bereft. Alone.

She learned the etymology of "viuda." She dissected the word, until she had opinions about the Greek root versus the Latin one.

She wore black. For a year. For a handful of years. For a decade. She would rarely wear anything bright again.

She cut her hair. She had cut it years before, but it had grown back. Now, she would never let it past her earlobes again. There was no need to be beautiful. There was only Anibal, his ghost. There was only his memory and a series of jovial portraits throughout the apartment.

She did not look at a man.

She could not trust a man.

She had children to raise.

* * *

She will stop using the word "widow." She is "the wife of the deceased." She is deprived of husband. She refuses "widow." She is concerned that once accepted, a state of matter will become permanent, and she likes to think that her frost is a choice. She is not transformed, she only wears the cloak of transformation.

She will never use her married name again, except on legal documents that require it. She is Esther Angarita Sarmiento. There is no Rueda to be uttered, but when she is asked, she will confirm she is married.

Her husband is dead. Enlarged heart. A failure to live.

She doesn't remember what day of the week it was.

My children, she'll say, *lost their father*.

As if there is a place he will be found.

And she closed the door. On her mother-in-law. On Sunday dinners.

She stopped seeing her brothers, who like her husband would one day die and leave her more alone in this world. She did not answer letters from her mother, who was growing older, and whose death she refused to even contemplate. She stopped answering phone calls from her sisters. She ripped out the new telephone Anibal had installed before he died.

She drowned in shame. She wallowed in it. She bathed herself in it. There were no speeches, only silences that deepened as she wore trenches into the sidewalk around her home. She was the widow duped, the woman scorned, the idiot who'd been married to a man who disrespected her for decades. She loved him more than the ocean loved the moon. She hated every contour of his face. She missed the way he smelled. She didn't want to live. She had to live.

*   *   *

No one plans to be a widow. No one plans to bury the person they love.

And the widows—no one wants to say this—there are ways in which they were lucky. Because they were seen and acknowledged. There were the lovers that never got a phone call, the "best friend" who never got to say goodbye. Those who wished to grieve in public. Who wanted to wear black but could never explain it.

My grandmother calls me a fool. *These lovers and friends and heartaches don't have to wear black*, she repeated, *that's for widows*.

She had changed states, she said. Become ice when she had started off steam. *Life is the act of cooling*, she told me once. She also told me that *fire* is how one fights back, but that an old widow like herself had run out of heat and only had her country to blame.

*   *   *

Anibal had left her a small empire, a legacy and trust for their children, and their children's children. Here were the cows—and the milk and meat needed for survival. Calves were born, and they needed to be weighed, branded, and logged.

She looked up one day and found that she had recommitted to living. Except, given the status of men, she'd instead committed herself to something that gave back more—her land.

It had been almost three years since Anibal's death, and those years hadn't been easy. The guerrillas had spread into the Magdalena, and soon threatened family lands. Cattle theft increased, as did casual robberies between neighbors.

Opportunists took advantage of the chaos to consolidate holdings, or to show off their wealth by leaving their fincas empty.

For Esther, seven children under the age of eighteen meant having to work that land and sell that milk. She tried to avoid offers of charity from the Rueda family, as the circumstances of his death, in the arms of another woman, had changed everything between them, and his family only reminded her of him, of his absence, of her pain. So, she became who she had always been—a dairy farmer and cattle rancher, with her children at her side as soon as schooling and ability permitted.

But the political violence of the guerrillas threatened that livelihood. Cows were no good without anyone to milk them. *Stolen cows were only good to thieves and the Devil*, she liked to say.

She'd spend her week in the city, calling the telecom office near the fincas often, getting reports on the milking, until the weekend when she could convince one of her older children to drive her out for three days of work, hopefully uninterrupted by revolutionaries (who harbored a deep hatred of landowners by definition).

My mother, Alba, loved the work, driving out with Esther in their Renault, going from finca to finca, and inspecting ledgers inscribed with small numbers. She enjoyed the long drives with her mother, catching up on family gossip and stories of who was where doing what.

Alba wasn't a perfect daughter, by any means. She'd attempted to elope with a much older man at sixteen, was kicked out of school, spent some time in a convent, and managed to graduate high school at a completely different school across town. But she'd gone to university to study law and took to it well, which made Esther proud. She had a daughter who was a professional, a first in a family that had always lived off the land.

A woman with a vocation, regardless of what she did with it, had options. And Alba always had options. Alba also always had a suitor; she laughed heartily, listened carefully, and danced joyously. Her vanity was as legendary as her aim—she has bragged often throughout her life of being a finalist in a national makeup contest as well as a part-time model and bocce ball champion. But even in full braggart mode, her charm persists. Alba's enemies and rivals would call her stubborn, blind in love, and difficult to persuade—all truths that Alba would hardly deny. She was also up for any adventure or trek, no matter how uncomfortable or difficult or long the task.

All this in stark contrast to her older sister. Lourdes wasn't really made for the finca in her youth. She'd go and make her best effort, but more often than not, she preferred the city. Her legs healed fully and quickly, although she'd struggle with hip and weight issues throughout her life.

But it was Lourdes, like her mother, who never fully recovered from Anibal's death. The first year, Lourdes existed in a state of shock. Her father was her world, and that world was over. Gone. Snatched from her. She did not know who to blame, but usually it was Esther.

Blame doesn't have to be rational to function. Blame is about having a clear villain. Don't get me wrong, Lourdes loved her mother. Tremendously. She always would. But in the first year after her father passed, Lourdes needed a target. There were others, of course. And Lourdes proved volatile whenever she encountered anyone with information on what really happened. But mostly, Lourdes did her best to survive, to keep going.

She knew she wasn't cut out for the finca, but she was good at keeping house. As she went to school for social work, after eventually completing high school, Lourdes took to raising her younger siblings, whenever her mother was absent. The eldest five (Lourdes, Alba, Jóse Alfredo, Edgar Anibal, and Alberto) could tend to themselves. But the younger two (Nidia and Elsa Yolima) needed attention. So, Lourdes set to helping run the household as Alba set out to help run the finca. As the boys got older, they joined Alba on the land.

My grandfather's land purchases proved wise. He left Lourdes and Alba two small fincas (Yerbabuena and Paratebien), Jóse Alfredo and Edgar Anibal shared a much larger finca (Las Mercedes), and the younger three shared a larger one still (Irlanda). Esther ran Galilea, largest of all and the stronghold that generated most of the family milk (and income).

Three days a week, Esther and her children braved the insecurity of their land to manage, upkeep, pay, and supervise the operation. Greater risks, of course, were taken by the farmworkers who lived there. But, in some ways, their poverty kept them safe. The landowners were the real targets. They fetched a better price if kidnapped.

The Rueda Angarita family were farm people while at the farm, but learned to become city people in the city. The girls went to dances at the Spanish Union and rubbed elbows at the country club. Large parties in elaborate hotel ballrooms were had for graduations, birthdays, and religious sacraments. Even though times were tough, the family thrived. And Esther, widow with seven children, ensured they all had the best chances she could offer them.

For the little ones, she had to be mother and father. Nidia, who was nine when Anibal died, at least knew her father. Elsa Yolima did not. Esther was the only parent she'd known, and Esther felt something akin to heartbreak when she saw his features in her baby's tiny face, the mirror image of a man Elsa Yolima would never meet.

Four daughters could be a curse, as many strangers offered to Esther when she mentioned such things at the grocery store or at church. But in her daughters, she saw herself, and in their choices, she saw all the different ways a life can play out. Esther wanted life to be fair to her daughters, and she told them this all the time: How important it was that they treated one another fairly, how important it was that they find professions before finding love—in case their man proved wrong.

* * *

The Colombian government survived its first two-party election after the National Front ended in 1974. Liberal Alfonso López Michelsen, son of a former Liberal president, received more votes for the presidency than any candidate every had.

Curiously, every candidate in the election was the child of a former president. López's father served from 1934 to 1938 and again from 1942 to 1945. Conservative Álvaro Gómez Hurtado was the son of Laureano Gómez (1950–1953), and María Eugenia Rojas de Moreno, running as a member of the Popular National Alliance, represented her father, the exiled Presidente Rojas Pinilla (1953–1957).

After his victory, Alfonso López proved himself to be a farmer's president, who cared about agrarian, fiscal, and spending reforms. His focus on agricultural improvements increased crop productions, expanded the power grid, and, incidentally, created the highest inflation Colombia had ever seen. Millions of Colombians who left the land had to pay high prices for food at newly opened grocery stores.

The president's government and soldiers attacked the cartels and the guerrillas with American dollars and weaponry. But every time one head was cut off, three grew in their stead, even more emboldened. The guerrillas began kidnapping members of the cartels. The cartels banded together and declared war. The guerrillas fought back. The farmers hired more paramilitary to fight the guerrillas, or the cartels, and protect their land. The guerrillas and the cartels then began to claim private fincas as their own, with the former claiming to expropriate from those who had stolen from the natives, even though those crimes had all been committed centuries before by the Spanish.

The guerrillas and the cartels wanted more power; the details were irrelevant. The fincas were no place for a woman on her own.

*   *   *

Slowly, she began to let people in again. Her brothers, their wives. She started calling her sisters too—visiting them whenever possible. The sisters agreed their mother needed to move in with one of them. Doña Eva offered Esther a chance to move back to Santander, and raise her children in their ancestral mountains. But Esther knew that was no option. Her cows were in the Magdalena River Valley. So she made her mother an offer instead. And that's how Doña Eva found herself in Barranquilla, a coastal transplant after sixty years of living on a mountainside.

And she wasn't alone. Sociologists marvel at this period in Colombian history, the internal movement and displacement of a people at the hands of violence. But millions of people shuffled into the new cities, new regions, while remaining utterly Colombian.

And yes, some left for Europe, the United States, or traveled deeper into South America, but most Colombians never left their country.

How could we? one of my uncles once told me. *We live in paradise.*

*   *   *

There is a coldness to my grandmother, just as there is a great warmth. She is a woman who could not return to Santander, but who could not leave her mother alone either. She is rigid, even as she sways into the wind.

There was nothing good in thinking about Anibal. Anibal was a broken promise. Anibal was everything she wanted and the one thing she could never have again. Anibal haunted her dreams. Anibal's betrayal was a nightmare.

She practiced forgiving him. But she couldn't. Just the thought of all the lies, all the omissions, all the juggling of women and children made her throat seize. What kind of man was he?

She stopped looking at televisions and magazines for long periods. She hated billboards and postcards. There was no good husband, there was no good man. They were all liars, thieves, thugs, bandits, and rogues. There were only good women, doing their best to raise children, while being tested at Jobian levels.

She cannot remember the last time he kissed her, the last time they made love, the last time he squeezed her hand. She did not know it would be the last, she did not know to record it, to memorize it, to hold it dear. She does not remember if they parted on good terms. Was she angry at him? Were they fighting? Had they embraced as he walked out? Had she turned away or followed him down the walkway? She loved him, without a doubt. But she could not forgive him. And so she decided to rarely mention him, a violence to his memory, a dagger to her love.

And then, to survive her own mind, she hardened her heart, she made herself a shield against anything that would hurt her. She protected her children, her aging mother, her siblings, and her workers. She became mother to them all, but in doing so, she gave up all except the very last of herself and her dreams, but that was the part of her that loved her cows. And she knew it would be enough.

* * *

At first, the workers called her the Widow. She did not love it, but she answered to it and got along with everyone well enough.

Happy workers meant happy land and happy cows. She believed in that the same way she knew that happy cows made the best milk. She worked hard, going home later than she needed to, getting up earlier than she had to, gradually bringing all the children along until everyone knew the trade, until they could all live off the land.

She was a widow. But she was also a teacher. And to the younger children, she was also a father of sorts. To her workers, well, eventually, they had a new name for her, one she liked better too.

"Patrona."

The Hacienda
(A SWIM IN BURLAP)

Nápoles, 1981

Pablo Emilio Escobar Gaviria found himself in the middle of coca-rich Colombia when the discos of the U.S. and Europe discovered cocaine in the late 1960s. By the mid-1970s, Escobar and a few of his cohorts and cousins were established drug barons, founding the Cartel de Medellín. By 1981, he was a millionaire in American terms, rich enough to take a five-star trip to Disney World and Washington with his wife and young children, snapping a photo of himself in front of the White House.

He'd purchased his hacienda a few years earlier, complete with a racetrack, zoo, and six swimming pools. Decorating the entrance was a small plane, the one Escobar had first used to smuggle cocaine into the United States in 1978. He boasted that his entire fortune was built in dollars, but he only spent in Colombian pesos, although his holdings abroad would prove otherwise. His nationalism was not misplaced, though. Given plenty of opportunities to flee the country, he never would—not permanently. He loved his land too much to live in exile. He loved his house, almost as much as he loved entertaining.

* * *

At a dinner party in his home, months after his return from Disney and before dozens of guests, Escobar ordered a man bound hand and foot after accusing him of stealing from his estate. Dinner at Hacienda Nápoles proved no small affair. On any given night, Escobar could comfortably serve three hundred people (with accommodations). There were plenty to witness his games.

Escobar had the man placed on the ground, near the edge of the swimming pool they all dined around. Then, to prove a point, Escobar kicked the man into the pool, saying "this is what happens to those who steal from Pablo Escobar!"

Escobar, and his guests, watched the man drown. Then they went back to their dessert.

To Escobar, the act was meaningless. He'd decided to teach a lesson, Colombian style, hurting the petty thief to send a message to his guests. After all, he trusted some of them with his safety, his money, his supplies, his power. The man he casually kicked into the water—this man's name is never recorded in any of the four accounts I find of the event. This man had no family, no identity other than servant and thief. He is a lesson—a metaphor for someone else to understand. This man was not a person to Escobar. And to history, he is only a line at the end of an obscure paragraph or two.

I read a version of this man's death where he is placed in a bag before he is kicked into the water. Would he have made a sound? When Escobar's foot came into contact with his body, did he know what fate awaited him? Did he think about struggling? Did he try to live?

Every outcome in this scenario is horrifying. Experts tell me how long it would have taken him to die. Assuming the man was not in a bag, he would be dead in two to three minutes. In the bag, depending on his position and movement, death would come as quickly as one minute, or as long as seven. His body, through instinct and reflex, would seal his throat, until the lack of air caused him to lose consciousness, at which point, his body would succumb to the inevitability of its death. The heart would go first, then other organs, and eventually, up to ten minutes after the heart has stopped, brain death. There is a poetry here, of course—the mind holds on just a bit longer even in the face of certain defeat.

Most drownings are quiet—people do not thrash or scream. A person is simply a bob in the water, mouth up, using what little strength they have to propel themselves upward. After the first twenty seconds, sooner depending on the man's reactions, Escobar's swimming pool would have been quiet.

They went back to dinner, Escobar and his guests. They ate dessert, laughing at all the right jokes, and pretended a man had not just died. They were complicit in their mirth, whether faked in terror or sincere in their sadism.

It's easy to think a man like Escobar did not value life. He took it far too easily for one to think it was a sacred thing—yet, when faced with the death of those he loved, he grieved loudly and avenged their deaths, burning down hospitals if he had to. He simply thought some lives possessed value while others did not.

When Escobar said "this is what happens to those who steal from Pablo Escobar," he meant it twofold.

First, the lesson learned: If vengeance and a cold-blooded death will be wrought upon those who commit minor offenses, imagine what will happen when someone who matters betrays his trust.

Second, when that trust is betrayed, the betrayer ceases to be human, ceases to be person, and is merely body—another corpse that will be fished out of the pool when polite company has left the building.

*   *   *

There were three major cartels in Colombia in the early 1980s—the Medellín Cartel, headed by Escobar, the Cali Cartel, and the Norte del Valle Cartel. All three oversaw the production of cocaine and its trafficking. Some used plane stops in the Caribbean, some used Mexico as conduit. All of them had complicated relationships with the guerrillas.

When the M-19 kidnapped and killed the children of a drug trafficker that fall, Escobar held a summit at Nápoles. On his birthday, in December 1981, he gathered over 223 capos and members of the National Army, as well as business owners and representatives of Colombian businesses under his financial control. It was rumored that CIA agents were in attendance as well.

By then, Escobar had agents and investments in most cities in Colombia. He controlled port authorities and policemen, bribing his way into open shipping containers and empty vessels.

Drug traffickers, Escobar argued, benefited Colombia. He had brought dollars and investment to this country. He employed people. He protected people. Drug traffickers like him had done something for Colombia, put it on the map—made the world afraid of slighting a Colombian.

Wealthy Colombians, Escobar argued, deserved protection. Local elites made the money that kept the nation moving, and by the 1980s, the drug traffickers had become the elite.

It was time to fight the guerrillas, Escobar said. It was time to kill the kidnappers. Pedro Marín and the thousands of other guerrillas were put on notice. They'd taken from the rich for too long.

*   *   *

El Jabón sees the irony: *We made money to be different than our fathers, obsessed with Liberal or Conservative. But we ended up being just like them—killing in the name of some false values.*

And now? Most of us are dead, running, hiding, or in jail. My God doesn't forgive. We stopped looking at the men we killed in the face. We stopped looking them in the eyes.

We ended up exactly like our fathers. But worse.

Our Lady of the Minefield
(A CONFIDENCE OF GUNSHOT)

Magdalena River Valley, 1982

Esther attended the meeting at her neighbor's request. He'd been invited by a man at the veterinarian's clinic, and he felt the need to include Doña Esther. The Asociación Campesina de Ganaderos y Agricultores del Magdalena Medio (Association of Middle Magdalena Ranchers and Farmers, or ACDEGAM) wanted to present their case to the cattle-folk of the upper Magdalena.

The movement had begun in Medellín, at the behest of Pablo Escobar, but Esther did not know that. She only knew that ACDEGAM promised to protect ganaderos, or cattle ranchers, like her from the guerrillas. She paid attention to the news, whether broadcast, printed, or simply repeated in line at the bank. The guerrillas had already taken several fincas in the greater Fundación area, they had commandeered, stripped, and mined the fertile lands in the name of the Cause. Esther shivered at the idea.

At the meeting, she could not help but remember her own father, listening to an impassioned speaker lecturing on how to defeat the enemy, the one here to end their way of life. And now, thirty-four years later, she was the one sitting in a cavernous hall, politely giving her time to a political salesman. But as the speaker began to discuss dismantling campesino rights, Esther listened more attentively. This was not a cooperative lobbying for willing farmers. This was a front for a paramilitary organization designed to destroy the guerrillas.

Esther supported her workers. She paid for their children's schooling. She wanted their families to leave poverty within a generation. She would never support the dismantling of their rights. She was a Liberal. And even though that effectively meant nothing as more and more political parties fractured the meaning of "left of center," Esther still considered herself a stalwart Liberal with clear pro-labor values.

When it came time for questions and answers, she tugged at her neighbor's sleeve.

It's too warm, she said. *Let's go outside where there's a breeze.*

* * *

Fundación had grown in the decade since Anibal died. It was still an ugly city, Esther maintained, but the sprawl and dust had become familiar. There was a joy to seeing her neighbors at the feed and supply store, stopping at the paper goods store for custom stationery, and visiting with the butcher to schedule the pickup of a newly fattened steer.

She got along with her many neighbors, some of them Ruedas, some of them old men who were as much a part of the landscape as the mangos that grew along the roads.

This ACDEGAM meeting had been ridiculous, and these protection schemes, however successful, amounted to hiring mercenaries to defend herself from revolutionaries. And as she well knew, that *when donkeys fought, only the donkey handler lost*. And these donkeys were proving quite deadly.

She said goodbye to her neighbor outside and met with Lourdes, who had already secured a table for eight at the restaurant across the way. Esther mulled over how to handle this whole situation. She would have to talk to Segundo, the only overseer she'd ever trusted, and the man currently in charge of her finca, Galilea.

*   *   *

Isidro froze in place.

What did you say? he yelled at Segundo, whose cry had stopped him in the first place. Isidro, the overseer of Las Mercedes, the finca that Anibal had left to his eldest sons, had just entered the finca on foot, and Segundo had pulled up behind the gate in a truck, honking like a madman.

You're standing in a minefield!

Isidro looked down at his feet. Where he was standing, it was impossible to discern what ground had recently been dug up, what step contained death.

How do you know? Perhaps Segundo's information was bad.

Some FARC son-of-a-whore bragged about it down the way. He said it was all mined. The whole finca.

When?

Last night.

The ground looked disturbed, that much was true. Isidro adjusted his hat with one hand, wiping away sweat with another.

Retrace your steps, shouted Segundo.

Of course. Isidro looked back at his footprints—a handful between him and the safety of the road. Carefully, he positioned his boot perfectly over the first print. Nothing happened.

"Ahí vas!" Segundo cheered him on.

Another step, backward, to make sure the soles aligned perfectly—Isidro began to work his way to Segundo.

One more step in, Isidro stumbled and lost his balance. He put out his arms, swaying, hoping to avoid anything too lethal. He regained his footing.

He took the last step, making it onto the road. Segundo, relieved, went to the back of the truck to pull out a beer or two.

Son-of-a-whore, I dropped my hat, Segundo heard Isidro say.

Let it go, said Segundo. *You're lucky enough.*

And as Segundo opened the tailgate, something exploded. The entire truck pushed back, knocking him to the ground. Segundo called for Isidro, but there was no response.

Isidro had tried to pick up his hat. He did not realize that the first land mine was right under the spot where the dirt road met the paved one.

The hat was all that remained of Isidro.

* * *

Segundo hitched a ride to Fundación, where he found his patrona eating dinner with her children, just about ready to head off to Barranquilla after a few days on the land. Segundo walked into the restaurant, filthy, still holding Isidro's tattered hat.

Mines. They mined Las Mercedes and Isidro blew up.

Who did this, Segundo? she asked.

The FARC, Doña Esther. The FARC. You have to pay up, or they won't dig them up.

* * *

Esther knew how to read the sky. She knew about storms hours before any rain or dark clouds. My grandmother says she feels the weather in her bones, and I believe her.

She knew the FARC would come one day. My grandmother saw the forecast clearly; she had heard rumors of the dark clouds approaching, long before any organization invited her to a meeting. Still, how does one prepare for an invading army?

She'd considered hiring the paramilitary, not the ACDEGAM, but maybe some other equally acronymic organization could provide support. But paid mercenaries were risky. If the FARC caught on that paramilitary were involved, if she called the police, everything could blow up in her face, like the cattle she was now certain had also been stolen. A small fortune in cows. Esther knew she could pay the FARC's extortion—but she hated even the possibility of having to do that. Esther had no intention of paying any guerrilla a penny of her hard-earned money.

Esther had done well. Her cattle numbered in the hundreds, her workers lived well, her children flourished—she'd paid cash for a wedding and several college degrees. My mother, Alba, married in Mexico City in 1981 and left Colombia, an immigrant on her own path, one that would eventually lead to Texas.

Esther walked my mother down the aisle. I love the image of my grandmother, arm looped through my mother's, giving Alba away.

In so many ways, Alba says, *my mother had to be my father.*

Esther managed the land as Anibal had—forever keeping the books on every operation.

She kept things professional always; Esther was never one to drink with her workers or play cards. But they loved her anyway, many of them bringing her small gifts over the years. She slapped their backs and gave their children generous dowries. She rode a horse well, and she knew the name of every cow. She established a cattleman's schedule—working three days on the finca, then driving home for four days of full-time mothering.

* * *

Often, her children would accompany her, and slowly, as they came into adulthood, she gave them their inheritance from their father.

Jóse Alfredo, her eldest son, technically owned Las Mercedes, although the workers still called her boss. It was his finca (shared with his brother Edgar Anibal) that was now without an overseer. He was twenty-five and hotheaded enough to make a mistake in dealing with the guerrillas. He could not be the one to negotiate.

But who? There was no man in Esther's life. Without a pater familias, Esther needed to be resourceful. What could she do to de-mine her son's finca? Or her own? How could she get the FARC out before they ruined everything she had built?

The solution she landed on was neither epic nor elegant. My grandmother, a woman of aphorisms, understood that some things in life are consistent—like wars, like personalities, like unfaithful men.

I once asked my grandmother how she processed all her trauma. *What trauma?* she asked. *Who has time for trauma?*

* * *

Esther consulted with her brother-in-law. Tito Edmundo, now a senator in the National Congress, understood Esther's plight immediately. Over the years, she'd defrosted her feelings about my grandfather's family. She could speak to Doña Rosa on occasion, and she liked his siblings, she decided, and made a point to keep them in her Rolodex. One of Tito's fincas in the same region had also been mined.

He had spoken with generals. The military had cautioned him to let things be for a while—he should seek other sources of income instead. Tito had enough in his savings to invest, but Esther was in a different situation.

She simply could not, and would not, walk away. Jóse Alfredo wanted to be married soon—and that finca would provide for his family. Without access to those lands, how would he earn a living? Most of the family's savings were in cows—the money fetched from the sale of one cow could support her family for a month—and right now, some of those cows were held hostage.

My grandmother was a woman of means, of privilege—her children attended universities and had traveled to Europe for their fifteenth birthdays. But any farmer will tell you that living off the soil means incurring debt. Milk prices fluctuated and different conflicts cut off distribution systems on a whim. Trucks carrying milk sometimes disappeared, taken as "taxes" by the guerrillas. She planned for losses, but how could she plan for this?

Tito Edmundo Rueda told Esther to wait. His intel as a senator said the guerrillas were merely passing through. He offered Jóse Alfredo a job—something to keep the kid going for a few months, maybe a year if necessary. Esther agreed, just beginning to grasp the size of the intrusion.

Months passed. The mines remained on her son's land. And then, the guerrillas came to her doorstep. Galilea, my grandmother's finca, is paradise. Its beauty does not disappoint or diminish as you walk through the lush pastures. The mountains loom to the northeast, but Galilea sits on a plain of tall grasses and tropical fruit trees. The temperature, while hot during the peak of the day, cools beautifully in the night—imagine hammocks swaying to the chirping nightlife as a gentle breeze kites through.

Esther liked to walk through the grass of Galilea, running her hands through the blades. She remembered when Anibal first found the property—the dreams he had for the place, the empire he wanted to build.

An old gangster once told me *everything is a chain*. My grandmother, a practical woman, knew this as well. When the guerrilla arrived in Galilea, asking for half her cattle in payment and a regular tithe, Esther had little choice in the matter.

If she did nothing, she would lose more income.

If she paid their bribe, it would hurt her soul.

If she fought them, she would lose. And that helped no one.

Her decisions became more complex as she considered the additional mouth she had to feed—Isidro's widow, Doña Carmen.

* * *

She hated giving the guerrillas anything, Alba told me. *With every bone of her body. She hated this more than she hated Conservatives. More than she hated Laureano Gómez. More than she probably secretly hated my father.* Alba looked upset for a moment before she continued.

But she paid that bribe. She paid it. They'd threatened to put mines in all our family's fincas—and she could not stand that either. Sometimes you pick between bad and worse. She gave up the cows and paid their tax, their toll, whatever you want to call it. Every week, they came, even after the government declared a cease-fire.

* * *

In 1982, the government, under newly elected Conservative president Belisario Betancur Cuartas, started to talk peace with the FARC. Smaller guerrilla groups had surrendered, choosing to demobilize. Perhaps, Betancur thought, the FARC could begin to transition into a different type of organization.

The obvious choice was to become a political party. With the ability to run for office, create legal coalitions, and lobby for change, the FARC had the opportunity to work within the system. The appeal was not lost on Pedro Marín. There was only so much a country could take, after all. In 1982, Escobar had achieved almost peak power. He'd begun using explosives and car bombs throughout Medellín, increasing the blood pressure of anyone just trying to get to work. The United States, after officially declaring the War on Drugs, poured a ton of money into training the Colombian military, supporting CIA/DEA missions into the jungle, and extradition proceedings for men like Escobar. A litany of capos and dons died. And now, with discussions of demobilization of the FARC on the table, President Betancur had an opportunity to significantly reduce the violence and normalize peace.

But the FARC had made millions holding people and land hostage. It wasn't easy for every soldier to put down their guns. It wasn't easy to give up the money.

*   *   *

Esther would not pay their bribe herself, of course, not in person. She'd leave the money on the front porch of the finca's house, in the care of the overseer, who was accustomed to the risk that Colombian stability provided.

It was crucial the cows remained milked, and the milk check kept arriving, but she wasn't taking any chances.

Initially, she tried to show the FARC that she did not care. My grandmother put on her boots and went out to the finca, but one day, after one of her neighbors was kidnapped, she decided to stay home. It was the same old man who had taken her to the meeting, the man who had also refused to pay for protection.

Esther was asked to come back to Barranquilla, to stay home from her finca. It was her children who convinced her. Lourdes and Edgar Anibal urged her to consider how young Elsa Yolima remained. She was only ten, too young to be orphaned by both her parents.

The neighbor turned up dead in a creek. Another friend from the milk cooperative lost an arm to a mine. Another man from the agricultural supply store had his tongue cut out for selling supplies to the wrong man. Within weeks, the families of all three began paying the FARC for protection from the FARC.

All kinds of business owners suffered this indignity. Some from the FARC, some from other guerrillas (the ELN or M-19, or any of the smaller guerrilla groups that sprouted throughout the country), some from the cartels, some from private militias. Sometimes, corrupt members of the National Police exacted "tolls."

But what were the owners of the land to do? They paid to stay in business, they paid for the right to work, they paid both for the revolution against their country and for the guns that defended their country.

My grandmother began to miss the Violence. The civil war had been over since 1958, but it felt like a less complicated time to her. *At least back then*, she tells me often, *there was a simplicity to the death count. Liberal against Conservative. It made sense.*

For her, the class warfare felt like a personal affront against her hard work. She wasn't one of the owners of the land who employed hundreds of people. She had twenty people spread over a handful of fincas. Esther had oppressed no one, she asserted.

She was a good boss, a fair landowner, she insisted. She had stolen her land from no one. It was paid for with money she inherited, sure, but that was money from milk and tobacco, from good honest work. The land only produces when it's worked right—everyone knows that, she said. To be told by some Communists that she had to give it back, that she owed reparations to the indigenous, to the worker, she could not contain herself.

This land was worked by my husband, she told anyone that would listen. *This land will belong to his children.*

*   *   *

Officially, a cease-fire was declared between the FARC and the national government in 1982. The FARC, the newspapers said, would put down their weapons. Money and training would be offered to the men, in exchange for the guns. *This is revolutionary!* said one newspaper.

Peace agreements take time to enforce, though. While the comandantes negotiated, foot soldiers kept at their tasks, cease-fire be damned. The FARC did not leave the Magdalena. They did not de-mine the fincas they said they would, including Esther's. They did not stop showing up, armed to the teeth, to collect their taxes.

To say Esther hated the FARC is an understatement. Just mentioning the FARC changes the current of her bloodstream. They are *pigs*, they are *sons of whores, even the women, especially the women.* They deserve *Hell, and whatever else my God has in store for them. May God forgive me for saying the truth.*

When I tried to explain that, initially, Marín's revolution made sense, my grandmother almost choked on her coffee. *It started off with a good idea—to protect the people,* I argued to her. I told her about the way people were caught in a system that prevented the poor from ascending. My grandmother's Colombian ears took in very little.

Everything the guerrillas ever said or did was a lie. They never wanted to make it better for anyone. They blew up the people they supposedly defended. Isidro, your uncle's worker, what did he own? Who did he oppress? He still died.

She remembered no cease-fire. All she remembered, all she needed to remember, was that the FARC held her land hostage. She had walked every inch of that land, rebuilding pastures even as the world collapsed around her. She did not care about the FARC's revolution. She did not care about their ideals or their mission statement. She did not care about the distribution of wealth.

My grandmother cared about her cows, about the hundreds of head of cattle and liters of milk she could not sell, because some asshole blocked the roads out of the finca and wanted to overthrow the government. The revolutionaries had humiliated her. The FARC had no values; in my grandmother's eyes, they were like every other gang or mobsters—trampling the people who merely wanted to live for their own enrichment.

There was no peace. And those animals never deserved amnesty. They deserved to be tried, like the criminals they were.

Some people, according to my grandmother, can never be forgiven.

*   *   *

In late 1982, an offshoot of the FARC sent my grandmother a letter. It arrived at Galilea and the overseer had someone deliver it to the telecom in Fundacíon. Someone there called my grandmother, reading it to her painstakingly slowly. In it, a declaration is made about the rights of the land. *These were indigenous lands*, the notice read. *These lands belong to the people that work the land, not to the people that own the land. Land ownership is a colonial concept, and we reject colonialism.*

My grandmother snorted when she heard that part. *They're a little late.*

But the end of the letter, the part that told her to leave, to stay away from her own land, the part that called her an *oligarch*—well, that was the part that pushed her over the edge. They asked her to continue paying her monthly quota, to "maintain the land's integrity," whatever that meant.

The milk cooperative was no longer picking up milk in the Magdalena River Valley. Fincas were being asked to handle delivery of their own milk, to lower the cooperative's risk. My grandmother, who could not ostensibly even go to her land anymore, had no way to handle the logistics. No deliveries meant no milk check. No milk check meant no income.

Esther did the complicated math—how much income loss could she take, before the situation got dire. She was a frugal woman with good savings. But that only allowed for a certain amount of time.

Against every piece of advice she was given, Esther drove out to the fincas after receiving the FARC's letter. There were three new checkpoints set up between Barranquilla and Fundacíon, each one manned by the military and meant to inspect for weapons. She brought her two oldest sons with her, twenty-five-year-old Jóse Alfredo and twenty-four-year-old Edgar Anibal.

At the first checkpoint, they inspected the car for guns. When they found machetes, my grandmother explained that they were ranchers and farmers, owners of fincas, and thus, entitled to such tools of the trade.

She was waved forward, and an hour later, as she turned inland and away from the sea, the second checkpoint emerged. The soldiers advised them not to go any further. *No one can guarantee your safety.* My grandmother insisted. She needed to step foot on her land. The language of the letter resonated in her head, *the lands belong to the people that work the land.* Well, she worked the land too, she argued. They waved her on.

The third checkpoint did not look like it was being manned by the military. The men wore fatigues, carried guns, and moved like they were military, but everything felt a step off. When my grandmother approached, they told her to turn around. She was not welcome past this point.

These lands, she was told, *belong to the revolution. They belong to the new republic.*

My grandmother protested.

One of the guards then, to show her he meant business, raised his weapon. But he didn't point it at her. No, he pointed it at Edgar Anibal in the backseat.

What price are you willing to pay?

Esther swallowed her pride. She had thought she could push her way through the guerrillas to Galilea. My mother will call it the blindness of Santander, all action and no thought. Even Esther wasn't immune to the stupid vengeance that ignited in her blood. But somewhere on that road, while staring at her son, she realized how naïve she'd been to leave the city at all.

She turned the car around and began the journey home, her two boys healthy.

She would come back, one day, she knew that. She felt it in her bones.

* * *

Esther stood in her bedroom for the last time, the bedroom she used to share with her husband in the house in Barranquilla. But the house had to be sold; she needed the money.

My grandmother, a woman not overly given to sentimentality, could not help but stop and examine every object before she carefully wrapped it and readied it for the move. Selling a home can bring up complicated feelings for anyone, but for my grandmother, this all had an extra weight.

She worked out the sale with the Ruedas. She laughed at the idea that it was the Ruedas who were saving her, the Rueda Guaríns. Her mother-in-law bought the house—with the understanding that in a year or two it would pass to Anibal's eldest, Jóse Alfredo, as soon as he married.

Over the years, nearly all of the Rueda Guaríns had moved to the coast. All of Anibal's siblings had joined Don José and Doña Rosa in Barranquilla. Inés and Francisco lived nearby, along with their two children. The Angarita Ruedas, her brother and his wife, maintained close contact with Doña Rosa.

In the ten years since Anibal's death, Doña Rosa and my grandmother only really saw each other at obligatory family events and milestones—a First Communion, a funeral, a wedding. Esther did not know how to talk to them about Anibal's death or his affairs, but it spoke well of the Ruedas in her eyes that they never engaged with Anibal's *natural* children (a Colombian way of saying "illegitimate"), they never contacted the blood of their blood. Esther, and her children, deserved that much respect.

When Esther told them of her financial troubles, of what the guerrillas had done to her, they offered to buy her home and keep it in the family. And while the offer seemed fair, it did not lessen the nostalgia that gripped her as she packed the bedroom she'd once shared with Anibal.

* * *

The bed, her bed, had once been theirs. Over the years, she had refused to change the mattress, keeping it clean with covers and slips. She swore she could still feel his shape next to her, enveloping her like the night.

She probably needed a new bed anyway. But for my grandmother, this moment was impossible to bear. The house was her biggest asset, or at least her biggest asset not currently invaded by the army of "the people." The milk deliveries had stopped, and with them the check. She had no cattle. She only had a piece of paper declaring her the owner of the land, a piece of paper that currently meant nothing.

With the money from the house, she bought herself an apartment in a building with security downstairs and a sturdy metal gate protecting the garage. It was half as big as her house, yes, but given the living situation, it would just be her, her elderly mother, and the two girls—Lourdes, approaching thirty and perpetually single, and Elsa Yolima, her baby, about to become a teenager. Alberto married. Nidia had moved away for college, Edgar Anibal had moved to Santa Marta with a girlfriend, and Jóse Alfredo had gone to live and work with one of his uncles on the Rueda side. Esther blinked and suddenly she had a new house that felt empty despite being much smaller.

There was enough money left over after the sale of her home that Esther bought a portion of an investment property, a commercial building in Bogotá she shared with more Ruedas. Her half of the profits from that rental weren't very much, but during hard times, and these were hard times, passive income in a secure location meant the difference between survival with dignity, and whatever other options existed. She refused to even consider the alternatives; she was an Angarita after all. Her pride carried her when even her legs could not. And with help and a solid foundation, she was able to maintain her household, *elegant and distinguished*, as my grandmother likes to say.

She did not want to sell the bed, though. And she did not want to leave it in this house. But there was a logistical issue: She could not get the bed out the door.

Esther remembered Anibal commissioning this bed, how she'd told him that building the bed inside the room meant they could never take it out. *Why would we ever have to take it out?* Anibal had asked, and in that moment, she had no answer. But here she was, waiting for a crew of workmen to destroy the last place she'd held and kissed her husband.

She didn't cry—she was herself, after all. She lay down before she had to leave and automatically reached for his hand, a hand that she knew would never come.

I needed you for this, she whispered to the heavens. *You son of a whore.*

*   *   *

After two years of occupying the finca, the FARC left. The Americans offered to send Colombia a new aid package to better enforce its cease-fire, and the FARC understood what that meant—new guns, new tanks, new de-mining equipment. Marín, finding himself potentially outgunned, ordered a strategic retreat, which pulled all his forces from the Magdalena River Valley. Overnight, the guerrillas disappeared.

My grandmother waited a few weeks after hearing the news. She'd decided, after confronting the guerrillas herself, that more prudence was required when dealing with the revolution. But when a month went by with no new sightings, my grandmother loaded up the old Renault and headed for Galilea. Jóse Alfredo accompanied her, still shocked that his mother would return at all.

He spent half the trip warning her about the guerrillas and the other half warning her about the cartels. The coast was in the middle of a marijuana boom, "the marimba bonanza," if you will—"marimba" being slang for marijuana.

It's the bank's fault, if you think about it. Jóse Alfredo spoke about the cheap and open exchange of dollars into Colombian pesos, with a policy of not asking where those dollars originated. *They're trying to stop the cartels from banking abroad.*

My grandmother, who does not trust institutions, remained silent for most of the drive, letting Jóse Alfredo outline the links between national economic policy and cartel finances. When they arrived in Fundacíon, Jóse Alfredo fell quiet.

The city was bustling. Every parking space along the main thoroughfare was taken, every café had patrons, every store boasted lines at every register. My grandmother rolled down the window and asked if there was a festival. She worried constantly about forgetting a saint's day, and she had been so preoccupied as of late, she could not tell up from down or Saturday from Tuesday.

No, ma'am. But the FARC is gone. The ranchers have returned.

My grandmother smiled her biggest smile.

Yes, we have.

El Rey

(A ROOFTOP IN STACCATO)

Medellín, 1993

Pablo Escobar was a talker, and to talk, as all Colombians know, is to *move the muscle without bone*—the tongue. Tongues are dangerous; an open mouth can get a man killed.

The mouth can make its own decisions sometimes. There are lifesaving mechanisms within us, coded into our DNA—the desire to close your mouth when drowning, for example. The yell you cannot contain when startled. The shortness of breath when afraid. The chattering of teeth when freezing. Our body knows when it's in peril.

We can choose to do a lot with the mouth. We swallow salt water, spit fire, vomit bile, break bone, gnash flesh, and wail history. We sob and we devour. We scream—when we should be silent.

*   *   *

The phone calls were his downfall. He couldn't resist. Even when he knew he was being bugged, even when he knew there were vans on the streets, signal-seeking helicopters in the sky, searching for the one telephone call that pulsed to the right cadence.

Here, a conversation with his boy. Here, a lecture to his minion. Here, a love whisper for his wife. Here, a bark for his lover. Escobar loved to phone up the police unit tracking him, late at night, telling one Lieutenant Aguilar just how Aguilar would die, calling the policeman *a gonorrhea, a hemorrhoid, a piece of shit*, always grounded in the body.

Escobar felt his mortality even as he flaunted that he'd live forever. But he sang to his hunters anyway. How could he not? To know the men that are hunting you, to know them by name and still taunt, to feel so secure, safe in your hubris.

He'd lost so much in the last two and half years. Then, he'd been on top of the world, ordering airplanes shot out of the sky after being expelled from the Colombian National Congress for ordering the murder of another congressman, making more money from cocaine than the national debt. He built neighborhoods, stadiums, and infrastructure. He was a president without being a president, he declared.

But in 1991, the extradition pressure from the Americans was too much, and Colombia needed to show the world it was not run by a narco, so Escobar was sent to a prison of his own choosing and design, where he was allowed to receive regular visitors as he lounged in a hot tub. After successfully running his operations from prison for over a year, he escaped.

His strategy for not getting caught? Changing houses every few days, keeping the police on their toes. Until he made one too many phone calls.

*   *   *

An hour-long chat with his son on a satellite phone cost Pablo Escobar his life, as he stood on the rooftop, clear of interference, above him only clouds. And in the clouds, the helicopters narrowing the perimeter, using the son's signal to track the father's position in the sky. He'd say it too, *we should hurry, they're probably listening*, but he'd keep talking.

A toad, is what they call tattletales in Colombia, slimy jungle creatures, the kind that get flattened by trucks on rural highways; the toad is slippery, hard to catch, but easy to kill—not unlike a tongue in some regards. A toad cannot help but tell on itself.

He'd been smoking weed all day, distracting himself from his own confinement. He went downstairs in his casual clothes, soon after smoking. He came back up. Made another phone call. He had another thing to say. Another thought. He had the time, right? How close could they be? How well could they track him?

Escobar was not betrayed by a lieutenant. He was not gunned down by a rival cartel. He was not extradited to the United States. He did not die in a prison. He did not die in the arms of a mistress. He had a weapon; Pablo Escobar always had a weapon. Not just his tongue.

As he stood on the rooftop, a shock of noise rang out. Escobar ducked immediately, trying to figure out where his assailants hid. There was one across the street on another rooftop. Another shot from below.

He shot back. He fled, or tried to, stopped on the rooftop. Pablo Escobar did not expect his fate. But that didn't stop it. He died, fighting the police, shot by Gonorrhea Aguilar, who had triangulated him perfectly, with a van's worth of equipment.

The man driving the van tells a story: He knew he was close to Escobar, but didn't know how close, so he started driving down streets in the designated area, until he saw Escobar through a window, pacing in a room as he spoke into his satellite phone.

The van had the audio from the phone playing, and the driver heard Escobar almost make him, knew that Escobar had paused speaking when the van drove by. But the driver also knew, a second later as Escobar resumed talking, that he hadn't been recognized as a threat.

Because Escobar's tongue—his negligent, arrogant tongue—couldn't sheathe itself, couldn't sit one out, couldn't stop.

Aguilar's bullet stopped the dance quickly enough.

And there, on the ground, with his belly out, vulnerable, without a single useful bone in his body, lay Pablo Escobar at the end of Colombia's greatest manhunt.

Some things are better left unsaid: a lesson to be learned from fish, from toads, and from the silenced dead.

Looking for El Dorado
(A RETURN TO THE MOTHERLAND)

Santander, 2007

In 2007, my grandmother, mother, and a handful of other aunts, uncles, and cousins took me on a tour of the remaining family fincas in Santander. One morning on the trip, I woke up late (at 7 a.m.), showered, and put on some jeans and a T-shirt. When I stepped into the foyer of the Casa Grande of a large finca belonging to an aunt on the Rueda side of the family, I ran into a short, mustached man. Behind him were camera crews, men with machine guns, and a priest. *Are you just getting up?*

Who is this guy? I asked my family. I was not ready for the level of volume this early in the morning. My uncle Alberto pulled me aside. *He's the governor of the department of Santander.*

I muttered an apology.

Did you know, my Aunt Tecla, a cousin of my grandfather's and our host, offered, *that he coordinated the Colombian side of the takedown of Pablo Escobar, he coordinated operations with the DEA, and he delivered the shot to Escobar's ankle.*

Only one of those three things was completely true. But it was the one that mattered. I recognized him once I stared at him for a second. Of course, he was the one giving the thumbs-up in the picture of soldiers over Escobar's freshly shot corpse—Hugo Heliodoro Aguilar Naranjo, the very man Escobar affectionately called Gonorrhea Aguilar.

Why is he here?

Ah, my aunt Tecla laughed a little, *he's here for breakfast. He's my neighbor. And I think he's inaugurating a bridge to his house, which explains the priest. Everything must be blessed in this country. Even the bridges.*

Lieutenant Hugo Aguilar looked me up and down.

Nice of you to wake up and join us.

This is my great-niece who lives in the United States, Tecla explained to Aguilar.

Americans . . . always late to the party, huh?

* * *

My grandmother and I sat in wooden rocking chairs on the long veranda that afternoon, watching all the people moving in circles to make the finca blessing happen next door. Aguilar sat underneath a small tent, with a woman holding a small, electric fan in his face, as she stood in the sun.

I told my grandmother about the reports from Escobar's son that Aguilar did not kill Escobar, despite the title of Aguilar's memoir, *This Is How I Killed Pablo Escobar*. Escobar's son insisted that the drug trafficker killed himself rather than surrender. A diagram had appeared on the news, explaining the bullet angles and trajectories.

My grandmother sighed. I had been working on a project about immigration, a book I wanted to write about why people moved, and my grandmother had spent the better part of the fifteen-hour road trip up trying to explain why she would never leave Colombia.

In the 1990s, the FARC came back to her lands twice more, and my grandmother waited them out twice more. Time, she learned, defeated all enemies.

The guerrillas grew, shrank, demobilized, deserted, reduced their attacks, retreated into rural areas, signed another cease-fire with the government, became a political party, and continued to engage in armed and illegal activity. But they also moved on.

She learned to diversify, to invest a little here, a little there, creating enough in savings to get her through the lean years. Planning came naturally to her. In this way, Colombia had made her resourceful. She had lived without a husband for well over three decades. And somehow, she'd become an old woman of moderate means listening to her granddaughter's theories about the death of Escobar. As far she could tell, history was an absurd joke. But here she was, alive on a rocking chair just footsteps away from the man who, allegedly, shot Escobar.

Colombia is a good story, Adriana. She looked at me pointedly. *Everyone has a version of the truth. The cop killed Escobar, or Escobar killed himself, or maybe both? There's still a dead narco at the bottom of the pile. People will simply choose which version pleases them most.*

*   *   *

Her eightieth birthday was a week away and my grandmother seemed as formidable to me as ever. She'd spent most evenings cheating her way to victory in cards and drinking small amounts of red wine, her *little vices*, she called them.

On the last morning in Santander, my grandmother asked my uncle Alberto to drive by Mancarique. It was no longer in the family; her siblings sold it eventually to pay for Doña Eva's private nurse. Still, my grandmother asked my mother and me to join her on a trip to the old finca.

There were fresh markers on the path to the entrance, commemorating an indigenous trail from Barichara to Cabrera. Now tourists took pictures next to the gates of a place she once called home. As we turned to leave, the new owners pulled up and recognized her.

You might not remember me, but my mother spoke of you often, cousin.

My grandmother did a double take. Something about them seemed familiar.

What ever happened to Leonor? she finally asked, placing them. *I fell out of touch at some point.*

My mother died in 1980. But it was a good death.

We can ask for nothing more.

The distant cousins offered us some coffee and dedos. My grandmother couldn't say no. And as the scent of freshly prepared tinto and fried cheese filled the hacienda, I tried to imagine it, and my grandmother, fifty years ago, suitcase in hand, saying goodbye to everything she knew.

* * *

There was more goat shit on the ground than I anticipated, and both my uncle and grandmother laughed at my discomfort as I walked through the far corrals. At some point, I found a good rock to stand on with a clear view of the valley below.

My grandmother and my mother sat next to me, and together, we took in the vista.

As the clouds shifted in the sky, the light played off the mountainside, revealing purples, blues, and oranges beneath the canopy of green, as the fruit trees and leafy shrubs swayed to the light wind.

My mother pointed toward a distant road, the way to Socorro, the town of her birth. We planned to reach it before lunch and had little time to linger.

My grandmother turned to me. Did I know, she asked, that one of her ancestors had laid down the cobblestone in Cabrera, with his bare hands? And did I know that my grandfather was the spitting image of a Rueda who had fought in the Comunero Rebellion in the eighteenth century?

Our blood has been shed in these mountains for centuries, she said, looking at me carefully. *Don't forget that.*

I promised her. I would not forget. I would bring my children back. She did not have to worry.

Love is in actions, not beautiful words, my grandmother said, one of her favorite aphorisms.

Those Dead Old Men
(A MALL OF NOSTALGIA)

Barranquilla, 2008

The Condor died in 1956. Pablo Escobar died in 1993. Pedro Marín in 2008. All those presidents, dead. All those bandits, those Birds, those guerrilleros? Their revolutions are the dreams of the dead.

*   *   *

Pedro Marín was the oldest guerrillero in the world in 2008, starting his war before the Cubans and waging it long after. He outlasted the Nicaragüenses, the Salvadoreños, and Bolivianos. For sixty years, Marín fought the oligarchs of Colombia, and for sixty years he'd remained on the margins, no matter how much his notoriety grew.

He was on the world's most wanted list—his involvement with the cartels and the Communist Party had ensured that. The Americans had put a $5 million ransom on his head, extradition orders had been filed for decades. This was his greatest achievement. He had recruited thousands to his cause, and thousands had died under his orders. But Marín never defeated his enemy, never effected the cultural and financial reforms he believed in. He died where he'd lived his entire life: the mountain jungles of Colombia.

Rumors had been circulating for months that he had cancer, that the succession of the FARC had already been worked out. And when, after three raids from the National Police, Marín suffered cardiac arrest, the grief in the ranks was real. Whatever he was—a legend, a terrorist, or both—he had finally surrendered his fight.

* * *

A year after his death, I saw his face on a teenage girl's shirt at the mall in Barranquilla. She was shopping at the H&M and carrying a bag from Zara, wearing tight black jeans and a white shirt with a picture of Marín in fatigues.

Not a single person batted an eye as she shopped. When I approached her and asked if she knew who was on her shirt, she shook her head and added, in a heavily, Medellín-accented voice, *some old guerrillero.*

After the fall of Escobar and the Medellín Cartel, the guerrillas filled the void, until they were replaced by the Clan del Golfo, or the Autodefensas Gaitanistas de Colombia (AGC), as the most powerful cartel in Colombia. The AGC took their name from the assassinated politician Jorge Eliécer Gaitán, whose death had only inspired another generation of violence.

But at the mall, that didn't matter. It was food courts and tattooed middle-class kids with too much money. The cartels and guerrillas fought in the mountain jungle or in cooled rooms filled with computers and logistics operations. The days of car bombs and kidnappings had passed, except for the occasional rich landowner or politician.

The nightly news paints two countries coexisting: the violent Colombia of drug traffickers and guerrilleros who refuse to surrender, along with the tourist-friendly paradise offering ziplining tours across jungled valleys.

There are just places you don't go, a cousin tells me. *But really, you wouldn't want to go there anyway. None of those places are worth it.* She laughs. *And, why would anyone leave the mall?*

She has a point. The mall is air-conditioned, and Barranquilla is sweltering.

*   *   *

In Barranquilla, the mall functions as a town square. The bank is in the mall, so is the bookstore and the clothing store; a fantastic steak house stands next to a phenomenal seafood bar in the upstairs food court. The playground offers excellent rides and entertainment that will never seem expensive to a person that earns in dollars.

The youth might protest their unfair wages in the cities, but when they're done, they're at the mall. Fewer and fewer are choosing to go to war against the rich, instead they all want to be rich. Or they want to go to America.

We're losing our boys, an anthropologist tells me over paella at a different food court, in a different and rival mall, across the boulevard from the first. *But now we're losing them to the United States or Europe instead of the jungle.*

As long as drugs remain lucrative, some will choose that path. But more and more want something else, borrowing another nation's dream instead of staying and fighting for their own.

*   *   *

There is no man strong enough to remake a country like Colombia in his image, not forever. There is too much wildness, too much of our snake mother and parrot father in the People of the Salt.

But in the end, the mall won. The comfort of progress, the mindlessness of consumerism. The people don't want eternal war; the people want nice things.

And the old men who lost? Well, they're on T-shirts now. Their names inspire cartels. Their children remain fatherless. Their wars remain unwon.

Marín dreamed of fighting for the campesino and ended up a drug dealer and kidnapper; in many ways, parts of him had died long before his heart gave out. Or as one old man, now dead, said to me once in a mall:

Those dead old men just kept dying. They were dead before they died, and they were dead after too.

La Dama
(AN EPILOGUE WITH THE SERGEANT)

Barranquilla, 2024

In 2016, to the shock of the civilized world, the people of Colombia voted against peace with the FARC, against forgiveness, in a national vote. The president disagreed with the people's vote, revised the deal, and pushed it through the national congress, this time without consulting the people. That peace, negotiated by that president, who won the Nobel, was undone by the time the next guy was sworn in. Some revolutionaries couldn't put down their guns. It's hard to end the fight.

Colombia is still paying for her sins.

*   *   *

Only one of my grandmother's siblings remains. The rest have been taken by time—one heartache after the other, like so many others in our family. Francisco and Inés, Doña Rosa and Doña Eva, and more—all gone. She's lost more people than she remembers. At ninety-seven, she remains sharp, cynical, and mean. I love her tremendously, despite her telling me every so often that I'll never be her favorite.

Every morning, my grandmother wakes up surprised to be alive. Surprised at what she sees—electric cars, streaming internet, and the robot vacuum I gifted my uncle astound her. She cannot work her phone, but she still answers when I call. She asks about my children, she laughs at my dumb jokes.

When I remind my grandmother that she's on track to bury all her enemies, she laughs for only a moment. Then, she turns sad. *I've buried so many.* And it takes everything for me to not start crying.

I visit when I can. But like all her grandchildren, I am gone. Two of us are in Germany, three others have moved within Colombia, complicated flights and schedules keeping them from her. We reunite for family events. Her great-grandchildren speak Spanish with German and American accents, and there's nothing I can do to undo the cruelty of history.

I simply try to make her smile when we're in the same room. I saluted her once a few years ago, and she smirked a little bit.

Your grandfather Anibal used to call me a sergeant.
I knew that one about you, Pita.
You don't actually know anything about me.
Truest thing she's ever said.

*   *   *

My grandmother isn't good at asking for forgiveness for her own peccadilloes, nor is she good at forgiving my grandfather's larger infractions. She's never moved on from his death, and a portrait of him looks down on her from almost every room in her house. She's been his widow twice as long as she was his wife. No one has romantically embraced or kissed my grandmother in over fifty years. No one. There were only twenty years of her life when she experienced that kind of affection.

She dedicated herself to her children—who blame her completely for her husband's infidelity. Her children who fight over money and inheritance, and who raised grandchildren who never look up from their phones.

* * *

I visited with my young kids the summer my grandmother's children finally parceled off her land into six pieces and left her an allowance that Lourdes would manage. Different siblings had different ideas and had split into different factions. The meeting had turned contentious within minutes.

It's like they already want me dead from all their talking, she told me.

She was tired. And sometimes, when she's tired, I can catch a glimpse of her real self, the self behind the mask of manners and injurious comments. My Aunt Lourdes brought coffee, and I gladly took the tinto and gave my kids over to Lourdes.

Sometimes, my grandmother Esther said abruptly, after Lourdes left the room, *I think God punished me for never forgiving Anibal. With my children.*

I could not move. She laughed. There was a bold honesty in admitting she'd never granted him clemency. Something that revealed her for what she truly was: a woman unforgiving as her nation. Until her laughter became something else, something much sadder—something closer to a quiet cry.

They all loved him more, my children all loved him more than they ever loved me.

My grandmother had never referred to my grandfather's infidelity in front of me. She'd never acknowledged any of her pain. And now she called her children a punishment from God.

My eyebrows could only go so high. But I understood.

The stories about Anibal centered on ice cream, laughter, and how he taught his daughter to walk again. Esther was the one who stayed home, who made rules, who forced them to eat their vegetables. Their father died perfect, and their mother remained critical. Of course they spoke of him fondly.

My grandmother walked to a bureau, dug for a minute, and pulled out a notebook. She flipped the pages and finally found what she was looking for, a small entry in a calendar from 1970.

Here, she said, *look at your grandfather's handwriting.*

I looked at it. His scrawl was clear, but childlike, with large, round letters. *My love, my love, my love*, it read.

He was the only man I ever loved. The only man I will ever love. I know, Grandma. I know.

She closed her eyes, and she smiled.

Acknowledgments

The summers of 2007 and 2008, I traveled to Colombia with a small digital camera and my mother. Over the course of two ten-week trips, I conducted over two hundred hours of interviews with family members, took hundreds of photographs, and visited the many villages and cities where this story is set.

Because I thought I was writing a book on immigration at the time, I interviewed people I met in my travels—some strangers, some friends of friends of my relatives—most of whom did not reside near the places where they were born, unlike generations and generations of Colombians before them. I cannot begin to thank them for the stories of why and how they left.

Many of the people I spoke to, now almost twenty years ago, are no longer living, including two of my dearest uncles: Alberto and (Edgar) Anibal. I hope one day our souls can meet again for a good whiskey and some gossip. Beto, Beto, Beto. I still hear your laugh. I miss you always.

My grandmother, Pita Esther, never really believed that I would write this book. Thank you, Abuelita, for answering and not answering the hundreds of questions I threw at you. Thank you for all your contradictions. As I write this, she is ninety-eight years old and angry at me, because my children haven't been to see her in four months. I am grateful that you are as mysterious and impossible to know today as you were when I was a child. And the kids will be there soon!

I could not have written this book without my family: My husband, Jesse Welch, the greatest human I know, who read every single draft of this book and made it possible for me to write it more than anyone else, and my children, Rafael Alejandro and Josefina Lyndon. I've been writing this book for the entirety of my children's lives, and I am grateful for their eternal patience with me. My father, who disagreed with this project ("family stories should remain in the family"), but also offered support and counsel when I needed it. Love you, French Fry.

And my mother. Oh, Alba. I started working on this book as long as I have a memory, from the first time she told me an old story. "This is ancient history, but . . ." is the most exciting phrase I can imagine. The parts of me that love a good story are all her. She's the one who taught me to recite and memorize poetry. She's the one who made sure I was always connected to Colombia, no matter how far away my journeys took me. She is the person who took middle-of-the-night phone calls to ascertain a year or an age or a location. And I'm sorry, Mama. There are dozens and dozens of stories that simply didn't fit. Don't be mad at me. I couldn't tell them all.

※　　　※　　　※

Thank you to my superstar agent, Bonnie Nadell, who over the course of a decade had to talk me off the ledge like a hundred times. To the entire team at Scribner and Kathy Belden, who was eternally patient with me as I delivered ten drafts that were not exactly right. Thank you to Charles K., and especially to Stephanie R., who helped me work out the structure that finally worked (thanks to John Steinbeck on that front too!).

ACKNOWLEDGMENTS

To my friends, the people who read drafts of this book at various stages and helped me figure out what to cut and what to keep: Carly Kocurek, Elizabeth Pienkos, Marissa Johnson-Valenzuela, Lizz Huerta, Jennifer A. Howard, Cara Masset, Laila Monteforte, Edward Banchs, Alejandro Nodarse, and Elizabeth Rodriguez-Fielder.

Thank you to Joseph N. Welch II and Debbi Welch, my in-laws, for being so generous with their time, especially to Debbi for her feedback and eternal enthusiasm. Thank you to my sister-in-law Becca as well.

Of course, this book would not work without the stories from my cousins and second cousins in Colombia. To all the Ruedas and Angaritas, I appreciate you from the bottom of my soul—especially Martha, Vanina, and Kevin. I will always consider your home my own, and vice versa.

*   *   *

Parts of this book were written during a residency in Brussels organized by City of Asylum Pittsburgh and the International House of Literature Passa Porta and the Flemish Literature Fund. City of Asylum, along with Henry Reese and Diane Samuels, have been constant cheerleaders and incredibly generous with their help, even just providing a place to sit and think. I also received support from the Carol R. Brown Creative Achievement Awards, The Heinz Endowments, and The Pittsburgh Foundation. Thank you to the VONA writers' workshop, including Elmaz Abinader, as well as the National Hispanic Institute.

Angie Cruz and my *Aster(ix)* familia held me down—and without Angie, I'd probably never have submitted this book to an agent in the first place. Thank you.

Thank you to all my writing teachers and mentors: Faith Adiele, Jeanne Marie Laskas, Susan Andrade, Lee Gutkind, Bruce Dobler,

ACKNOWLEDGMENTS

Chuck Kinder, Carl Kurlander, Shalini Puri, Marsha Recknagel, and Peggy Mott. Thank you to the August Wilson House, Terrance Hayes, Yona Harvey, Deesha Philyaw, Damon Young, and Brian Broome, who all make being a writer in Pittsburgh more fun. To Scott Morgenstern in the Latin American Studies Department at Pitt, who let me borrow books on the Violence and never return them. Thank you to my cohort of Pitt Creative Writing MFAs, 2006–2009.

Thank you to my therapists (Dana and Brianna), neighbors (Lauren Brown, Liz Dell, and Rachael Kelly), and colleagues at the University of Pittsburgh, Chatham University, and the *Pittsburgh Post-Gazette*—Brandon McGinley and David Mills. To La Escuelita Arcoiris, Rocio Ruíz, Charmaine Moore, Kelly Trautman, Dave and Silas—and the village of support that enables a working mother to write.

Thank you to Svetlana Alexandrovna Alexievich, who let me argue with her about politics and violence far too long at a dinner long, long ago. To my friends I have yet to mention: Kirsten Strayer, Dan Buchanan, Shannon Reed, Carolyn Kellogg, David de Give, Brenda Giraldo, Lindsay Cashman, Rebecca Spiess, Darrell Kinsel, Ashley Cecil, Jean Guerrero, Nathan Tyler, Javi Perez, Christina de la Garza, and the rest of the Group (McAllen Memorial Class of 2001). Thanks to my OQL team, my QuiP team, my J! mates, the Biddies at Bigfoot, and everyone else that helps keep me sane.

To all the authors and books that inspired me. I am eternally grateful.

And to Colombia. May this book be a love letter to my mother's country and its extraordinary history.

Works Consulted

El Colombiano (newspaper), n.d.
Aguilar Naranjo, Hugo. *Así Maté a Pablo Escobar*. Bogotá: Planeta, 2015.
Alape, Arturo. *Tirofijo: Los Sueños y Las Montañas, 1964-1984*. Bogotá: Planeta, 1994.
———. *Manuel Marulanda, Tirofijo, Colombia: 40 Años de Lucha Guerrillera*. Buenos Aires: Txalaparta, 1998.
Alfredo, Cardona Tobón. "La Masacre de Ceilán—Valle del Cauca." *Historia y Región* (2018).
Arenas, Jacobo. *Cese el Fuego: Una Historia Politica de las Farc*. Editorial Obeja Negra, 1969.
———. *Diario de la Resistencia de Marquetalia*. Editorial Obeja Negra, 1965.
Bowden, Mark. *Killing Pablo: The Hunt for the World's Greatest Outlaw*. New York: Penguin, 2001.
Brittain, James. *Revolutionary Social Change in Colombia: The Origin and Direction of the FARC-EP*. New York: Pluto Press, 2010.
Bushnell, David. *The Making of Modern Colombia: A Nation in Spite of Itself*. Los Angeles: Universty of California Press, 1993.
Caballero, María Cristina. "Mapiripan: A Shortcut to Hell." The Center for Public Integrity, May 19, 2014.
Castillo, Fabio. *Los Jinetes de la Cocaina*. Bogotá: Editorial Documentos Periodísticos, 1987.
Centro de Pensamiento. *Violencia Política en los Años 30: De Capitanejo a Gachetá*. Bogotá: Universidad Sergio Arboleda, 2015.
Copolitica (newspaper), n.d.

Davis, Wade. *Magdalena: River of Dreams, A Story of Colombia*. New York: Vintage, 2020.
Deas, Malcolm. *Intercambios Violentos: Y Dos Ensayos Más Sobre El Conflicto en Colombia*. Bogotá: Penguin Random House Grupo Editorial, S.A.S., 2015.
Echeverry Nicolella, Juan. "Un Día con Tres Presidentes." *El Informador*, June 13, 2013.
"El Día Que los Conservadores Incendiaron Rionegro." *DiariOriente* (2019).
"El Sabor Amargo del Conflicto en San Vicente de Chucurí." *Verdad Abierta* (2016).
El Tiempo (newspaper), n.d.
Fernández L'Hoeste, Héctor, and Pablo Vila. *Cumbia!: Scenes of a Migrant Latin American Music Genre*. Durham, NC: Duke University Press, 2013.
Fluharty, Vernon L. *Dance of the millions; military rule and the social revolution in Colombia, 1930-1956*. Pittsburgh: Univ. of Pittsburgh Press, 1957.
Fundación Cultural Nueva Música. *Barranquilla: Historia, Cronicas y Datos Esenciales*. Barranquilla: Escala Impresores, S.A., 2009.
"Gaitán, el Gaintanismo y la Efervescencia Política de los Años 40." *Historia y Memoria*, n.d.
García Márquez, Gabriel. *Living to Tell the Tale*. New York: Vintage International, 2003.
———. *News of a Kidnapping*. New York: Vintage International, 1997.
Gómez Hurtado, Enrique. "Balcón Sobre el Abismo." *El Tiempo*, June 13, 1993.
Gómez Zea, Leonardo Javier. *Biografía, Contexto e Historia: La Violencia en Colombia, 1946–1965*. Santiago de Cali: Universidad del Valle, 2014.
Gossaín, Juan. *La Memoria del Alcatraz: La Realidad Colombiana Vista por Uno de Sus Más Grandes Cronistas*. Bogotá: Intermedio Editores S.A.S., 2015.
Gunson, Phil. "Manuel Marulanda: Obituary." *The Guardian*, May 26, 2008.
Gutiérrez, Francisco. *¿Lo Que el Viento Se Llevó? Los Partidos Políticos y la Democracia en Colombia, 1958–2002*. Bogotá: Grupo Editorial Norma, 2007.
Herlinghaus, Hermann. *Violence Without Guilt*. New York: Palgrave Macmillan, 2009.
Human Rights Watch. *The "Drug War" in Colombia: The Neglected Tragedy of Political Violence*. New York: Americas Watch, 1990.

WORKS CONSULTED

Kirk, Robin. *More Terrible Than Death: Massacres, Drugs, and America's War in Colombia*. New York: PublicAffairs, 2003.

LaRosa, Michael J., and Germán R. Mejía. *Colombia: A Concise Contemporary History*. Lanham, MD: Rowman & Littlefield, 2012.

Leech, Gary. *Beyond Bogotá: Diary of a Drug War Journalist in Colombia*. Boston: Beacon Press, 2009.

Lewis, Paul H. *Authoritarian Regimes in Latin America: Dictators, Despots and Tyrants*. Oxford: Rowman & Littlefield, 2006.

"Los Secretos del 'Rey de los Pájaros' de La Violencia." *El Colombiano*, August 10, 2013.

Martin, Gerald. *Gabriel García Márquez: A Life*. New York: Alfred A. Knopf, 2009.

Martin, Gerard. *Medellín: Tragedia y Resurrección Mafias, Ciudad y Estado, 1975–2013*. Medellín: La Carreta Editores E.U., 2014.

Oppenheimer, Andrés. *Ojos Vendados: Estados Unidos y El Negocio De La Corrupcion En America Latina*. Buenos Aires: Sudamericana, 2001.

Palacios, Marco. *Between Legitimacy and Violence: A History of Colombia, 1875–2002*. Durham, NC: Duke University Press, 2007.

Paternostro, Silvana. *In the Land of God and Man*. New York: Dutton, 1998.

———. *My Colombian War: A Journey Through the Country I Left Behind*. New York: Henry Holt, 2007.

Posada Carbó, Eduardo. *Una Invitación a la Historia de Barranquilla*. Bogotá: Fondo Editorial CEREC, 1987.

Rabasa, Angel, and Peter Chalk. "Colombian Labyrinth: The Synergy of Drugs and Insurgency and Its Implications for Regional Stability." RAND Corporation, 2001.

Ramírez Tobón, William. *La Guerra y el Contrato Social en Colombia*. Bogotá: Penguin Random House Grupo Editorial, S.A.S., 2015.

Redacción Judicial. "La Ingrata Huella de las Masacres en Colombia." *El Espectador*, August 23, 2020.

Rodríguez Machado, Mateo. *Los "Pájaros" y la Violencia en Colombia: Un Análisis desde la Historia y la Literatura*. Medellín: Universad de Antioquia Facultad de Cincias Sociales y Humanas, Departamento de Historia, 2018.

Rojas Contreras, Ingrid. *The Man Who Could Move Clouds: A Memoir*. New York: Doubleday, 2022.

Safford, Frank, and Marco Palacios. *Colombia: Fragmented Land, Divided Society*. Oxford: Oxford University Press, 2002.

Sancho Larrañaga, Roberto. "Memoria Histórica y la Decisión de 'Irse al Monte.'" *Problemas de la Formación del Estado: Annuario de Historia Regional y de las Fronteras No. 6*, n.d.

Sarmiento, José Felipe. "La Verdad Sobre la Carta de 'Tirofijo' al Presidente Valencia." *Colombia Check* (magazine), July 11, 2019.

Semana (magazine), n.d.

Sifton, John. *Violence All Around*. Cambridge, MA: Harvard University Press, 2015.

Simón, Pedro. *Noticias Historiales de las Conquistas de Terra Firme en las Indias Occidentales*. Bogotá: Medardo Rivas, 1882.

Skidmore, Thomas E., and Peter H. Smith. *Modern Latin America (fifth edition)*. New York: Oxford University Press, 2001.

Taussig, Michael. *Shamanism, Colonialism, and the Wild Man: A Study in Terror and Healing*. Chicago: University of Chicago Press, 1987.

Vallejo, Virginia. *Amando a Pablo, Odiando a Escobar: La Increíble Historia de Amor entre el Narcotraficante Más Buscado del Mundo y la Estrella Más Famosa de Colombia*. Madrid: Ediciones Península, 2017.

Vargas Velásquez, Alejo. "Tres Momentos de la Violencia Política en San Vicente de Chucurí (De los Bolcheviques del Año 29 a la Fundación del ELN)." *Análisis Político* (1989).

Villar, Oliver, and Drew Cottle. *Cocaine Death Squads and the War on Terror: U.S. Imperialism and Class Struggle in Colombia*. New York: Monthly Review Press, 2011.

Wade, Peter. *Music, Race and Nation: Música Tropical in Colombia*. Chicago: University of Chicago Press, 2000.

Williamson, Edwin. *The Penguin History of Latin America*. New York: Penguin, 2009.

About the Author

Adriana E. Ramírez is a writer, critic, and poet based in Pittsburgh, where she writes a column and edits "InReview" for the *Pittsburgh Post-Gazette*. She is the winner of the 2015 PEN/Fusion Emerging Writers Prize for her nonfiction novella *Dead Boys* (Little A, 2016), as well as a former critic-at-large for the *Los Angeles Times*'s book section, and the cofounder of *Aster(ix) Journal*. Her writing has also appeared in *The Atlantic*, *The Boston Globe*, *People*, ESPN's *The Undefeated* (now *Andscape*), *Literary Hub*, *Guernica*/PEN America, *Nerve*, and elsewhere. She once lost terribly on *Jeopardy!*